*Routledge Revivals*

# Hindu Customs and their Origins

*Hindu Customs and their Origins* (1937) primarily examines the topic of caste in India, looking at the ancient ideas of the origins of caste and testing modern theories through a critical examination. It also looks at the veneration for the ox and cow, a custom that is unique to India.

# Hindu Customs and their Origins

Stanley Rice

First published in 1937
by George Allen & Unwin Ltd

This edition first published in 2025 by Routledge
4 Park Square, Milton Park, Abingdon, Oxon, OX14 4RN

and by Routledge
605 Third Avenue, New York, NY 10017

*Routledge is an imprint of the Taylor & Francis Group, an informa business*

© 1937 George Allen & Unwin Ltd

All rights reserved. No part of this book may be reprinted or reproduced or utilised in any form or by any electronic, mechanical, or other means, now known or hereafter invented, including photocopying and recording, or in any information storage or retrieval system, without permission in writing from the publishers.

**Publisher's Note**
The publisher has gone to great lengths to ensure the quality of this reprint but points out that some imperfections in the original copies may be apparent.

**Disclaimer**
The publisher has made every effort to trace copyright holders and welcomes correspondence from those they have been unable to contact.

A Library of Congress record exists under LCCN 38000730

ISBN: 978-1-032-93242-2 (hbk)
ISBN: 978-1-003-56508-6 (ebk)
ISBN: 978-1-032-93251-4 (pbk)

Book DOI 10.4324/9781003565086

# HINDU CUSTOMS
## AND
# THEIR ORIGINS

STANLEY RICE

*With a Foreword by*
H.H. THE MAHARAJA GAEKWAR
OF BARODA

LONDON
GEORGE ALLEN & UNWIN LTD
MUSEUM STREET

Dedicated to
## H.H. THE MAHARAJA GAEKWAR OF BARODA

---

FIRST PUBLISHED IN 1937

*All rights reserved*

PRINTED IN GREAT BRITAIN BY
UNWIN BROTHERS LTD., WOKING

# Preface

SOME years ago while trying to write an essay on South India, I found myself drawn almost inevitably into a discussion of caste, which is admittedly at its strongest there. And the more I thought about it the more convinced I became that the accepted theories were unsatisfactory. If it be true, as it is, that ancient ideas of the origin of caste are fantastic, it is equally true that modern theories are also open to so many objections that none of them will bear critical examination. The idea that the beginnings of caste are to be found in aboriginal customs is not new, but so far as I am aware it has not been discussed hitherto in any detail. It has merely been suggested as a possible hypothesis without any attempt to co-ordinate it with other ideas. Dr. Schweitzer in a recent book on *Indian Thought and its Development* brushes aside the theory that the ideas of "world and life negation and magico-religious ideas were originally foreign to Aryan thought" and were borrowed from the aborigines, on the ground that "we know nothing of the thought of the aboriginal inhabitants." This, it is true, is not the same thing as a denial of the origin of caste to the pre-Aryans. Although the idea of "world and life negation" may be connected with magico-religious notions, it does not follow that they had not separate origins, and caste in its origin has little to do with the former but is closely concerned with the latter. If we know nothing of the thought of the "aborigines" we do know something of their customs and of the customs of other races in the same grade of civilization. We are entitled to make reasoned inferences from these.

This inquiry led me to the question of untouchability and to that of the peculiar veneration for the ox and the cow. These customs, which are special to India, are too often taken for granted, however inconvenient they may be and however distasteful to European ideas, but it is evident that they must have had a beginning. Neither is a custom which would spring up naturally in the course of the evolution of history. The chapter on Maratha customs is the outcome of certain researches in the Maratha country and is largely founded on information given to me by Maratha Brahmans. I do not know whether or how far these same customs are to be found in other parts of India.

My thanks are due to Dr. Ramjee Shahani, who has read the manuscript and has made some valuable suggestions.

## Contents

| | | PAGE |
|---|---|---|
| | Preface | 5 |
| | Foreword | 8 |
| i. | Introduction—East and West | 11 |
| ii. | Caste—The Racial Purity Theory | 35 |
| iii. | Caste—The Occupational Theory | 47 |
| iv. | Caste—The Aboriginal Theory | 56 |
| v. | Caste—The Vitality of the System | 81 |
| vi. | Caste—Professor Ghose's Suggestion | 86 |
| vii. | Untouchability | 104 |
| viii. | The Brahmans | 117 |
| ix. | The Cult of the Cow | 133 |
| x. | Some Maratha Customs | 154 |
| xi. | Esoteric Hinduism | 194 |
| | Index | 215 |

# Foreword

THIS year India enters into a new phase of her long career. Though there were certain democratic institutions in the dim past, never before has she tried democracy on the Western pattern with all the machinery of the ballot box, the party system, and government by the people. Never before has the idea of a federated India, in which all component parts share, come so near to realization. There were those who prophesied disaster—culminating in blood, internecine strife, and possibly chaos. It is a view which no educated Indian shares. But there were also those who thought that she would gradually slip back into ancient ways, reviving or perpetuating customs which are rooted in the traditions of a bygone age.

Mr. Stanley Rice's book does not touch politics directly, but in attempting to explain some of our customs and how they arose, he does throw light upon the problems of to-day. For customs, even those which are unsuited to modern conditions, must have seemed good to those who lived at the time of their birth, and no one should hastily judge them who has not at least an intelligent idea of their object. The theme of the book is highly controversial. No one can adduce exact proof, for many of our customs have arisen silently and there is no record of their inception or early growth. Mr. Rice cannot therefore expect everyone to agree with him or to accept all his conclusions. But he has served under me for a period in a position of responsibility. I know him to be a conscientious worker with much sympathy for all things Indian and he has always been interested in the subjects of which he writes.

It has long been my endeavour to do away with the restrictions which caste imposes upon social intercourse and I am happy to think that my efforts have not been unsuccessful. The idea that men cannot enjoy the pleasure of conversation while partaking of food and drink lest they should incur some kind of pollution, has long ceased to have any usefulness, if ever it had any. In Baroda the educated classes,

## FOREWORD

for the most part, have no scruples in this respect. Restrictions on marriage present a difficult problem, for they are so very deeply rooted that compulsion is not to be thought of. My own feeling is that the wisest solution is to open the way by legislation removing restrictions and preventing victimization, and then to allow education to bring about a gradual improvement. Child marriage is another custom which is gradually becoming modified by the force of modern circumstances and in the light of modern knowledge. Indeed, the position of women, in which the Maharani and I are deeply interested, is rapidly changing, and with the change the estimation in which women are held.

Untouchability is generally allowed to be a stain on our record of progress. But here again it is exceedingly difficult to eradicate the habits of centuries. It is at least a plausible conjecture that the custom arose from early religious ideas of pollution, carried to extremes. The extent of its survival even in these modern days is, however, remarkable. I am doing what I can for these unfortunates, but unhappily it has to be admitted that progress in the villages, all over India, though perceptible, is disappointingly slow. To this and to other aspects of social legislation I have given much attention of late, but there are limits to what a ruler can do. It certainly cannot be laid to his charge when the people do not freely respond to what is intended for their good. But it does emphasize how important is the growth of education in the development of a broader outlook.

I am myself a Hindu, possibly because I was born one, but I hold that the same fundamental truths are inherent in all religions. Provided a man brings those truths to bear upon his relationships with his fellow men, I care not what religion or creed he professes. There is, however, much misconception about the nature of the Hindu religion. As it is, it is never taught to the people and they pick it up by hearsay or tradition. It would be a very good thing if they could be taught the history of their religion and enabled to compare it with other religions. This would broaden the minds of the people, lead to greater liberalism of thought, and stimulate progress. Mr. Rice has tried in this book to explain the leading tenets of Hinduism which, contrary to a popular belief in the West, have nothing whatever to do with idolatry. He has done so in simple language, and has wisely not confused the issues by entering into complexities. What is needed by readers such as those for whom Mr. Rice has written, is an understanding of fundamentals, for no one who is ignorant of them can judge Hinduism.

SAYAJI RAO GAEKWAR

*March 1937*

# i

## Introduction—East and West

BY common consent the civilized world is divided into East and West. Outside these two main categories lies the greater part of the vast continent of Africa and the many islands that dot the Pacific. The genius of the European races, and especially of the Anglo-Saxons, has carried the Western line further into the two Americas and southward into Australia and to some extent into the more favourable quarters of Africa. But broadly speaking a line drawn through the Ural Mountains from the White Sea to the Suez Canal separates the East from the West, for the American stock, with the exception of the imported Negroes and a remnant of the aboriginal people, is drawn from Europe, and Australia may be regarded as an outpost of the West, peopled, like the United States, with European blood with a small aboriginal sprinkling.

This arrangement of the earth, which practically resolves itself into the continents of Europe and Asia with additions on both sides (since the whole coast of North Africa is predominantly Asiatic), is convenient, and since it follows the path of the sun it is geographically correct. Everyone knows what is meant by a voyage to the East; you have only to take a map of Asia to enumerate who are, in common parlance, Eastern peoples. But, unfortunately, it is not scientific, and the word Oriental, like the word native, has acquired a special connotation which has led to misconceptions. While the distinction is largely one of colour, the word now means—except in travel advertisements and similar publications—a peculiar type of civilization.

But colour is clearly a false guide. Colour alone cannot account for the difference of characteristics which are supposed to separate East from West—cannot indeed account for any part of it. Nor is it accurate. If Europe is predominantly white, Asia is almost any colour appropriate to

## HINDU CUSTOMS AND THEIR ORIGINS

humanity except white and red. There was, in fact, as everyone knows, a time when Asia was superior to Europe in the arts and sciences, not excluding the art of war. Nor does creed help us, for creeds are exclusively Asiatic, and though they have naturally taken on the impress of the civilizations with which they have come in contact—in Europe the Greco-Roman, in India the ancient Aryan or Dravidian, in Japan and China the ancient Japanese and Chinese—the stubborn fact remains that no religion has the monopoly of either continent. Creeds, with their varying ethical conceptions, may help to mould a civilization, and the misuse of them may help to retard it, as happened in Europe in the Dark Ages and in the Near East up to the time of the Great War. But creeds do not make a civilization. We are what we are, not alone because we are Christian but because we are the heirs of Greece and Rome.

Civilization implies culture and culture involves characteristics. And these last are largely the result of a slow evolution determined by environment coupled with opportunity. We need not elaborate the point at any length; it is sufficient to instance the nomad Arabs whose notorious reputation for hospitality and for fierceness is traceable to the conditions of the desert under which they live. It was, then, an easy transition or extension which applied the term Western to what were or were supposed to be special features common to European and the term "Eastern" to similar features common to Asiatic culture. It is, however, manifest that these apparently common features are not common at all when you begin to break up either continent into its component races and nationalities. What is true of the Englishman is not necessarily true of the Bulgarian; what is true of the Spaniard is not necessarily true of the Swede. And in Asia the Arab is as wholly different from the Indian as the Indian is from the Japanese. That is so obvious that it would not be worth saying were it not for the fact that though the differences are even more marked in Asia than in Europe we have attached the label "Oriental" to characteristics which are probably true only of certain countries at certain times and are not—and never were—true of all countries at all

## INTRODUCTION—EAST AND WEST

times. We talk of Oriental duplicity, Oriental cunning, Oriental luxury, and Oriental patience as if these features were common to the whole continent, though it is very doubtful if any of these, given the country and the period, could not be matched out of European history.

Nevertheless, though the character of a continent may not be susceptible of labels, even if we are prepared to apply sub-labels to specific peoples, we can discern general differences in the cultural outlook as manifested in the art, music, and literature of the two, as well as in the attitude towards life as we see it around us to-day. How did this arise? And what were the forces at work? What is it that differentiates Asia from Europe? We have seen that colour and religion do not carry us very far, though it may be urged that the ideas of Love and Service, which may be called the keynotes of Christianity, have coloured European civilization and, therefore, ought to have coloured the treatment of races who are subject to European rule. It may be similarly urged that Renunciation, which is the keynote of Hinduism, and Submission, which is the keynote of Islam, have contributed to the acquiescence in foreign government, because, however little you may believe in dogmatic creeds, you cannot wholly escape from the atmosphere in which you were born and bred. But generalizations like these do not serve to explain differences which occur on each side of an imaginary and arbitrary line.

Clearly, then, we must look elsewhere for the main forces which influence the national character of a people. Except for purely geographical reasons, we must give up thinking of the world in terms of Longitude; and if we are to get rid of our misconceptions, which have been induced by the extended connotation of the word "Oriental," we must accustom ourselves to think in terms of Latitude. For while the zero parallel of longitude may equally well be drawn through Greenwich or Tokyo or any other place,[1] the parallels of latitude mark definite differences in climatic conditions. From the Poles to the region about latitude 60°

[1] Broadly, but not quite, true. "Monsoon conditions" do not appear to depend on latitude.

the climate is very rigorous and the population consequently scanty, though in the Southern Hemisphere this latter fact is due equally to the want of land. From 60° to 35° it becomes increasingly milder, gradually bordering on heat, and from 35° to the equator it is very hot and enervating. Within these two latter regions are included in the Northern Hemisphere the greater part of Europe and Asia and nearly all North America as well as a piece of South America. The Southern Hemisphere we may disregard as not relevant to our purpose, merely remarking that Patagonia is alone excluded.

It may be asked why we should choose this particular parallel of latitude. Why should we not take the Tropics of Cancer and Capricorn, which are well-marked divisions recognized by geographers? Climate being a matter of almost insensible gradation, any line must be arbitrary; surely it would be better to accept the obvious lines laid down, rather than adopt one of your own choosing? We are, however, here concerned with Europe and Asia, and the map will show that whereas the Tropic of Cancer cuts right through the desert of Sahara, through India, and leaves Persia, Afghanistan, and nearly all China to the north, the parallel 35° coincides on the whole more nearly with political divisions as we know them. The 35th parallel runs through the Mediterranean, barely touching the continent of Europe; to the north of it lies only the smallest fraction of Africa and India; the whole of Arabia, the greater part of Persia and Afghanistan and of the Chinese Empire proper lie to the south of it, and when we are dealing with national character and progress it is of great advantage that we should have these well-marked political divisions, inasmuch as they must have more influence than the very indefinite division on an imaginary climatic line. It is true that the Tropic of Cancer runs through Mexico and to the south of Florida, thereby leaving the whole of the United States to the north. But this does not really affect the argument; you cannot expect an imaginary line to coincide exactly with political divisions, and the 35th parallel which runs through North Carolina and the lower part of California does, in fact, leave the greater part of the States to the north of it.

But whatever line you take "there can," to quote a writer in *The Times*, "be no hard and fast rule and no quite clear-cut line . . . but the broad statement can be made that an individual may defy climate but a race submits to it." The urge to work, the need to maintain existence by the sweat of the brow, was not there. When Nature was most prolific, life in early times was the easier; the gathering of food was not difficult when primitive man had, as it were, but to stretch out his hand for fruit, when the crudely cultivated soil would yield rich harvests and when animal life was so abundant that little trouble was found in hunting. Hence it is that we find the Brahman enjoined in the third and fourth *asramas*, or stages of life, dwelling in the forest and pure asceticism, to submit to what Nature had provided for him, an injunction which in less luxuriant regions it would have been difficult, if not impossible, to obey. Consequently, with the abundance of provision the acquisition of wealth became easy, and with it there came naturally the desire for leisure and the employment of others to do the work of providing food and other necessaries. Society began to take shape: the richer became the employers of the poorer; the food-producing class required leadership and protection; the leisured classes employed their minds in speculation, which in the conditions of life just described was not unnaturally concerned with the great forces of Nature round about them. The universe was to them evidently controlled by gods, each of whom had his special function: one to rule the sun, another the moon, a third the rain and storms. And so these speculations, as they developed, gave rise to other ideas concerning the one Supreme God who controlled all the rest and, by analogy, to the attribution to the various gods of domain over moral and metaphysical departments.

All the early religions—Judaism and Christianity, Hinduism and Buddhism, Islam and Confucianism—took shape and almost all early civilizations flourished round about or rather south of the 35th degree of latitude. Sumeria,

Babylon, Egypt, Northern India, and Greece all fall within this zone. It was almost inevitable that should be so. It was here that Nature was most abundant without being too enervating. There was no special virtue in the East; she merely obeyed the laws common to all evolution and could not help herself. The virtue was in the exuberant South which scattered with both hands the gifts which the colder North denied. To one nation, however, it might be said, this reasoning does not apply. The Chinese Empire, being so vast, stretches right up to and beyond the 50th parallel, but the exception is rather apparent than real. For the Empire of China in early days excluded Mongolia and Manchuria, and Nanking is at latitude 32°. It is clear that the greater and more important part of the ancient empire lies like the rest between the equator and the 35th degree.

The East, then, had evolved states and empires, a rational system of government and religions at least plausible, not because it was the East but because it was the South. By degrees these empires disappeared, primarily because as society became more organized, armies were set free from the labour of getting food and kings began to feel the spur of ambition, the poorer and hardier attacked the richer and more luxurious and destroyed them generally at a time when the autocratic ruler was weak or incompetent. But secondarily they obeyed the law of human nature. As the world progressed those to whom Nature had not been so bountiful invented means whereby they could overcome the difficulties. They became strong, not because they were Western, not necessarily because the others were in decay, but because they had become relatively stronger through the exercise of energy which life demanded. Hence, when the ancient empires came in contact with races made hardier and more resourceful by the struggle for existence, they succumbed. The empire passed first to Greece and then to Rome. Both were fortunate in that they were the heirs of what had gone before and each enriched the heritage. Greece left the priceless possession of her art and her philosophy but she owed much to the older empires, especially to Egypt. It is significant that in the Iliad it is the more essentially Greek conceptions of deity who fight for the Greeks, while the Asiatic types are to be found on the side of the Trojans. Even more significant is it that according to modern authorities, Indian music is the only key left to us of the lost art of the Greeks. It is not for nothing that they included in their modes the Lydian and the Phrygian. Greek music, in fact, came from Asia, and it is not unlikely that the earlier drama with its predilection for lyrics was also influenced by Asiatic conceptions. These things, slight as they are, at least suggest a close cultural connection between Greece and Asia. And then came Rome with her genius for war and administration. The tide of empire seemed to be flowing westward, but it was also flowing northward, and it was the North and not the West that mattered. Long before the Romans had reached the period of decay that led to dissolution, the North was threatening. The Roman Empire fell to pieces in the hands of effete rulers. Hired soldiers were brought in from the North who put the empire up to auction. The Empire of Charlemagne succeeded to that of Augustus and the tide of civilization again flowed northward. Rome sank into insignificance save for the Papacy. The priests employed all their arts to preserve ecclesiastical supremacy and to maintain the throne of power which the policy or the conviction of Constantine had erected. But the ghostly power waned before less spiritual arms. The sovereignty passed to France and England—always northward—except for the brief and fortuitous ascendancy of Spain during the sixteenth century. Further, it seems, Nature will not permit man to go. To the northern nations of Europe she was not so kind as to those early pioneers of Asia. They had to work hard for their living; they had to overcome the forces of Nature, and, living as they did in a bracing climate, they developed a determination and a power to overcome obstacles which the peoples of the softer South never acquired. To them, because of this, was given the spirit of adventure and the practical gift of invention; to the South, dreaming in her vines and her sunny lands, was given the gift of imagination and artistic beauty. The materialism of which Europe is accused is the outcome of her training and her environment.

To her the phenomenal world was no illusion, but a stern and hard necessity, of which she had to make the best she could. Food, light, warmth, clothing, were matters of paramount importance. The "urge to rule" of which the writer in *The Times* spoke, meaning, evidently, rule over the less developed peoples, was a much later result of this struggle for existence. It was based upon the unquestioned superiority of Europe in material things. It did not manifest itself till after the spirit of adventure had been awakened and it grew with the desire for the acquisition of wealth. Those who learned in the harder school were imperceptibly moulded into the sterner stuff of a material civilization.

Asia, on the other hand, prides herself upon her spirituality. It is not India alone which makes this claim. The philosophies of life, contained in all the greater extant religions, came from Asia. This does not mean that she had the monopoly of thought. Long before the Christian era Greece had produced her Plato and her Aristotle, to mention only the most eminent names, and Rome too had her philosophers. But it was in Asia that originated the religious system out of which arose such a flood of literature in an age when Europe was dominated by theology. But as we have seen, the Northern nations were compelled by the rigour of Nature to wring from the soil what the gentler South was ready to give with both hands. And when once the process had begun, there was no telling where it would end. And so when primitive man took to agriculture under difficult conditions he began to cast about for the means of lightening his burden. One thing led to another until we have the scientific discoveries of to-day. There was no such urge in the South. If you could get a tolerable crop by merely scratching the surface, and if that tolerable crop sufficed for your needs, why should you go to the extra labour of inventing and of using more efficient means? Consequently the North, preoccupied with the struggle for existence, developed a material civilization; the more it invented the easier became the acquisition of wealth and the greater the appetite for it. Not that Asiatics were indifferent to wealth, as the histories of Eastern peoples abundantly show. Without wealth they could not

## INTRODUCTION—EAST AND WEST

have set up the empires of which we have such abundant evidence to-day. But after the overthrow of these empires, India, Persia, and China were left as the greatest countries on the continent. Persia fell before Alexander, but India and China remained, the former not homogeneous but as yet the heritage of her own sons. Both fell before invaders from the North. The Manchus conquered China and established a long-lasting dynasty. The Hindu States fell before the successive onslaughts of invaders from the North-West, and at last, in the sixteenth century, after the Arabs, Turks, and Afghans had ruled her for some five hundred years, came Babar with his hardy Central Asians dwelling about the 35th parallel and established the Mogul Empire. Thus Asia too followed the rule of the Northern Hemisphere that the tide of conquest flowed from South to North. Indeed, the only exception to the rule was that of the Moorish conquest of Spain, which was so far enduring that it lasted for nearly eight hundred years.

In the earlier times the white races were so far from being the superior of the dark that they were overwhelmed by floods of invasion from Asia. These were generally spasmodic; they were seldom sustained to the point of colonization, though they have left a mark upon Eastern Europe. It can hardly be said that these invaders—Turks, Huns, Tartars—who came from that intermediate belt which we call the temperate zone (though the Turks were deflected southwards and actually entered Europe by way of Asia Minor) brought with them any high degree of civilization, nor did they, in fact, show any superiority except in arms. We are accustomed to look upon these invasions as the devastating whirlwinds of savages, but they were only the normal expression of the primitive ambitions of men who had got beyond the stage of the nomadic search for food and were attracted by the lust of plunder and the greed of power. It is indeed very doubtful whether these hordes were more ruthless, more avaricious, more destructive, than the hordes of Northern Europe who swept down upon Rome or the Vikings of Scandinavia who harried the coasts of England and France. The great Timur, who led his hosts from the confines of China to the shores of the Mediterranean and wasted Persia and Irak with fire and sword before overthrowing the great Sultan, turning aside to inflict upon Delhi the most terrible sack she has ever known, was nevertheless a leader endowed with military talents and well-defined ideas of government. He, however, belongs to a later period when the various influences at work had already gone far to mould Western Europe into something like her present-day geographical form.

But it is clear that climate, however important, is not the only factor in the moulding of national character. If it were, we should expect that races occupying lands in the same degree of latitude would be more or less in the same stage of civilization. It is notorious that they are not. Central Africa cannot be compared to India or China, and in Asia as a whole, compared with Europe, the whole position is reversed. There the centre or temperate zone is still in the early stage, whereas all the civilizations of the continent are crowded into that tropical zone where they originated. India, China, Persia, even Irak and Arabia, have advanced further than Southern Siberia and other parts in the same latitude. Evidently, then, we must look for other causes.

If we examine the topographical map of Europe, we shall find that there is a great plain that stretches from the Pyrenees to the Yenesei River, very little of which is more than 600 feet above sea-level and which is broken only by the chain of the Urals. The highest land occurs in Spain, the Alpine system (which includes parts of France, Austria, Germany, and Italy, besides the whole of Switzerland), the Balkans, and the Carpathians, including Transylvania, and much, even, of the high land is under 3,000 feet above the sea. If, then, you draw a line obliquely across Europe and continue it into Asia you will have travelled over easy country with hardly any exception from the Mediterranean to the Arctic, across land of varying, but on the whole of great, fertility. But, as we have seen, there is a point beyond which man cannot go because the forces of Nature are too strong. The map of Asia is the exact antithesis. The whole of the centre of the continent is from 1,500 to 6,000 feet in level,

## INTRODUCTION—EAST AND WEST

rising in the plateau of Tibet to 12,000 feet. The only really low-lying parts (excluding the Great Siberian Plain) are coastal strips and the valleys of the great rivers, the Tigris, Euphrates, Indus, Ganges, Irawadi, Yang-tse, and Hoang Ho. This does not, of course, mean that all land marked below a certain range is the only land that is cultivable, nor does it mean that all land below that range is fertile. On the contrary both Asia and Central Africa abound in deserts and forests—intractable deserts and impenetrable forests—which are as hostile to advance in civilization as mountain ranges. Now in Europe the whole of the plain and high table-land is within those latitudes which most conduce to energy both of mind and body, whereas in Asia the valleys of the great rivers are either in the tropic or the arctic zones. It is, perhaps, superfluous to remark that the distribution of population follows a universal law and that the same relative proportions are found wherever hilly country and fertile lowlands exist side by side. What is perhaps not so obvious as a general law is that the more hilly and broken the country, the more ignorant and backward is the population. Thus, writing about 1860 of the Highlanders of Scotland in the seventeenth and eighteenth centuries, Buckle says:

That barbarous race thought with regret of those bygone days when the Government had not only allowed them but had ordered them to plunder and oppress their southern neighbours —war was their chief amusement; it was also their livelihood; and it was the only thing they understood . . . their only notion of right was to do what those [chiefs of the clans] commanded.

So far, then, we have found that whereas in Europe climate and topography have combined to create the most favourable atmosphere for the development of civilization, in Asia each is counteracted by the other. To some extent these conditions would be modified by the migrations of pastoral and nomadic peoples who roamed about under the spur of hunger, abandoning one exhausted tract for another giving greater promise, but when they reached the agricultural stage, these wanderings would either cease or would tend to become more circumscribed. The great invasions, though they might have been induced rather by lust of plunder and greed of conquest, and though when these desires were satisfied the waves receded, generally left behind them a residue which to that extent brought new blood. But since a tropical climate tends to a physical lethargy and degeneration, and since that degeneration tends to increase and to become more marked as time goes on, such races drop behind, not altogether because they have lost in stamina but also because they are unable to keep pace with the hardier nations who have advanced in knowledge and capacity more nearly to their level. Nowhere was this better illustrated than in India. The army of Ibrahim Lodi, whom Babar defeated on the plain of Panipat, came from the same stock as those fierce warriors who swooped upon India five hundred years before. Five centuries of the Indian heat and the Indian luxury had so worked upon them that they could not stand against the hardy men of Central Asia.

If these things stood alone, the Central Asiatic, in spite of topographical difficulties, should have been on much the same cultural level as the Swiss, but, as everyone knows, they are nothing of the kind. Wherever men are gathered together they are able to exchange ideas. Life becomes more subdivided; labour is allotted to special classes and tends to become specialized. Each man concentrates upon his own work and, his mind being active, evolves ideas which he communicates to others. And this advance by contact tends to increase in geometrical progression as contact becomes closer and ideas stimulate and suggest others. The consequence is that as men congregate in towns they become more and more sophisticated, and it is of universal experience that the town dweller is mentally in advance of his fellow in the country. But contact is impossible, or at least very difficult, in rugged and hilly country. The configuration of the ground prevents the growth of cities and even of towns, and though there may be assemblages of men in the valleys, the nature of the country makes them comparatively inaccessible to others. Hence even in a country like Switzerland the general life is simple and the contribution to thought and art is negligible except in that corner where access to the outer world is relatively easy.

## INTRODUCTION—EAST AND WEST

What applies in a moderate degree to the Swiss applies in acute measure to the Tibetans, who not only live at extreme altitudes in difficult country, but have added an artificial barrier to contact by forbidding the country to foreigners. There is, it is said, in the Cameroons a tribe who, living themselves in almost inaccessible jungle, are so suspicious of strangers that a visitor must go naked and must have a black skin lest he should discover himself by wearing clothes. Where contact, already difficult, becomes impossible by the deliberate action of man, no progress can be expected.

But there are other ways of contact besides mere juxtaposition. Ideas are communicated through books—through the written as much as and even more than by the spoken word. It was by this means that Macaulay hoped that Indians would in time become English in everything but colour, and he instanced the Tartar, who had become civilized through the medium of French. Here Europe is at an immense advantage. For although there are many languages, those in Western Europe at any rate fall into groups, so that there are affinities between German and Dutch, between English and Danish, between French, Spanish, and Italian which considerably lessen the difficulties of mastering them. Similar affinities are no doubt to be found in Asia. In India, for example, there is the Sanskrit group, the Dravidian group, and Urdu, which is a member of the Semitic or Arabic group. It is not, however, upon the structure of the language but on the script that emphasis must be laid. The use of the Roman script has been of immense service to the Western nations of Europe, and it may even be accounted one of the reasons why Eastern Europe has lagged behind Western that the difficulties of mastering such languages as Russian or Czech are greatly enhanced by the initial obstacle of learning an entirely new alphabet—a difficulty which is only reduced in the case of Greek because that has become part of a classical education and it learned at an early age. Naturally enough, as civilization progressed, as some nations increased in power, wealth, and population, and as the desire grew for closer contact, the smaller peoples who had a universal message to give found it necessary to express themselves in a widely understood tongue, first in Latin and later in French and English.

The languages of Asia abound in scripts. Arabic, Persian, and Urdu, Chinese and Japanese, are about the only two groups which use respectively the same script, if indeed they are the same and not merely cognate. Siberia is chiefly peopled by Russians, while most of the greater languages of the Indian Empire, Gujerati, Tamil, Telugu, Canarese, Malayalam, Oriya, and Burmese, all use different scripts, though Hindi, Bengali, and Marathi—all three important—use the Nagari character. Yet even so they cannot be understood beyond the confines of India. There was thus no easy means of communication between the nations of Asia, and contact with Europe was almost entirely shut off. There was, of course, trade between Venice and the Levant and the Moors of Spain have left their mark on the country to this day, not only in the names but also in the culture; but it was not until a group of savants arose and with European curiosity and industry began to study the literature of the East that there was any real consciousness of Asiatic culture. In fact, owing largely to this difference of scripts—a difficulty enhanced by their complicated nature—each Asiatic nation was sufficient to itself in the sphere of literature. It was not until Asiatics began to write in Western tongues that they began to speak effectively, either to the world or to one another. The remarkable progress in all directions which we see in India, in Japan, and doubtless in Annam is due in part at least to the mastery by the educated of a European tongue. We must not, however, lay too much stress on this question of script; it cannot have had an influence comparable to that of climate and topography, for script is after all a man-made thing which can be overcome by diligence and application and if it had been suspected that any hidden treasure was to be found men would have been forthcoming to discover it. What is here contended is not that it is of primary importance but that it had at least a secondary influence in keeping the nations apart and in denying that contact which is necessary to the growth of civilization. The forces of Nature must be always stronger

## INTRODUCTION—EAST AND WEST

than the forces of man, and since man's life is developed by effort, it is those nations who by their effort have successfully overcome the obstacles which Nature has placed in their way who have developed the strongest national character. And to these forces must be added yet another, no less formidable.

For to this contact with the outer world and to this spread of a convenient medium of communication the greatest of all contributors is the sea. For the sea is the natural and the easiest means of transport before the coming of railways and aircraft. Armies did not usually travel by sea (unless, of course, the attacking country or the objective was an island, as in the case of the English wars against France, the Athenian expedition against Sicily, the Turkish attack upon Rhodes, and Hideyoshi's expedition against Korea) because their objective was generally more easily reached by land and in the case of the early invaders because they conquered as they went and apparently never had any main objective except the one immediately in front of them. To use ships for transport implies a considerable knowledge of shipbuilding and this the Tartars, Huns, Goths, and Vandals do not seem to have had, no doubt because if they were not actually inland tribes they set little value on the sea. Hence we find that nearly all maritime enterprises began in what we should now call the Near East, for it was there that the early civilizations flourished. The Phoenicians were notoriously a sea-faring people, the Persians fitted out a huge fleet against Greece, the Athenians sent a fleet to Sicily, a daring enterprise for those days, and later the Carthaginian fleet was a thorn in the side of the Romans, until the fortune of war turned in their favour. It is remarkable that from the date of Actium to the battle of Sluys we hardly hear of a naval fight in the West and the chief maritime nations were the Venetians, Genoese, and Turks—a fact which indicates that no nation was bold enough to venture far out of the narrow seas. And so the Mediterranean became the chief, if not the only contact with the East and then only for purposes of trade. No one was much interested in the East except for what material gain they could get out of it. Palestine, it is true, for obvious reasons attracted Europeans, then under the fanatical domination of the Church, but otherwise the non-trading community had no interest in Eastern countries.

Nor was the East entirely oblivious of sea advantages. Arabs, Indians, and Chinese put to sea very early, but they too were afraid to venture far beyond the coast, and while the Arabs for the most part confined themselves to the narrow waters or sailed along the southern coasts, Indians did not venture far beyond the same routes and among the islands of the Archipelago further east, and the Chinese trade was largely coastwise or among the same islands. There was, of course, no rivalry with Europe, which was effectually cut off by the Isthmus of Suez.

But during the fifteenth century events occurred which geologists might have called catastrophic. Between 1419 and 1446 Prince Henry of Portugal, greatly daring and inspired by the hope of gain, made his African discoveries; in 1492 Columbus discovered America, and in 1498 Vasco da Gama sailed to India. It is suggested that these famous voyages first took shape out of the desire to find a westward, or at least a sea route to India, because the Mediterranean was becoming closed to European ships owing to the activities of the Turks who by tradition and temperament had always been moved by military adventure rather than by the love of commerce. We should like to think that though this may have been the motive which first set men's minds to work, the adventure was prompted also by the mere love of it. Whatever may have been the impelling motive, it is important to notice two things. The countries who were first in the field of discovery were not those who afterwards disputed the mastery of the seas. They were neither England, France, nor Holland, but the Iberian Peninsula, which lies as near the Equator as any part of Europe, and while Spain had profited by direct contact with the Arab civilization which had been so far in advance of Europe during the eclipse of the Dark Ages, it is hardly possible that Portugal, not separated by any natural barrier, could have escaped its influence.

## INTRODUCTION—EAST AND WEST

The second point which deserves attention is that this period of maritime adventure coincides in time or rather forms part of the great movement called the Renaissance. That the spirit of maritime adventure should first have been evoked in the Iberian Peninsula would, therefore, of itself prove very little, for by the time of the Renaissance, the beginnings of which are discernible towards the end of the twelfth century, European civilization had taken definite shape, at any rate in the western part of the continent, and the traces of Asiatic influence are scant because they have been overlaid by a new form of culture. But the higher forms of civilization as represented by Literature and the Arts had hardly begun to trickle northwards. Italy still took the lead in painting and sculpture and music. England has little to show except Chaucer to balance the great names of Dante (1265), Petrarch (1304), and Palestrina (1526); France has only Ronsard and Villon. The blossoming time of the Northern nations had yet to come. The general trend of culture as of power was from the South and East to the North and West.

The maritime adventures of the fifteenth century were made possible by the invention of the compass and astrolabe. The origin of the first seems to be doubtful; the mariner's astrolabe is attributed to Behaim, a German from Nürnberg, but it was originally an Eastern invention and was probably brought to Europe by the Arabs. Such things as these were due to the new spirit of inquiry embodied in the Renaissance. It was the resultant of forces which were combined in Europe alone and therefore it was that in Europe they received their fullest expression. The hand of the Church still lay heavy upon the land, but to the great advantage of the world Liberalism triumphed over the ecclesiasticism to which religion had sunk.

The example being set, the challenge was taken up by the maritime nations, with what result every schoolboy knows; and here again geography came to the help of Europe. For no continent possesses so broken a coast-line, so greatly out of proportion to the size of the land area, unless it be the north of North America where we begin to enter the Arctic seas. Both Africa and South America are devoid of anything more than indentations of the coast at the mouths of rivers, and in Asia, which no doubt contains the Persian Gulf, the Red Sea, and the Sea of Japan, there is nothing to correspond to the training grounds of Europe except the waters of the Archipelago in the South, which stretches out to Australia, and where, incidentally, navigation was so difficult that Drake was very nearly wrecked there after crossing the Pacific. There was, therefore, no incentive to Africans and South Americans to build ocean-going ships, for except on the North the Africans had nothing in front of them but vast masses of water, while the South Americans had only the Pacific and Atlantic oceans; they could and perhaps did venture for short distances along the coast, but the only two civilizations worth the name which the Southern Hemisphere has produced had little temptation to the sea. On the other hand, the land-locked seas of Europe were specially adapted for apprenticeship in ocean adventures. The Mediterranean became a recognized trade route very early; the long peninsula of Italy and the scattered islands, especially in the Levant, ensured that no ship need ever be very far from land, while the Black Sea, too closely barred to be of great service, was matched by the Baltic in the North, and the barrier of Britain diminished, if it did not quite destroy the terrors of the North Sea. And so all Europe became sea-faring, first in the North the Danes and Scandinavians and Normans, then in the South the Venetians and Genoese and Catalans, later the Spanish and Portuguese—and where Spain and Portugal led the way, England, France, and Holland followed. Maritime supremacy fell to England and France with the Dutch securely seated in the islands of the Further East. It is significant that neither Russia nor Germany ever attempted such enterprises and that both states were comparatively uncivilized, Germany at any rate in the East.

There is, then, nothing inherent in the mentality of Europe that has given her predominance in the world of to-day. She is the darling of Nature. Climate gave her the energy to act; topography gave her the contact necessary to progress;

## INTRODUCTION—EAST AND WEST

her seas, the nursery of her sailors, encouraged them to apply their energies to far-distant adventures, and finally the Roman Empire—the only man-made factor—gave her an easy medium of interchange of ideas. Asia, having little incentive to feverish energy, preferred the contemplative life. She invented religions and philosophies, neglecting the material part of this life. Her topography, never conducive to contact, was reinforced by rules and regulations which shut her off from the world. In India caste was invented with the corollary that to cross the black water was to forfeit that most prized possession; in China an exaggerated idea of their own importance kept visitors away. Tibet too was inaccessible until the intrusive European forced his way in. These things might be put down to the evolution of history, since they are all the voluntary acts of man, but it would probably be more accurate to ascribe them to temperament out of which the history arose. The East was not indifferent to the acquisition of wealth, but she did not regard it as of primary importance. In accordance with her environment she preferred to accept what was easily won, but she was not prepared to make any special effort to obtain it. Asia was Asia not because she was the East but because she was the South.

But there is one "Eastern" country on which history seems to have had so direct an influence that it cannot be ascribed to temperament or to any other of the factors which we have been considering. Japan stretches from latitude 45° to 31° but the most important section is between 40° and 33°. She is thus a little south of nearly all Europe, Tokyo and Yokohama being parallel with North Africa and slightly south of New York and Lisbon. The climate is conducive to energy, and though the Pacific may have been too hard an enterprise for her sailors, she had the narrow sea for a training-ground and the mainland for an objective. There is good evidence that the Japanese merchant flag searched the coasts even as far as Siam and India, but for some reason not altogether apparent the Japanese fleet was not up to the standard of its neighbours. There was, of course, a Japanese civilization which was largely borrowed from the Chinese, but in 1639 any progress by way of contact with the outer world came to an end by the voluntary action of the Japanese themselves, brought about by the meddlesome interference of foreign missionaries. These Jesuit priests were, of course, very much in earnest; all fanatics are—from Samuel to Lenin. They justified the defiance of the civil government by the usual excuse that they were serving a higher Master and in doing so they arrested Japanese progress for two centuries. There is no other recorded instance of a people so highly cultured severing themselves from the rest of humanity for two hundred years. Whether the Japanese were wise in this self-denying ordinance may well be doubted; they, like the rest of Asia, were probably unaware what they were doing and did not realize that by this act of segregation they were stunting their own growth. But when at last the barriers were burst and Japan, looking over the broken barricades, found herself face to face with the outer world, the law asserted itself. They set themselves to repair whatever mistake there was in this loss of contact and to make the most of the advantages they had. Art they evolved for themselves; that they took on the Western form of civilization was due first to the fact that the Western peoples had been most insistent on forcing the barred door and so impressed by their power, and secondly (what is perhaps the same thing) that Western civilization was dominant in the world.

And because the inferiority of Asia in the military sphere had been so often proved, because the very word "Oriental" had become so generalized that it was almost a synonym for inefficiency, the result of the Russian War was greeted in Europe with astonishment, in Asia with jubilation. Asia had beaten Europe; the East had beaten the West. A French writer has gone so far as to explain that the Japanese are really Western and the Russians really Eastern, so galling was it to the pride of the West that it should own itself defeated by Orientals. India rose to the slogan "What one Oriental race can do, another can do." No one saw that when Japan had freed herself from her self-imposed shackles she would begin to assert herself and to move forward towards the destiny for which Nature had marked her out. She made

## INTRODUCTION—EAST AND WEST

the most of her advantages; she saw where the springs of power—political and economic—lay. She copied; she adapted; she perfected herself upon the best models she could find and these things she was able to do because of the genius that was in her people, but also because of the gifts with which Nature had endowed her.

This sketch does not profess to do more than to indicate in the broadest outline the main factors which have influenced national character. That indeed is too narrow a word, for what we have been considering is rather continental character without any attempt to differentiate between nationalities. These latter have undoubtedly been influenced by social and political, economic and religious cross-currents, as well as by institutional tradition. An American writer holds that the chief difference between "East" and "West" is to be found in their political institutions. Even if this be so, the question remains: how did it come about? The earliest forms of government were those of the king or tribal chief who commanded implicit obedience from his people and had the lives of individuals at his disposal. Constitution-making is notoriously a difficult thing and it requires not only the competent brain to devise but also the active practical man to put it into practice. The Chinese again evolved for themselves an eminently practical, non-proselytizing religion, which in spite of the quietist teaching of Buddha has left its mark on the people, and Islam, fanatically devoted to the Prophet and strong in the austerity of the desert, produced the one nation in Europe which is before all things a military people. Turkish misrule retarded progress in the Near East; Russia and Spain were too long under the unenlightened despotism of the Church. But these things came later; they were like the branches of a tree which had grown to maturity from quite other causes. It is perhaps difficult for us to project ourselves into the distant past, to realize that the growth of continental character was so slow that beside it an oak grows with almost incredible swiftness.

The background of India was a country sufficient unto itself, full of mountain ranges of varying heights, of wide and, in the rainy season, impassable rivers, of extensive and impenetrable jungles, of rich and fertile valleys where the soil needed only the minimum of labour to produce at least a subsistence. The climate was and is hot and enervating over a considerable period of the year. In such conditions it was only to be expected that sedentary occupations would find favour. There does not seem to have been much incentive to the pursuit of gain. The kings waged their petty wars and conquered one another's territory, taking all they could get and extracting from the peasantry all that could be spared from bare necessity. The soldiers followed the king with no idea of patriotism, but chiefly in the hope of plunder, the only kind of gain which appealed to them. But the business of life had to go on. The people were not interested in and had no time for speculation; they were content to obey their rulers and to follow the lead which the rulers gave them. The population was scanty; but what was much more important and what specially influenced daily life was not the visible human beings but the invisible spirits. Man had to walk warily; there were pitfalls everywhere, of which the demons were always ready to take advantage. Rules and regulations had to be framed to circumvent them, for the priests taught that the least deviation from the ritual of sacrifice would divert the offering from the intended god to the unintended devil. And since the priest alone knew all the minutiae, it was natural enough that the people to whom it was all-important to propitiate the evil spirits as well as the good should have willingly granted what they thus claimed.

This insistence upon the importance of the unseen world is illustrated by the four *asramas* of the Brahman life. He was to pass twelve years as a learner or Bramhachari—that is to say that during the time when a more material civilization was cultivating the physical body, the Indian youth was enjoined to cultivate the self-discipline of the mind, the emotions, and the passions. The next stage was that of the householder or Grihasta, for the insistence on the unseen did not reach so far as the total disregard of the seen. The world had to be peopled; there had to be some sort of concession to man's "lower nature." But there was an element of religion here too, for the birth of a son was most important—in fact necessary—to the salvation of a man's soul, and if no son was born of his body the place was supplied by the device of adoption or of delegation to a near relative. Then came the stage of the Vanaprastha, the forest dweller. The ascetic was required to live in the forest, to clothe himself in bark, and to eat nothing but what Nature provided in the shape of roots and fruit. This was the kind of person who figures in such plays as Kalidasa's *Sakuntala*, and, if the poets can be trusted, the enforced austerity had a bad effect on the temper. But the important point is that such a life would only have been possible amidst a luxuriant Nature and that it was to be accompanied by intensive meditation. Surely it was only a people to whom the active life made no appeal and to whom the material blessings of the world meant little or nothing who could have conceived such an idea. And when this stage was over, there came the purely ascetic stage of the mendicant, the Sannyāsi, who must not be distracted even to the extent of fetching the forest food and drawing water from the brook, but having renounced the world altogether must beg his bread from door to door.

This, then, was the typical life of the South but not necessarily of the East—a life in which there was no desire for intercourse with others, in which the disputations of philosophers seemed of the first importance to kings and princes, in which the activities of colder climates would have been regarded as a pandering to an unworthy materialism. Out of these conditions grew caste, untouchability, and other institutions peculiar to the country. For these institutions were mainly designed not so much to preserve the purity of the race as to maintain the purity of the family, which was the unit. It was of small consequence that such things interfered with social growth, by shutting up communities into watertight compartments. The all-important goal was to counteract the mischievous influence of the evil spirits. If punctilious observance was necessary to the sacrifice, it was equally—perhaps more—necessary to the conduct of human affairs, and what could be more inviting to the evil spirit than a polluted man—ceremonially polluted because he had strayed from the right, that is, the orthodox path? The ideal of the spiritual life could not be wholly maintained; occupations grew with material needs, and finding an institution ready to hand moulded themselves on the same lines. The contact which was earlier shunned was forced upon India by the intrusion of foreigners; much disappeared, but enough remained behind and even what was lost stamped itself upon the character of the people. Subtle in dialectic, exceedingly quick in argument, yet with a certain incapacity to put into practice decisions reached, the Indian is the true son of the South.

## ii

## Caste—The Racial Purity Theory

"THE attempt to solve the problem of origins requires, as Renan has said, a keen eye to discriminate between things certain, probable, and plausible, a profound sense of the realities of life, and the faculty of appreciating strange and remote psychological situations. And even with all these rare qualities, it is very difficult to attain certitude in the problem's solution. There must be always wide gaps and interspaces where one can only measure possibilities, draw certain inferences, note half-seen indications, and where, after all, one can but choose the least unlikely clue among many."[1] Sir Alfred Lyall's warning was never more needed than when one sets out to explain the origin of caste in India; the most careful inquirer will probably never attain certitude in the solution of this problem, and all that seems possible is "to choose the least unlikely clue" by reference to probabilities. The task is rendered doubly difficult because we have no positive record to guide us; all that can be said is that from the internal evidence of the Rig-Veda there was a time when the institution was unknown to the Aryan invaders, and that the only reference in the collection is the famous passage in the tenth book, which is admittedly of much later date, and which evidently shows caste as already established and grown to maturity. Unfortunately, too, the possibility that it was of non-Aryan origin cannot be explored by reference to literature, because we do not now possess it, if, indeed, it ever existed in conditions which must have been primitive, when men thought more of doing things than of writing about them. And this absence of literature has perhaps led to a rather one-sided investigation; scholars have been over-prone to assume that, because it is only in Aryan records that we find mention of caste, because it became a useful weapon in Aryan hands,

[1] Lyall: *Asiatic Studies*, vol. ii, p. 286.

## HINDU CUSTOMS AND THEIR ORIGINS

particularly to the Brahmans, and because of the Sanskrit word *varna* which was used to denote it, the whole institution must have been Aryan in origin.

The approach to the question has undoubtedly been modified, if not completely changed, since it was established that the Dravidians, like all other conquerors, entered India from the North-West, and not, as had been previously supposed, from the South. This new theory opened up possibilities, for it suggested that the Dravidians, instead of merely colonizing the South and subduing or repressing the aboriginal inhabitants there, had been the true predecessors of the Aryans in Northern India also, and, what is perhaps even more important, it also suggests that the Aryans came in contact, not with the aborigines, who, secure in their jungles and in their mountain fastnesses, had been left severely alone, but with the Dravidians, whose civilization was little, if at all, inferior to their own. The general situation was, in fact, with reservations, not unlike that of the waves of invasion which swept over Britain, so that the Normans when they arrived had to contend, not with the ancient Britons, but with the much more formidable Saxons.

It is clear that so long as it appeared that the Aryans had to contend with a vastly inferior civilization, if it could be called civilization at all, there was good ground for preserving the purity of the race and even for reserving the more attractive trades and professions to the ruling people. The Dravidians, it was assumed, were content to remain in the South, while the Aryans were deterred not only by the business of mastering the country but also by the formidable obstacles in the shape of mountains, forests, and rivers, which had to be overcome before any approach could be made to the Peninsula. If, however, it be granted that the Dravidians entered India from the North-West and spread over the country just as the later Aryans did, the problem becomes at once more complicated, and the arguments must be modified. The impulse to preserve the purity of the stock against admixture would be much weaker if the conquered race was comparable to that of the conquerors, the possibility of achieving the desired end would be more remote, and the desire to keep to themselves all the more lucrative and better esteemed trades and professions would be far more difficult of attainment.

Three assumptions are commonly made, unconsciously, perhaps, for it is very difficult to rid oneself entirely of preconceived opinions, but none the less to be avoided if one approaches the problem dispassionately. Relying largely on the word *varna*, and also to references in Sanskrit writings to the "black" Dasyus, the demons who are contrasted with the fair Aryans, scholars argue that caste was invented to preserve the purity of the race, which was based upon its most obvious manifestation, and this is on the whole the most generally accepted theory. Thus an American writer, Mr. Lothrop Stoddard, whose views on such matters may not be scientific but at least reflect what is popularly taken for granted, writes dogmatically:

> Fearing to be swallowed up in the dark Dravidian ocean, the fair Aryans tried to preserve their political mastery and racial purity by the institution of caste, which has ever since remained the foundation of Indian social life. Caste was originally a colour line.[1]

And, again, Mr. O'Malley, of the Indian Civil Service, says:

> Anxious to preserve their racial purity, their culture, and their standards of living, the Aryans relegated to a lower status the children of mixed marriages and those who were engaged in base pursuits, and the latter adopted similar lines of demarcation among themselves. There were thus divisions based primarily on race and partly on occupation.[2]

Nearly everybody who writes on this subject, whether with or without authority, whether French, English, or German, has adopted this view almost as if it were axiomatic. But, in the first place, it does not necessarily follow that because the Sanskrit word for caste is *varna* the Aryans intended to draw a strict colour line between themselves and their predecessors. If the Dravidians came into India through the North-West Frontier (where they have left

---

[1] Lothrop Stoddard: *Clashing Tides of Colour*, p. 284.
[2] O'Malley: *India's Social Heritage*, p. 10.

traces in the inconvenient Brahui tribe) they may be presumed to have come from that part of the Northern Hemisphere where colours are light. No one who holds this theory of the Dravidian invasion can suppose that they were a Southern race who somehow found their way into the Persian Gulf, and so advanced into India by way of Persia and Afghanistan. But the temperate zone ends somewhere about 40° and the greater part of India is classed as tropical or sub-tropical. Practically all the really dark-skinned population is to be found between the latitude of 20° and the equator. What effect long residence in a foreign country—residence of perhaps one thousand years or more—may have had upon the colour, and how far interbreeding may have affected it, is probably impossible of proof. It is quite certain that, at a time when caste restrictions were unknown, or were at least undeveloped, there was a very considerable intermixture of blood, which may well have produced a race as dark relatively to the original Dravidian as the present Anglo-Indian is to the pure Anglo-Saxon. It is, therefore, not impossible that the Aryans coming in contact with a race which was darker than themselves, and also with aborigines who were very dark, classed the two as "black men" in the same loose way that English people to-day will talk of Indians as black men, though the great majority are only a few shades darker than they are. For some reason, based perhaps on civilization or culture, a fairer race always tends to hold a darker in some contempt, and it is noticeable that in India itself even to-day a fair skin is considered desirable. A conquering race, moreover, will always tend to despise the conquered, especially in early times when military prowess transcended any ideas of ethical superiority. This would of itself have been sufficient to preserve the purity of race as a whole, without the aid of rigid caste rules, just as it has largely served the English in India; in both cases there was the inevitable spill-over which accompanies the impact of one race upon another.

There is, however, so far nothing impossible in the theory of race purity, nor even improbable, if we accept the fact

## CASTE—THE RACIAL PURITY THEORY

that nowhere else in the world, except among savage tribes and then only in certain aspects, has a social barrier been set up so closely guarded as caste has been, and no social barrier approximating to it has ever survived intact for some thirty centuries, to put it no further back. But what I am now concerned to show is that the theory of race-purity is not a necessary deduction from the Aryan word *varna*. For if, as suggested, the Dravidians were themselves lighter-coloured than the aborigines, it may well be that they invented caste for the very same purpose of race-purity, all the more because there is reason to suppose that their civilization was relatively to that of the aborigines on a much higher plane than was the Aryan relatively to their own. Nothing would be more natural than that the conquerors, finding an institution ready-made and based on colour, should have adopted it, and used it for their own purposes, even accepting the colour signification by which it was known. Or, again, caste may have started in quite a different way, and later have become incorporated into the Aryan system as a colour bar, and so acquired the name *varna*. If that were so, the theory that the Aryans invented it would fall to the ground, though it would still be possible to argue that it was an Aryan institution, inasmuch as it was developed by the Aryans to the extent of losing its original character. A further objection, which is more difficult to answer, is that on the hypothesis that the three higher or twice-born castes were Aryan while the conquered race were all relegated to the Sudra category, there could have been no question of the purity of race as between the Aryan castes. Why should not an Aryan Kshatriya not have inter-married (to say nothing of inter-dining) with an Aryan Brahman? Why should a Vaisya not marry a Kshatriya? What is there to show that these prohibitions were more rigid as between the three higher castes on the one hand and the Sudras on the other than as between each other? It is clearly insufficient to reply that caste was not so rigid in the early days; if that were a satisfying answer, what becomes of race-purity? It is, I believe, of universal experience that when an institution is designed for a particular purpose, rigidity tends rather to relax than to increase. This is especially the case when two races live in close contact with one another; artificial religious sanctions become weakened by the pressure of human relations, and it requires all the force of religious orthodoxy to prevent backsliding. If, therefore, the institution were based upon race as differentiated by colour, we might reasonably expect that it would become less rather than more rigid, until, with the disappearance of the motive, it disappeared altogether. Not only did it become more rigid, but in essentials it is as strong as ever.

Next, we must not too hastily assume that the Aryan civilization was superior to that which they found established. Professor Berriedale Keith no doubt says:

> Of the stage of civilization attained by the aborigines we know little or nothing. They had, it is certain, large herds of cattle, and they could when attacked take refuge in fortifications called in the Rig-Veda by the name of "pur," which later denotes "town," but which may well have then meant no more than an earthwork strengthened by a palisade or possibly occasionally by stone. Stockades of this kind are often made by primitive peoples, and are so easily constructed that we can understand the repeated references in the Rig-Veda to the large numbers of such fortifications which were captured and destroyed by the Aryan hosts.[1]

By using the word "aborigines" Professor Keith seems to exclude the possibility of an intervening stratum, which may be called non-Aryan, between the Aryans and the true aborigines such as still exist in the jungles and the wilder parts of India. The suggestion that the so-called towns may have been no more than "earthworks strengthened by a palisade" really begs the question; if we take our stand upon the theory that the Aryan civilization was definitely superior, it is no doubt convenient to believe that their enemies were incapable of building towns or any works in advance of mud walls with facings of wood or stone. But that is to put the cart before the horse. It is only on the assumption that the civilization was markedly inferior

[1] *Cambridge History of India*, vol. i, p. 86.

that the guess is permissible that these towns meant only flimsy villages. On the other hand, the excavations at Mohenjo-daro and Harappa have shown that some ten or twelve centuries before the time of the Aryan invasions or irruptions there was in the Indus valley a people perfectly capable of building substantial houses and therefore walls and ramparts which would ordinarily be adequate for the defence of a city. It is true that up to date there are few if any signs of destruction by an enemy such as have been found in Mesopotamia, but that of itself does not preclude the supposition that the walls may have been there. Indeed, we are told that after the examination of the two sites in Sind, "but in the narrow corridor between the Indus and the Baluchistan border," Mr. Majumdar has discovered "on rocky ground two large settlements each protected by massive stone fortifications. These two sites have not yet been thoroughly examined, but it would seem that one at least was guarded by a double wall built of rough boulders; at the other settlement the wall was built of roughly dressed blocks of stone averaging 2 by 1 feet in size."[1] We must remember that even on these sites in Sind there is still a great deal of work to be done, and we should certainly not be justified in assuming that what was known in Sind was quite unknown in districts further east. The idea that the fortifications "may then have well meant no more than an earthwork strengthened by a palisade, or possibly occasionally by stone," seems to be an unfounded surmise which strikes one as in the nature of *a posteriori* reasoning. The finding of these walls or double walls, built long before the Aryans arrived, certainly suggests that we must revise our views about the military capacity of these pre-Aryan tribes. No doubt it can be argued that this civilization passed away completely and that the "aborigines" had, as it were, to start again. That might well be true as regards culture and the arts; it is hardly likely to be equally true of so elementary a subject as self-defence. An attacking mobile army might have forgotten the art of fortification; it is far less probable that a settled community would have done so, and we can

[1] Mackay: *The Indus Civilization*, p. 62.

but argue on probability. So far as the large herds of cattle are concerned, they would show that the "aborigines," or, more accurately, the predecessors of the Aryans, were well advanced in the pastoral stage, and that from the obviously nomadic character of the Aryans and from the frequent references in the Rig-Veda to cattle in the sense of wealth is about all that can be said for the Aryans themselves.

This brings us naturally to the third of the assumptions against which we must guard. The Aryans did not—at any rate, there is no evidence that they did—pour into India in a mighty flood like that of Genghis Khan or Timur. On the contrary, there is general agreement that they occupied only the North-West corner of India at first, where they settled down and took time to establish themselves. For it is one of the frontier problems of to-day that the tribes, unable to obtain more than a scanty subsistence from forbidding Nature, are forced to supplement their resources by raiding, and it is the boast of the British Government that they have turned the arid and dusty plains of the Punjab into smiling grain-fields. It would have been impossible in those early days for great hordes to have moved with their women and their flocks and herds over such inhospitable country at the rate which was determined by the methods of transport available. At what stage, then, did this new idea dawn upon them of establishing caste to preserve the racial purity of the stock? Evidently not at the time of the first nine books of the Rig-Veda, which contain no reference to it. We have no ground for thinking, as some people seem to do, at any rate by implication, that caste was the invention of some brilliant brain, which caught the imagination of the brethren and came into being in an early though basic stage within the course of a few years, or that it was imposed upon the community by a fiat of ecclesiastical authority, like a Papal Bull or the Laws of Moses. M. Senart, it would seem rightly, opposes any such idea. He considers that the germ of the caste system is to be found in the constitution of the Aryan family, that it grew up insensibly during many generations, and was influenced, though only partially and in a secondary sense, by the magical and other

## CASTE—THE RACIAL PURITY THEORY

existing customs. It is true that on this hypothesis the gradual evolution of the institution depends upon the gradual evolution of the family system, for M. Senart accepts the general opinion that the Aryan civilization was superior and also that the origin of caste was essentially Aryan. "Les Aryens s'avancent," he says, "dans leur nouveau domaine. Ils se heurtent à une race de couleur foncée, inférieure en culture qu'ils refoulent." He seems to relegate all the rest of India—the non-Aryan races—to the category of "autocthones" or "aborigènes," and while admitting that the customs of the aborigines have had some influence, he rejects with scorn the notion that that influence could have been great, much less fundamental.

Si l'on songe uniquement ou même principalement à l'organisation des tribus aborigènes de l'Inde, si l'on admet qu'elle ait réagi avec une force décisive sur la constitution générale du monde hindou qu'une classe ambitieuse de prêtres s'en soit emparée, en ait fait une arme de combat, on retourne le courant probable de l'histoire, on prête à des mobiles trop minces une puissance disproportionée. Tout indique que dans la marche de la civilisation indienne l'action determinante appartient aux éléments âryens; les éléments aborigènes n'ont exercé qu'une action modificatrice, partielle et secondaire.[1]

This quotation has been given in full, because it is unfair and unscientific to drag a particular passage out of its context, just because it happens to suit a theory. It will be seen that M. Senart still clings to the Aryan tradition, though on grounds differing from those usually adopted, and that he definitely rejects the idea that the germ of caste can be found in non-Aryan customs which, owing to the assumption of a superior civilization, "could not have had more than a secondary influence." His whole argument, indeed, rests upon that assumption, for if we grant an inferior culture, then the theory that the inferior had a decisive influence over the superior may well be said to be contrary to the teachings of history. Quite apart, however, from this reasoning, it does seem to conform with probability

[1] Senart: *Les Castes dans l'Inde*, p. 196.

that the caste system was gradually evolved from some primitive custom or organization, Aryan or other, and did not spring into being either at a single bound or over a relatively short period of time. That is not the way in which customs destined to last for centuries do arise. But if the system was the final expression of a custom which had been embryonically in existence for a long time—perhaps even for centuries—what, again, becomes of the theory of racial purity? As long as the Aryans were settled in the Punjab and were making their slow and painful way towards the East, there was bound to be miscegenation which, in the absence of a religious tabu, would only be checked by the reluctance of a successful invader to inter-breed with those whom he regarded as his inferiors. This has, of course, happened wherever the white race has come in contact with or has overcome the coloured; there is a definite colour bar in South Africa and in America as well as in India, though even then it may be doubted whether the force of public opinion or of instinct has had quite the same rigid effect as the caste system. Yet in the cases of Africa and America there was the extra incentive, not only that the two races were at the opposite poles of colour, but that they were also at the opposite poles of civilization, and that the white man was marked out as the master, the coloured man as the servant. The Aryan could not have differed in colour to the same extent; it is quite unlikely that he differed so markedly in civilization, and there is nothing to show that, for a very long time at any rate, he was obviously the master reducing the so-called aborigines to slavery and relegating them to the menial position. Had this been the intention, there would surely have been two castes as there are in South Africa, the Aryan and the non-Aryan. The Aryans would then have been free to inter-marry and inter-dine among themselves, being restricted from mixing the blood by religious sanction as well as by instinctive repugnance. There can be no good reason for forbidding an Aryan to marry an Aryan—still less to dine with him—on the ground of racial purity. It is true that later on these main castes might have been subdivided, just as, while an Englishman

## CASTE—THE RACIAL PURITY THEORY

might regard with abhorrence a union with a negress, he would think it beneath his dignity and altogether inconvenient to marry a woman of a lower class of society; that might be a *mésalliance* but it would not be tabu. It may, of course, be argued that that is exactly what the Aryans did; they reserved the first three (or twice-born) castes to themselves and relegated the "aborigines" to the fourth caste, the Sudras. In other words they divided themselves according to class and fenced off the rest according to race. That is hardly the sort of classification we should expect of a primitive tribe who were clearly not far removed from the pastoral stage. We need not expect anything scientific, but surely even a primitive people, bent on preserving the purity of the stock, would not naturally mix up two separate principles in this curious way. Moreover, it does not account for the existence of the no-caste men. For if racial purity was their object and they were willing to admit their late foes, the non-Aryans, into a lowly place within the system, if at the same time they held them all in supreme contempt, they would have relegated the whole lot to the fourth caste, leaving them to arrange class distinctions among themselves. So long as they attained their supposed object there was no need to trouble themselves with further subdivisions of the despised aborigines.

These three assumptions, then, do not seem to be justified by the evidence, which is based upon the Aryan literature. But the literature of every people tends to be coloured by self-glorification. The Jewish writings with their contempt for the heathen, the Greek with their classification of Greeks and barbarians, the English, the French, the German—all tend to exalt themselves and their civilization at the expense of their foes. We require—and usually we get—other evidence in order to check this partiality; and in these more critical days we are able to see even comparatively ancient peoples in truer perspective. The picture of a host of fair-skinned warriors sweeping across the plains of India, subduing the black enemies as they went, and holding themselves aloof by the most rigid of religious sanctions ever known from a civilization, if such it may be called, which they not only despised but which was markedly inferior to their own, is one which might pass as a description of the clash of black and white in South Africa, but is obviously distorted when we are speaking of the Aryans and their predecessors. Even if the case rested upon these assumptions alone, there would be good ground for accepting the theory with caution, if not with hesitation, but there are objections even more weighty.

# iii

## Caste—The Occupational Theory

IT is common knowledge that the caste system, as we know it to-day, flourishes in the Dravidian South better than in the Aryan North. It is in the South that Brahman ascendancy is at its highest. It is in the South that the treatment of the "no-castes" is most oppressive, and it is in exactly that part which was sheltered from Aryan and other invasions by the Western Ghats and the Arabian Sea that caste reaches its highest development. Upon the orthodox Hindu theory that caste is not based upon ethnic separateness but is "the result of a divine grouping according to actions and tendencies,"[1] one would naturally expect the more highly Aryanized North to be its proper home; the European idea that the North was more subject to invasion and so to disintegrating influences is liable to be challenged by the argument that the Hindu religion has remained intact through all the storm of successive invasions, and that persecution only tended to draw tighter the bonds of a system which was so ardently cherished. It is clear that the Dravidian South had not the same grounds for a desire to preserve racial purity; in any case it would have been far too late, for admittedly caste was not invented or did not come into being until some considerable period after the Aryan invasion, and whatever mixture of blood had taken place in the South, it must have been at a time long before this. The mischief had, therefore, been done. We can only conclude upon this hypothesis that the people of the South—the non-Aryan races—only adopted the system in order to copy their betters, or to be in the fashion; in doing so they lost sight of the main object—the purity of race—and confined themselves to class distinctions in which they eventually surpassed their prototype. Such explanations as these are clearly unsatisfying, and, combined with the other objections to the

[1] Ramaswami Sastri: *Hindu Culture*, p. 159.

theory of race purity, have led to the alternative theory that the origin of caste must be found in occupation. The theory may be thus stated. In early, and indeed in all, civilizations there is a tendency for occupations to become hereditary, and as each art slowly became the exclusive occupation of certain artisans, they jealously guarded the secrets of the trade, as is occasionally done in India to this day. And since sexual maturity comes earlier in a tropical climate, boys and girls are mated at a time when they themselves cannot be trusted to choose. But since the selection falls upon the parents, they would naturally choose one of their own craft. Magic and religious ceremonies assist to build up the exclusive caste, so that marriage outside that caste becomes one of the things that are not done. The Aryan invasion, therefore, was not the cause of caste, but modified it in two ways: (1) by strengthening the tendency for castes to be graded in a fairly definite scale of social precedence; (2) the prohibition of inter-dining follows the prohibition of marriage, since feasts are the accompaniments of the three great stages of human life, and the ordinary private entertainments of the West are by no means so common in India. The outcaste class arose as a natural result of the division of labour, and, being extended to various forms of manual labour, justified itself by unclean habits.

It is, of course, true that caste has tended to develop on the lines of occupation, although in later times these lines have become blurred. As the struggle for existence became keener, as opportunities for education became more accessible, and as the desire to rise in the social scale became more insistent, a tendency arose to break away from the occupational tradition; Brahmans took up the law, goldsmiths and others entered Government service; Sudras were no longer confined to agriculture. Nor was this change confined to the time when the more liberal English ideas had opened up new opportunities and when Western conceptions had invented new sources of livelihood. The Maratha Peshwas were Brahmans, and it was a Sudra who commanded the forlorn hope covering Sivaji's escape in one of the most dramatic episodes in Maratha, if not in

## CASTE—THE OCCUPATIONAL THEORY

Indian, history. But, of course, this later deviation does not of itself prove that caste was not originally founded in occupation. On the other hand, there are many objections to the theory, whose stoutest supporter is Nesfield. The fact that castes do tend to split up on occupational lines is no safe guide, because institutions often change their character; that which was once secondary and subordinate becomes by the atrophy of the primary causes principal and dominant.

The occupational theory, taken by itself and regarded as an explanation of origins, assumes that caste arose only after the society had become highly developed, as is shown by the division of labour into various skilled—some of them highly skilled—crafts. That, however, is an objection which can be explained away, for it may plausibly be said that even primitive tribes become subdivided upon a more or less crude division by trades and crafts, and that as skill developed caste developed with it. The earliest division may still have been by trades, though these may have been primitive and few in number. A more serious objection is that it lays too little stress upon the religious sanction which is so marked a feature of caste, not only as we know it, but also in the sacred writings of the Hindus. Dr. Slater, in his work *The Dravidian Element in Indian Culture*, has seen this difficulty and has tried to explain it, but his explanation is not convincing. There have been other peoples among whom the division of labour was precisely similar; crafts are almost equally hereditary and secrets are jealously guarded; but they have not introduced caste except in a modified and quite indefinite form. Dr. Slater therefore suggests that the inertia of the tropics prevents a man from seeking more than one occupation: a goldsmith's son becomes a goldsmith, a labourer's son a labourer, because it never occurs to him to seek to be anything else, and he has neither the energy nor the enterprise to strike out a new line. That does not carry us very far. Even in individualistic countries like our own, environment and experience combine to urge the son to follow the father; men will tell you with pride of a naval or military tradition in the family, a parson's son will enter the Church, miners have almost a close preserve of mining, and seafaring men will follow one another to the trades of the sea. No doubt many sons, owing to the individualistic influence, will break away from the tradition, and in countries where the unit is the family such a tradition would be stronger, but not to the point of a stern and unyielding religious sanction. So it is further argued that the precocious sexual maturity makes it imperative that marriage should be arranged by the parents, and the parents will naturally choose brides from the families of men who follow the same craft. They would do this not only because it is natural, but because they want to preserve the secrets of the craft. Now it is not apparent why this conduct should be natural. The argument is on general lines. What is natural is common to human nature always and everywhere. It is true that because of environment such marriages do very often take place. The father's friends may very well be those of his own profession, and so the parson's daughter meeting mainly parsons will very likely marry a curate. The only deduction to be made is that men can only mate with the girls they meet in any society where choice is free, and since the girls often belong to a family of their own profession they tend to establish a tradition. Nor does the argument from trade secrets stand on any firmer ground. For the secrets of the trade are not disclosed to females, and nothing is put in jeopardy by union with a woman of another guild; and the choice of brides is strictly circumscribed even now when tradition has largely broken down. We are thus no nearer an explanation of the rigid rule of endogamy and exogamy by which caste is bound. And yet it is the essence of the argument, for it is contended that inter-dining follows naturally upon it. Why should it? If, for the sake of argument, we allow that in a highly sublimated form of the nervous desire to keep trade secrets intact men will only be invited to the house who can be trusted not to reveal them, we are still at a loss to explain why the cooks who prepare the food and the servants who draw the water must not fall below a certain grade of caste, nor why you must not accept a drink of water from a man of lower caste, even on a casual occasion when perhaps your need is great.

## CASTE—THE OCCUPATIONAL THEORY

I once had occasion to call on an Indian gentleman of high education, an intimate friend and a colleague, to ask his advice on a certain matter. I was told he was at breakfast. "Oh, very well, then; will you take a message to him?" "I cannot do that," said the secretary. Thinking that he did not wish to be disturbed by his secretary, I suggested that an attendant might take in the note. But it appeared that no one could enter the room except, perhaps, the Brahman cook. How can such an episode be explained by the theory of occupation or trade secrets?

Seeing this difficulty, Nesfield suggests that caste began long after the Aryan invaders had been absorbed in the mass of the native people and all racial distinctions had disappeared. Different occupations grouped together men from different tribes into guild castes, which then borrowed the principles of endogamy and exogamy and the prohibition of commensality from the customs of the old tribes, and thereby solidified themselves into isolated units. This seems to be nothing more than a guess. How came the aboriginal people to have these customs? Why did the Aryans in inventing caste upon occupational lines introduce the customs of the despised aborigines? The objections just stated to the occupational theory remain in full force, and the argument to meet them is merely a conjecture, founded upon an assumption which has no basis in reason. As Senart says, "To grant to community of trade a place among the motive forces active in shaping the destiny of the caste is a very different matter from claiming it to be the all-sufficient origin of the system," and to close the gaps by suggesting that the Aryans dragged in quite unnecessary customs relating to marriage and eating is not a method which fulfils the canons of probability.

While Dr. Slater, laying the greater stress on the economic aspect of the problem and so ascribing the larger share in the origin of caste, yet holds that race was not without its influence, Professor Dutt of Bengal takes the view that "the *varna* division of society was mainly Aryan in character, though accentuated by the peculiar conditions of the early Aryan conquerors in India, and that the formation of the

Jati castes, many of which were tribal in origin, together with some of the practices like untouchability, infant marriage, etc., was largely due to aboriginal influences."[1] He has come down decisively upon the side of racial purity: "Thus we see that the development of inter-caste marriage restrictions was principally due to the racial difference between the white conquerors and the black natives, and the desire of the former to preserve their purity of blood."[2] The arguments by which he supports this thesis, regarded as an explanation of origin, are not entirely convincing. Laying the usual stress upon the word *varna* and the references in Vedic literature to the "black" foes, he argues that as there was less difference of colour between Aryans and non-Aryans in Europe, caste did not come into existence; it owes its birth, largely at least, to the more violent contrast of white and black, or, to be more accurate, of fair and dark in India. The order of the main castes took shape according to the measure of intermixture with non-Aryan blood; the Brahmans, keeping themselves entirely aloof, remained white, the Kshatriyas became red, the Vaisyas yellowish "like the mulattoes of America," and the Sudras black, as described in the Mahabharata. So it went on. At first the three higher castes inter-married freely enough, but as the Kshatriyas and Vaisyas became more and more polluted with non-Aryan blood the marriage of a Brahman with either of them was frowned upon, and the greater the pollution the more the abhorrence, so that while the son of a Brahman by a Kshatriya woman was still held to be a Brahman, the son by a Vaisya woman was a Vaisya. The source of these statements is the Anushushana Parva of the Mahabharata, but "negative evidence in India," according to Washburn Hopkins, "makes it improbable that any epic existed earlier than the fourth century B.C."[3] The date of the Rig-Veda is more or less guesswork, but there is general agreement that it is many centuries before that. The argument, therefore, does not prove that the basic origin of caste was racial purity, but

---

[1] Dutt: *Origin and Growth of Caste in India*, p. 31.   [2] Ibid., p. 23.
[3] *Cambridge History of India*, vol. i, p. 258.

## CASTE—THE OCCUPATIONAL THEORY

only that by the age of the Mahabharata the castes had settled down into a definite order of precedence in which admixture of blood may or may not have had a predominating influence. In other words, it is not incompatible with a non-Aryan origin, but shows that in the course of the centuries it was modified to suit Aryan ideas. Professor Dutt, however, adds to the two popular theories of race purity and occupation a third ingredient. The non-Aryan tribes had certain customs of totemistic exogamy and tribal endogamy, and "these tribal and cultural divisions of society could not be shaken off even after their conquest by the Aryans, and under the changed circumstances they became hardened into caste divisions." Hence it is that the caste rules are more rigidly observed in the Dravidian South than in the Aryan North; and the "practices of the conquered aborigines contributed as much to the development of caste as the racial or class prejudices of the Aryan conquerors." The conclusion is, therefore, that caste originated with the Aryans as a method of preserving race purity, but that it was then influenced by the division of labour and by the tribal differences of the non-Aryans which survived the spread of a common Aryan culture, the product being the economico-socio-religious institution which we know to-day.

There is much to be said for this theory of the rise and development of caste. If we assume the Aryan origin and compare the picture thus conjured up with what we know of caste in later centuries and with what we know certainly to-day, it would seem that only in some such way can we account for occupational divisions, and especially for its predominance in Dravidian India. But the two main features of caste to-day are the prohibition of inter-marriage and the prohibition of inter-dining, which latter must be extended to include the taking of food handled by a low-caste man and the casual acceptance of water from an inferior caste. We know that even where untouchability has not gone to the lengths it has reached in the Madras Province and especially in Malabar, the rural villages, still barely touched by European ideas, regard the untouchables with aversion, refuse to allow them to enter temples, or attend caste schools, or to draw water from caste wells, even when ordinary humanity suggests the relaxation of such rigid rules. A short time ago I had occasion to visit a village in Gujerat where there was an outbreak of cholera. On the outskirts of the village was an encampment of low caste but not untouchable folk. Their huts, such as they were, had been burnt down accidentally. That day there was an incessant downpour of tropical rain, and half-naked men, quite naked children, and very lightly clad women were huddled, drenched through and through, in such meagre shelter as the fire had left. I believe they had been allowed to shelter at first in outhouses and verandahs in the village, but the inconvenience was too great, and they were doing the best they could in their own quarters.

Now, as I have already pointed out, inter-marriage may well be prohibited on grounds of race-purity, and inter-dining might conceivably, though not very probably, have been interdicted as too dangerously leading to such marriages; but what is to be said of the other prohibitions? How are we to account for prohibition by touch, or of entering the house, or of sitting down to table on casual occasions? Mr. Dutt seems to follow M. Senart's contention that aboriginal customs can only have had a partial and secondary effect, though we concede that he allows them more weight. But apart from the occupational divisions, which are by no means universal, these are the main characteristics of caste as we know it to-day. Racial purity, in the sense that a given family can trace unbroken descent through pure Aryan blood, has long ago disappeared; it has lost all practical effect. A man may call himself an Aryan, and it may flatter his pride to do so, just as in England it may flatter the pride of certain families to boast of their Norman descent; but no one cares to inquire if the claim be true, because on the whole it does not matter. Occupations, as has been pointed out, cut right across the line of caste. But the marriage and the feeding restrictions remain as strong as ever, at any rate amongst the rural population, though as regards the latter European influence has induced some laxity among the educated. And these have obviously very practical results. We arrive at the conclusion that it is the "secondary and partial" ingredients which now dominate the system, and though it is not unknown that secondary characteristics may remain when the primary have disappeared, yet when we are dealing with an institution which has more than any other governed and moulded the whole life of a people or peoples it is not the probable result which we should expect to find.

## iv

## Caste—the Aboriginal Theory

IN dealing with primitive peoples and their customs we are on much safer ground if we look to religion rather than to economics or to a rationalism much more suited to a later age as the basic origin of such an institution as caste, which is no doubt an integral part of the social structure but which is practically regarded as a religious tenet. I must repeat that the stages of early Indian civilization were not one but two.[1] It was not a question of Aryans, whether they came in successive waves of invasion or not, conquering a more or less heterogeneous population of dark-skinned Danyas, Asuras, or Dasyus, but of an Aryan civilization imposed upon or blended with a Dravidian civilization which had ousted or at least driven underground the aboriginal cults, though these, too, had not been without their influence. We are, of course, not to imagine one civilization piled on top of another in distinct layers, but the gradual modification of the later by the earlier, as the Israelitish cults were influenced by those which they found in Canaan and neighbouring countries.

Now it is generally admitted that the Dravidians were and still are well skilled in magic. Numerous first-hand instances could be given of the belief in charms and amulets, of the efficacy of mantras, of devices for keeping off evil spirits or for curing snake-bite. No one ought to overlook the fact that the cult of the village deity, so marked a feature of the South, as Bishop Whitehead has shown us, is altogether alien from the Aryan ideas reflected by the Rig-Veda, and that the superstitions which are so closely allied to magic or quasi-magic and play so large a part in village worship are in all probability a survival of very ancient customs, either Dravidian or pre-Dravidian or a

[1] Possibly more; for the purpose of the argument it is enough to employ the general terms.

## CASTE—THE ABORIGINAL THEORY

blend of the two. But magic in primitive tribes is often found in conjunction with totemism, and a people so addicted to charms and incantations may well have adopted the principle of the totem. We may remark in passing (for it will be necessary to revert to the subject) that the Atharva Veda, admittedly later than the other three and, in the words of Professor Berriedale Keith, "long not recognized as fully entitled to claim rank as a Veda proper," is "a curious repertory of most mingled matter, for the most part spells of every kind, but containing also theosophical hymns of considerable importance."[1]

Now the aborigines, who must be distinguished from the Dravidians, and who are represented to-day by jungle tribes, have never advanced far on the road of civilization, and they still have totems.[2] There is, therefore, at least *a priori* reason for supposing that they were originally totemistic. The totem has been defined to be "the object, generally of a natural species, animal or vegetable, but occasionally rain, cloud, star, wind, which gives its name to a kindred actual or supposed."[3] Your totem may be the crow or the snake or the frog; it does not seem to matter much what. But whatever it is, it is held in some kind of reverence, which may or may not amount to a prohibition against killing that particular species, for the custom seems to vary a great deal. The degrees of religious regard for the revered object increase in proportion as it is taken to contain the spirit of an ancestor or to be the embodiment of a god, and socially the totem as found in Australia has a very distinct influence on marriage customs, and particularly on the practices and limitations of endogamy and exogamy.

Nor is the custom of totemism and exogamy confined to the primitive jungle folk, "vagrant savages with no house over their heads and little or no clothing on their backs." On the contrary, it is widespread throughout the peninsula of India, and even among people where it might least have been expected, people who are by no means to be classed

[1] *Cambridge History of India*, vol. i, p. 115.
[2] O'Malley: *India's Social Heritage*, p. 86.
[3] Article, *Encyclopaedia Britannica*, "Totemism," by Andrew Lang.

with the jungle tribes and who are indistinguishable in ordinary intercourse from the general population. The Komatis, who are described as "the great trading caste of the Madras Presidency," but more particularly of the Telugu-speaking part of it, and are well known both as traders and as money-lenders, the Bants, an important caste in South Canara on the West Coast, and the Kapus or Reddis, "the largest caste in the Madras Presidency, the great caste of cultivators, farmers, and squireens in the Telugu country . . . and next to the Brahmans the leaders of Hindu society," are all declared to practise forms of totemism and, in common with the rest of Hindu India, exogamy.[1] All this seems to show that the original practices have survived through all the vicissitudes of Hinduism, and that they are to be found even among castes which are professedly Hindu, though they are non-Aryan. It suggests, though it does not prove, that in such cases as these caste arose quite independently of any ideas of racial purity or even of occupation.

A further development of the idea is found in Samoa, where there are customs of burying and lamenting dead animals which are regarded with reverence by this or that family or clan, and the animals which once were sacred on their own account are now regarded as the vehicles of the gods belonging to the "family" or "clan." There is a curious resemblance here to Indian custom or religious observance. There is no doubt that animals play a considerable part in the ancient Indian mythology, both as vehicles for the gods and also as incarnations of the deity. Thus Garuda is the vehicle of Vishnu, who is also guarded by the cobra, Sesha; Siva rides upon the bull Nandi, Hanuman is the monkey, Ganesha the elephant, while Vishnu has appeared as a tortoise, a fish, and a boar, even if we exclude the *avatar* of Narasimham, the Man-Lion. These are evident traces of totem worship; the analogy with Samoan custom is obvious. The inference is further strengthened by the known inviolability of the cobra, the bull, and the monkey, to which may be added the peacock in some parts but not in all. The

---
[1] Frazer: *Totemism and Exogamy*, vol. ii, chap. 10.

sacredness of the kite is not quite so obvious, though it must be remembered that Garuda is the kite—it may be, too, that the kite, soaring aloft on extended and steady pinions in the heavens, seldom comes into direct contact with human beings, and, hanging as it were suspended in the heavens, suggests something of the supernatural. *A propos* of this sanctity of the kite, I may mention a curious custom which I personally saw in a village near Chingleput, not far from Madras City. A Brahman lays out food for the birds, and every day two—exactly two and no more—come from nowhere and take it. You strain your eyes into the brilliant sky and for a long time see nothing. Then at last two specks appear, coming nearer and nearer until they take shape as the birds. As this custom is said to have been in existence for generations, it seems that there is a kind of freemasonry among the kites, for it cannot be the same two who have come for a century or more to take the offering. We may perhaps note in passing the association in Greek mythology of Zeus with the bull, Hera with the peacock, and Athene with the owl. This proves nothing, but it is significant, and it suggests that the custom was widespread.

We are now to consider whether there is any connection between the sacred character of these animals and totem worship, or something akin to it, in the conditions of ancient India. Dr. Oldham,[1] who has been at great pains to discuss serpent worship in India and to establish its connection with the worship of the sun, remarks:

"Who was Garuda? We find from the Mahabharata that the Garudas inhabited one of the provinces of Patala. . . . A list of forty-eight Garuda chiefs is given, and it is said that only those are mentioned who have won distinction by might, fame, or achievement."

And he thus answers his own question:

"Garuda or the eagle was therefore the totem of one of the Solar tribes of Patala. . . . Garuda is described as tearing the bodies of the Yakshas and devouring the Nishadas; also as destroying the elephant and tortoise, which represent Solar tribes." Krishna, he points out, is distinguished by

[1] Oldham: *The Sun and the Serpent.*

the auspicious sign Srivatsa, which is also the sign of the Garudas, and therefore the adoption of Garuda as the *vahanam* (or vehicle) of Krishna, and as his ensign in battle, is only a figurative way of saying that Krishna led into battle a tribe of warriors whose totem was the eagle or kite. Similarly, it may be argued that the army of monkeys which Rama led to Ceylon and whose leader, Hanuman, was the monkey, or, again, the squirrels who built the bridge across the Gulf of Manaar, represent tribes whose totem was respectively the monkey or the squirrel. All that we know of totem worship suggests that this interpretation is correct. Most of these ancient legends, which seem to us to be fairy tales, have a foundation in fact if we can but discover the secret, and nothing is more likely than that the tribe should be identified with its banner or that the banner should represent the totem.

"In Australia the aboriginal tribes are divided into sections or phratries, which again are subdivided into totem clans. In some parts it appears that the phratries have no names, the original plan having been superseded by the greater importance of the totem clans. Thus phratry A will contain the tribes of the Crow, the Snake, and the Lizard; phratry B those of the Owl, the Wolf, and the Bat; and so on. In a savage state of society which remained unprogressive either in culture or in numbers, this arrangement would still hold good; but amongst a vigorous and energetic people it is bound to have become modified—all the more so as it came into contact with other communities. The spirit of tribal unity would assert itself, and so in time would be formed kingdoms or principalities, like those of Israel and Judah, separate in themselves but claiming descent from a common ancestor. Mr. Andrew Lang has advanced the hypothesis that the phratry, far from being the segment of a larger group, was itself formed as the result of an alliance of two groups, already exogamous and inter-marrying." Thus he would build up from below, and by an extension of the same principle the phratries thus formed would tend to coalesce into a single tribe which owned the same totem.

It is significant that the Tamil word for caste is *kulam*,

## CASTE—THE ABORIGINAL THEORY

which means a clan or family, and, as an Indian friend pointed out, suggests a common ancestor after the pattern of Jacob and the Israelites. This indicates that, in the mind of the Dravidian, caste was associated not with colour but with that division of the tribes into clans and families which we now find in totemistic societies. The word *kulam* is Sanskrit in a Dravidian language which does not contain, by comparison with others, a very large proportion of Sanskrit words. But this is not a serious objection. The Sanskrit word on which so much reliance has been placed is *varna* or colour, and this contrast of ideas in the North and in the South rather suggests what was prominent at the time when they were adopted. The suggestion made earlier that the word *varna* may have been adopted as a distinction between the Dravidians and the black aborigines was intended to show that the word is not conclusive proof of Aryan origin, though its value as evidence is not destroyed. It may well be that when caste was adopted and adapted by the Aryans they gave it the name of *varna* as the outward and visible sign not of race purity, but of distinction between the higher and lower castes. As, however, Aryan ideas filtered through to the South, the Southerners, holding to the original idea of a common ancestry, translated the vernacular word into the more elegant Aryan, as the Anglo-Saxon sheep became French mutton when it became food for the higher, more elegant, or more fashionable classes.

Now all the information we have—and it is derived from Aryan sources—shows that caste in early days by no means followed the rigid lines which we are accustomed to associate with it. Thus, in the age of the Brahmanas, Professor Berriedale Keith says that, on the scanty evidence available, "a change of caste was not impossible," and it also appears that at that time, "while we have no reason to doubt that priesthood and nobility were hereditary, these castes seem to have been free to inter-marry with the lower castes, *including the Sudra*."[1] And in the later age of the Sutras, "the only test when one seeks a wife," according to Professor Washburn Hopkins, "is that of the family; 'they ask the girl in marriage

[1] *Cambridge History of India*, vol. i, p. 126.

reciting the clan names.' "[1] The evidence is valuable; it indicates, as far as it goes, that the important point was the family—that is, in totemistic phraseology, the totem clan, and not the phratry. M. Senart, after giving elaborate reasons for rejecting both the racial and the occupational theory, advances a theory of his own which is based upon the ancient conception of the family. And, again, Lyall says:

> In the combination of modern European society it [the feeling of kindred] is of little importance even within the narrow sphere of families, and throughout the greater part of India it is merely an important social element; but among the clans it is the supreme consideration. It must be remembered that in all pure Hindu society the law which regulates the degrees within which marriage is interdicted proceeds upon the theory that between agnatic relatives connubium is impossible. And as by an equally universal law no legitimate marriage can take place between two members of two entirely different castes or tribes, we have thus each member of Hindu society ranged by the law of intermarriage, first as belonging to an outer group within which he must marry, and, secondly, as belonging to an inner group of agnatic kinsfolk among whom he may not marry.[2]

It is reasonable to suppose that this agnatic prohibition is based upon the idea of a common ancestor, the line being continued through the males, who are thus blood-brothers, while the females, being regarded as transferred to their husbands' families and hence into a different tribe or family, have no such blood relationship with the ancestor. This is exactly what we find in totemistic tribes where the ideas of endogamy and exogamy are very strong.

Mr. O'Malley, in his little book *India's Social Heritage*, takes us a step further in this direction. Speaking of tribes of the interior, by which he means those aborigines not admitted within the Hindu pale, he says:

> The tribal organization is now chiefly seen in the social divisions within or outside which marriage takes place. They are of an unusually complex character, for they are based on religion as well as totemism. . . . There is no intermarriage of

[1] *Cambridge History of India*, vol. i, p. 235.
[2] Lyall: *Asiatic Studies*, vol. i, p. 170.

## CASTE—THE ABORIGINAL THEORY

members of the same group, i.e. a member of one group must marry into another group with a different number of gods. This rule is subject to a further condition imposed by a system of totemistic septs. Each group is divided into septs which also have totems, and there is a similar rule of exogamy based on the totem; according to this a member of one sept may not marry into a sept in another group if it has the same totem, even though it worships a different number of gods.[1]

Neither Lyall nor Mr. O'Malley seems to have had caste in mind when they wrote these passages; indeed, Mr. O'Malley has already been quoted as an exponent of the Aryan or racial theory combined with the occupational. We shall have to revert to M. Senart's ideas later.

We may, then, take it as established that the cult of the aborigines was totemistic in character, and that this cult survived in a modified form after the coming of the Aryans down at least to the age of the Epics. We have also seen that the family, that is, the tribe descended, or thought to be descended, from a common ancestor, was all-important, and had an immense influence on endogamic and exogamic customs. These conclusions are fortified by modern observation. The aboriginal tribes still have their totems, having advanced little beyond their primitive stage, and the family, which is recognized as a unit throughout Hindu India and which has an important bearing on public morals as we understand them, is conspicuous as a social idea among the clans of Rajputana, where, perhaps more than anywhere else in civilized parts, Hindu ideas have best survived the contact with various invaders. We are now dealing with a time long anterior to any written record. In the course of centuries the arts were developed; cities and towns came into being; tribes coalesced into nations or territorial units; religious ideas became more elaborate and wars more highly organized. Cultivation on some approach to scientific lines took the place of the primitive idea of burning the jungle, which still persists among aboriginal peoples. Consequently, the old notion of the family totem died out, and the totem of the tribe now became emblematic, so that armies marched

[1] *India's Social Heritage*, p. 86.

under the standard of the eagle or monkey, just as at Barnet the Star of the de Veres was opposed to the Sun of Edward of York. But though the family totem died out, the idea remained. The religious sanctions were not lost, but the tribe now tended to crystallize into families or clans rather than on totemistic lines. Occupations tend to be hereditary, owing especially to the notion of the family as the social unit, and also to congregate round a centre, as happens to-day in England and other highly civilized countries. Thus the Wolves tended to become weavers, the Owls carpenters, and the Hawks blacksmiths. The caste, then, was not the direct product of occupation, but was adjusted later to suit the new conditions. It may be objected that this does not account for its rigidity; you cannot expect all Owls to become carpenters so that the totem clan exactly coincides with occupation. That is, of course, quite true; to imagine otherwise would be contrary to all human experience, and it is just this difference which, as already pointed out, exists to-day. Not all Brahmans are priests, nor have they been for a very long time. Not all goldsmiths work in the precious metals, nor are all carpenters workers in the trade. But while there are many exceptions, it is true to say that different occupations are generally associated with different castes, and hence, while the exceptions are fatal to the occupational theory, considering the rigid restrictions of caste, these differences are quite compatible with a theory of evolution which is based upon a gradual transition from a religious origin.

But, next to the drastic rules which govern marriage, the most prominent feature of caste is the prohibition of inter-dining and of drinking together, extending so far as to shadows polluting food and the uncleanness of water offered, though untouched, by a man of lower caste. "The test of caste," says Professor Washburn Hopkins, "is not marriage alone, but defilement by eating and touching what is unclean."[1] This passage no doubt refers to the age of the Sutras, and it may fairly be argued that as the purity of the stock became the dominant consideration more drastic

[1] *Cambridge History of India*, vol. i, p. 234.

sanctions were applied to prevent mixed marriages, and that one of these would be the religious prohibition of intercourse involved in inter-dining. But, apart from the obvious criticism that the argument does not explain the interdict against the acceptance of food or water casually offered, nor the defilement which was the consequence of touching unclean things, the context of the passage shows that Professor Hopkins was not suggesting any connection between marriage and defilement. On the contrary, he seems to indicate that the defilement was analogous to that suggested by the famous passage in the Acts in which at the instance of James the Gentile converts were advised to "abstain from meats offered to idols and from blood and from things strangled." Such defilement seems to have been in the nature of a tabu, one of the objects of which is, according to Mr. Thomas, "provision against the dangers incurred by handling or coming in contact with corpses, by eating certain foods, etc." Sir James Frazer thus explains the meaning of tabu:[1]

> In primitive society the rules of ceremonial purity observed by divine kings, chiefs, and priests agree in many respects with the rules observed by homicides, mourners, women in childbed, girls at puberty, hunters and fishermen, and so on. To us these various classes of persons appear to differ totally in character and condition; some of them we should call holy, others we might pronounce unclean and polluted. But primitive man makes no such moral distinction between them; the conceptions of holiness and pollution are not yet differentiated in his mind. To him the common feature of all these persons is that they are dangerous and in danger, and the danger in which they stand and to which they expose others is what we should call spiritual or ghostly and therefore imaginary. To exclude these persons from the rest of the world so that the dreaded spiritual danger shall neither reach them nor spread from them is the object of the tabus which they have to observe.

We gather from the numerous instances given by Sir James that the underlying principle of tabu is a belief in evil spirits which infect the body by sympathetic or contagious magic and so cause pollution. And this pollution can only be

[1] Frazer: *Golden Bough*, p. 223.

exorcised, or in some cases the infection itself be avoided, by certain ceremonies. The objects of tabu differ from country to country and from tribe to tribe; it is not to be supposed that all countries go, or have gone, to the lengths of some of the customs described.

Now when we consider that in India the belief in evil spirits is till very general, and that the music in marriage and other processions is intended to drown inauspicious noises, when we remember that in Malabar, which was largely protected by geography from Aryan penetration, the very shadow of a low-caste man pollutes the food, when we recall that the victim of pollution must cleanse himself by ceremonial washing, and that magic was a special attribute of the Dravidians, the analogy is too striking to be disregarded. I once asked a Hindu friend, "Why do you make such a fuss about food?" He replied, "The body and the soul are the two parts of a man. They are inseparable. To take polluted food into the body is therefore to infect the soul." I did not pursue the inquiry further, but it is clear to me that what infected the soul was the invisible infection of the food derived from a lower caste on magical principles, and that this in modern days may have some relation to the metaphysical doctrine of the three *gunas*, Sattva, Rajas, and Tamas—Purity (or truth), Passion, and Darkness—the goal being to attain to Serenity through the intermediate stage of Human Passions in which the great majority find themselves. A person plunged in Tamas would communicate some of the inferior element to the higher castes by means of the material food which would transfer it to the soul by way of the body.

This view is further borne out by the extreme sanctity of the kitchen. It has already been said, on the authority of Mr. Andrew Lang, that in Samoa the totem animals have become the vehicles of the gods, but these gods are "clan" or "family" gods. This custom of the family god is well known in India, and it is usual to keep one room of the house especially for this god. In fact, the worship of the family god, together with the prevalent ancestor worship, is exactly analogous to the worship of the Lares and Penates in Rome. The analogy is, indeed, so remarkable that no apology is needed for a lengthy quotation from Sir James Frazer's article on "Penates":[1]

The store-room over which they presided was in old times, besides the atrium, the room which served as a kitchen, parlour, and bedroom in one, but in later times the store-room was at the back of the house. It was sanctified by the presence of the Penates, and none but pure and chaste persons might enter it, just as with the Hindus the kitchen is sacred and inviolable. . . . Closely associated with the Penates were the Lares, another species of domestic deity who seem to have been the deified spirits of deceased ancestors. . . . In the household shrine the image of the Lar (dressed in a toga) was placed between the images of the Penates, who were represented as dancing and elevating a drinking horn in token of joy and plenty. . . . The shrine stood originally in the atrium, but when the hearth and the kitchen were separated from the atrium and removed to the back of the house, the position of the shrine was also shifted. . . . The old Roman used in company with his children and slaves to offer a morning sacrifice and prayer to his household gods. Brefore meals the blessing of the gods was asked and a portion of the food was placed on the hearth and burned.

And then, after considering and rejecting various ancient theories of the origin of these gods, Sir James makes this significant remark: "A comparison with other primitive religious beliefs suggests the conjecture that the Penates may be a remnant of fetishism or animism."

This description of old Roman custom applies almost exactly in its two essential features to the Indian practice. In every house, where there is room for it, not only is the kitchen sacred but a room is set apart for the worship of the family god. At least once a year, if not oftener, the ceremony is kept of offering worship to the ancestors, or, if worship is too strong a term, at least of performing a rite which bears a strong resemblance to it and which seems to have had its origin in such worship. The prohibition of interdining could not then have arisen, as Dr. Slater suggests, from the simple custom of only asking people of the same caste or craft to dinner, neither could it have arisen from

[1] *Encyclopaedia Britannica.*

the desire of the Aryans to keep the race pure. If it could be traced to such common-sense origins, there seems no reason why the kitchen should have been regarded as sacred, nor why it is necessary to employ a caste cook. Following up the common-sense theory, we can see no conceivable reason why the guests of a single community should not partake of food cooked by a respectable man, whatever his caste, or how the sacred character of the kitchen can have any effect whatever on the choice of brides. So long as the proper young people are thrown together, why should they not eat food that is wholesome, however prepared? If you, an Aryan or a carpenter, wish to marry your son to an Aryan or a carpenter girl, by all means invite nobody to dinner but Aryans or carpenters; but the girl is not going to marry the cook, nor the boy the cook's daughter.

If, on the other hand, we adopt the racial theory, we are confronted with the same difficulty, for it seems almost fantastic to suppose that, to guard against a possible *mésalliance*, it was necessary that the household staff should be of the same caste as the master, especially when we remember that the choice of a mate was not so uncontrolled as it is in England. For if racial contamination is what was in their minds, why should not an Aryan Vaisya serve an Aryan Brahman, seeing that side by side with caste there existed here, as everywhere, the social distinctions between kings and commonalty, between servant and master, between employer and employed? What conceivable reason is there for keeping the kitchen sacred in order to preserve the purity of race? But the moment you regard the kitchen as a holy place the case is altered. Unclean, that is, ceremonially or religiously polluting people, are not admitted into holy places, since they are thought to communicate by contagious or sympathetic magic an evil influence to what they touch, and food would thus acquire qualities of pollution to those who partook of it.

It cannot be argued that this kind of ceremonial pollution is enough to cause defilement, because the whole rationalistic argument is based on the material conceptions of the mixture of blood and of the material idea of the indirect effects of

## CASTE—THE ABORIGINAL THEORY

food pollution. Three illustrations out of many may be given of the extent to which tabu plays its part in the life of India to-day. So important is the ceremonial purity of food, at any rate in the South, that Brahmans, before eating, change their clothes to a silk cloth which should be free of defilement by the excreta of the body, and do not break their fast until they have purified themselves by ablution and prayer as signified by the putting on of the so-called caste mark or *namam*. Next, the use of iron as a charm against evil spirits is quite common; in the extreme South —and probably elsewhere—you can see an iron bar laid across the threshold just inside the door for this purpose. So confident was the Indian friend who showed it to me that he walked up to the first house he saw, and there, sure enough, was the bar. An iron ring is also worn or some piece of the metal carried on a journey to keep off ghosts and robbers. Sir James Frazer, with his usual wealth of instances, points out that iron was at first "perhaps" regarded with the suspicion and dislike which savages have for something new and therefore awful, but that the very "disfavour in which iron is held by the gods and their ministers . . . furnishes men with a weapon which may be turned against the spirits when occasion serves."[1] Iron, therefore, can be used as a charm for banning ghosts and other dangerous spirits, and he quotes instances from the Highlands of Scotland, Morocco, Ceylon, and the Slave Coast. Lastly, it is common for Brahmans in the South to shave off all the hair of the head except one lock (called the *kudimi*), and this, unless a man be so emancipated as not to care, must be retained. I well remember how a friend, coming to England to attend the Round Table Conference, parted with this lock of hair as almost the last evidence of having shaken off the external trammels of caste. Here, again, Sir James comes to our assistance. He gives instances of primitive peoples amongst whom a lock of hair is left on the shorn crown, to which the soul can retreat when the hair is cut. It is possible that the legend of Samson has traces of this superstition mixed up with the sun-myth which it seems to be.

[1] Frazer: *Golden Bough*, p. 225.

## HINDU CUSTOMS AND THEIR ORIGINS

We have now advanced to this position. The ancient tribes were totemistic, and as such divided themselves into phratries, again subdivided into families, with strict rules of exogamic and endogamic marriage. On this foundation there grew up not only the belief in evil spirits which is common to all primitive and savage tribes, but also a system of tabu, with equally strict regulations as to what does and what does not cause pollution, and what remedies may be taken against it. Then came the Dravidians with their notions of magic, obviously already inherent in the system of tabu, and in order to preserve not perhaps so much race purity as social divisions and the superiority of the conquering race, they erected this system into some form of caste. It is quite possible—and indeed probable, seeing that History usually works by evolution rather than by revolution—that this early form of caste was not what we know now, nor is there any means of speculating what form it took. But that the seeds were sown in some such way as this seems far more likely than the supposition that caste was invented by the Aryans to preserve the blood, or that it arose from the desire to keep trade secrets and to make sure that the girls only married within the professional community.

But, it may be argued, none of these things is really incompatible with the Aryan theory. Though the Aryans were superior in civilization, they were not above practising magic, and the survival of totemism among the aboriginal tribes shows no more than that they have not advanced, while all the others have grown out of it and have left it behind in the course of progress. The very fact that totemism is to be found in the mythical stories of so late an epic as the Ramayana is some evidence that it was not unknown even to the Aryans, and it is admitted even by M. Senart that the ancient customs had a partial and secondary influence. The absorbing desire to keep the race pure led to all sorts of extravagance which commended itself to the primitive mind, for the keynote is the word *varna*, and everything else must be regarded as subsidiary. The germ of the four great castes is to be found in the Iranian divisions, which roughly correspond, even in nomenclature, to the four great

## CASTE—THE ABORIGINAL THEORY

Indian castes, and to build up a theory based upon Dravidian practices is to ignore all outside influences from Iran, Egypt, Mesopotamia, and other places with which ancient India was in contact. If you appeal to the present-day prevalence of magic by referring to superstitions, that only shows that in the course of the centuries the purest Aryan ideas became overlaid and inoculated by the grosser superstition of the less instructed masses and by the natural tendency to elaborate, and thereby to cause degeneration, as happened in the Christian Church.

If that is a fair presentation of the Aryan case, it must be remembered that we are to "discriminate between things certain, probable and plausible." M. Senart, strong advocate though he be for the Aryan origin of caste, has pointed out that, since in no other country is the caste system to be found, at any rate on the Indian lines,[1] it is in India itself that the origin of it is to be sought. It is common ground that the Aryans did not bring it with them, and that for a long time after they had settled in the Punjab they never thought of it. It has been suggested that there are points of resemblance between the Indian castes and the social arrangements of early Greece and Rome. In Greece the family, the phratries, the phyle; in Rome the gens, the curia, the tribe; in India the family, the gotra, the jati. The Roman analogy of the sacredness of the kitchen has already been noticed, and there were other customs concerning marriage, sacrifice, and food which have their counterparts in Indian caste. Professor Dutt, criticizing these analogies, points out that marriage and dining restrictions were unknown to Rig-Vedic Indians, nor had they any idea of pollution by touch. He looks upon the Greek and Roman divisions of society as the "natural product of the evolution of human society, especially when the king and the priests gather round them a kind of sanctity and divinity." He is, therefore, driven to the conclusion that if the Aryans ever knew of

[1] It is sometimes said that there is caste, too, in Europe; to a certain extent this is true, but it exists on wholly different lines. There is nothing to prevent a countess from marrying a chauffeur, or a gentleman from dining with a sweep. The objection mixes up class and caste.

## HINDU CUSTOMS AND THEIR ORIGINS

these Indo-European customs and social uses, they had forgotten all about them, and only remembered them in some inexplicable way. An argument based upon analogies which can only be explained by improbable assumptions can hardly be regarded as weighty. Professor Dutt, however, concludes that "for the time being we shall have to remain satisfied with the view that the *varna* division of society was mainly Aryan in character, though accentuated by the peculiar conditions of the Aryan conquerors in India, and that the formation of Jati castes, many of which were tribal in origin, together with some of the practices like untouchability, infant marriage, etc., was due largely to aboriginal influences."[1] And he summarizes his conclusions thus:

The most important factors in the development of caste were the racial struggle between the fair-skinned Aryans and the dark-skinned non-Aryans; the division of labour leading to the formation of occupational classes and the tribal differences, especially among the non-Aryans, which survived the spread of a common Aryan culture. These were aided by the superiority claimed by the priests and witch-doctors in all primitive societies; by the natural desire to follow hereditary occupation with a view to keep trade secrets; ... and by the inherent disinclination of a man to marry outside his own folk, especially when there are racial or tribal differences involved.[2]

Confronted with the question why caste cannot be found among other primitive races where most, if not all, of these factors are present, he argues that this was due to the want of political supremacy able to enforce uniform laws and customs, to the peculiar nature of the Indian religion, which is cosmopolitan in outlook and is concerned more with the preservation of social order than with the development of a unifying creed; because of the law of Karma, which engendered a spirit of resignation to the various lots assigned by Providence to different classes; and, finally, because of the abnormal development of Brahmanical rituals, ensuring the position of the Brahmans.

All this is plausible but hardly probable, especially when considered in the light of origins. It must be noted that

[1] Dutt: *Origin and Growth of Caste in India*, p. 31.   [2] Ibid., pp. 34–35.

## CASTE—THE ABORIGINAL THEORY

Professor Dutt uses the word "development," and his argument from the law of Karma and from Brahmanical rituals must certainly refer to a time when caste had taken definite shape as the body of a boy develops into the body of a man. His explanations, even when we allow for development, sound too much like the excuses of one who is faced with insoluble riddles and is hard put to it to find an answer. He sees that the Iranian system was not imported into India, and so has to invent a theory of the revival of memory of forgotten things; he sees that much that has survived and is still living must be referred to aboriginal influences, and so he postulates that such customs died hard and became incorporated with the Aryan creed. He is obliged to adopt this excuse, because otherwise he must forgo the superiority of Aryan civilization, which is the corner-stone of the whole theory. He sees, finally, that caste is unique in India, and, still clinging to the Aryan idea, he is loath to admit that they found it there in some form or another, and so he explains its vitality on Indian soil, and there alone, by somewhat vague statements, most of which relate to much more modern times. He is, however, right in ascribing caste to various ingredients, to purity of race, to division of occupation, and to tribal custom. But if there is any force in what has already been written, the seeds of caste were sown in the tribal custom, and it is to that that we must first look for an explanation. The other two came later by evolution, and it is difficult to say which came first; in such cases as in determining the periods of history, no date can be definitely assigned. It is far more probable that they grew up together, insensibly hardening into the rigidity of the system which we find in the laws of Manu.

We may now enter upon the final stage of our journey from the beginnings of caste to its consummation as we know it to-day. When the Dravidians—or pre-Aryans—arrived in India they found there a people who were in a low—if not the lowest—state of culture. They themselves were in all likelihood only a few degrees higher, but the difference was enough to ensure conquest, and the primitive folk were driven into the hills and jungles, which were then very extensive. These primitive folk were totemistic, and greatly impressed by the existence of evil spirits, against which, and often, too, in the service of which, magic charms and spells were thought to be an effectual remedy. But the pre-Aryans were themselves addicted to very similar beliefs and practices, which, moreover, involved various forms of tabu—all carrying with them some notion of bodily injury or death to be avoided.

The restrictions on marriage are specially significant. They are perhaps the most prominent feature of the caste system, and even those who have consented to relax the rules relating to inter-dining and do not scruple to sit at meat with Europeans, Mussulmans, and other "unbelievers," still adhere to the old rules concerning marriage. But Sir James Frazer says: "So far as I am aware, no other Aryan people besides the Hindoos is certainly known to have regulated marriage by a rule of exogamy. Can it be that the ancestors of the Hindoos borrowed the institution from the aborigines with whom they came in contact when they settled in India?"[1] The answer to this tentative suggestion which I have been trying to give is that there is every reason to think that exogamy was so borrowed, and, considering that it is the core of the whole system, we are justified in ascribing the origin of that system (whatever its development) to pre-Aryan cults. The whole idea of race purity is founded upon this very principle of exogamy—a principle unknown to the Aryans and never practised by them except in India, but a principle, combined with totemism, which is "widespread among the swarthy, black, aboriginal race called Dravidian. . . . Indeed, the evidence seems to justify us in inferring that at one time or another totemism and exogamy have been practised by all the branches of this numerous and ancient people." Totemism is not practised by the Aryan races in India; it is now confined to the jungle tribes, the real aborigines, and to some classes or clans of the Dravidian family. The Aryans, therefore, having a purer or higher form of religion of their own, never adopted totemism; but they did adopt exogamy, not so much from the futile desire

[1] *Totemism and Exogamy*, vol. ii, p. 330.

## CASTE—THE ABORIGINAL THEORY

to keep the race pure as from the intuition that by this means they could best preserve social distinctions and keep occupations on lines more or less hereditary. It is surely a very remarkable phenomenon, if not unique, that the higher culture should have invented a custom which was so largely followed by the lower but which was entirely foreign to their own scheme of life, and yet the suggestion of borrowing seems to be the only one which really fits the facts.

On such a background of ideas, restrictions upon marriage and conventions of ceremonial pollution, especially in connection with food, since these appear to be most widespread, would naturally arise, and after some centuries would harden into regular custom. These ideas would be reinforced by the very intelligible repugnance to avoid close contact either by matrimonial union or by physical touch with the aborigines, who would also be debarred from taking part in religious exercises, and, partly owing to their low intelligence and partly to the superiority complex of the ruling race, would be relegated to the humbler, though not necessarily degrading, occupations. These ideas once established, it became a matter of time and evolution to extend them to social classes among the ruling race themselves. It would be seen that no very sharp line could be drawn between the higher aborigines and the lowest of the rulers, and the higher social ranks, being averse from too intimate a connection with obvious inferiors, would apply the same maxims to the extent of marriage restrictions and food tabus; but since these inferiors were of the same race and the same religion, their touch would not involve pollution, neither would they be denied the rights of worship, except to the extent (which is not uncommon in other communities) of being debarred from entry into the holier parts of the shrine. By degrees, as these ideas became hardened, those who were relegated to the main caste of the Sudras would adopt the principles of their betters, and, still with notions of totemism and tabu, would split up into subdivisions or minor castes. And these castes, finding no other means of distinction, and observing —instinctively perhaps—that people of the same trade were drawn together into intimacy for obvious reasons, tended to split up on the lines of occupation, so that castes became multiplied with the multiplication of trades.

While this process was going on, the Aryans flowed into the Punjab, which they conquered and colonized. They were people of a culture possibly some degrees higher than what was by this time the general level of Indian culture, but this is not certain. They brought with them, however, a somewhat highly developed Nature worship, the main gods being Varuna, the god of the sky, Indra, the god of rain, and Agni, the god of fire. There seems to be no trace of totemism or tabu in this system, and if they practise magic, as did practically all the earlier peoples, it does not seem to have figured largely in their compositions. It is, indeed, the positive quality of their religious ideas, as expressed in the hymns of the Rig-Veda, and the negative quality of the absence of those ideas which we associate with savages and other low-grade civilizations, which induced the belief in their great superiority to the Indians. They had, of course, no caste, nor any thought of it. Marriage was apparently free; there were no restrictions of pollution in the matter of food, and they both ate beef and sacrificed cattle. From the evidence of similarity of names and of social divisions, they may very well have brought with them reminiscences of the Iranians, but they did not act upon them until a much later date.

They remained as colonists in the Punjab for a long time —how long it is useless to speculate—and during this period many of them filtered across the borders of the settlement and came into contact with the Indians. By degrees, as they increased and multiplied and were perhaps reinforced by others, they found the arid plains of the Punjab insufficient to maintain them with their primitive methods of agriculture and their need for pastures. They felt themselves strong enough to make a move forward, and were impelled to do so by their nomadic habits. They came in contact with the Indian tribes and overcame them, either because they were the stronger and the more virile, or possibly also because there was greater unity amongst them, since they were not divided by those feelings of totemism and tabu which to-day

## CASTE—THE ABORIGINAL THEORY

would have a powerful influence in keeping African tribes apart should there be any question of their uniting in a common cause. Thus, first by infiltration, and later by conquest, they reached the banks of the Jumna, and may even have penetrated into the Ganges valley, but there seems to be little or no direct evidence that they came into armed conflict with what is now the Province of Bengal, or with any part of India south of the Vindhyas or west of the Western Ghats. The early history of the Marathas is a case in point. As we shall see later, scholars differ as to the make-up of these people, but, whatever view may be taken, Aryan conquest does not figure in the evolution of Maharashtra. If it were the object of caste to preserve the purity of the race, it was singularly unsuccessful there, for the Marathas are as mixed a race as we are, and yet caste is as strong amongst them as anywhere else, except in the South, where it is admittedly strongest.

These Aryans, then, having come into contact with the older inhabitants, discovered that they had an institution which, however it may have differed in detail, resembled the caste which we know to-day. They found also that one of the main objects of it was to keep the Dravidians apart from the older aborigines and, if progress had advanced so far (for here we are in the region of guesswork), to preserve social distinctions among themselves. The analogy appealed to them. They saw that by adopting a similar custom they could keep themselves apart from the Dravidians; and, as the obvious distinction was between the fair-skinned and the dark-skinned, they named the institution, when it had taken root among them, *varna*, or colour. We need not suppose that this came to them as an inspiration; still less that they invented caste for a specific purpose. Their natural instinct would have been to keep themselves to themselves, particularly as they practised what to them at least must have seemed a higher form of religion. But as the years passed and the inevitable intermingling of the population had taken place, what had at first started as an instinctive convention gradually took shape as a semi-religious sanction, and so crystallized into a full-blooded religious prohibition. They would quite naturally extol the military prowess of their own people, as we do to-day, and as all peoples have done since man first appeared, and there is nothing surprising in their christening their foes "black devils." They did not forget the Iranian prototype, nor is there any reason to suppose a revival of memory in some unexplained way; all that happened was that as caste settled down upon social lines the precedent of which they had had experience came into play and naturally suggested a division which also conformed to the existing estimation in which the classes were held. In an age when religion was predominant, and especially after the virtue of sacrifice, of spells, of incantations, and of magic generally, had been more and more fully accepted, the priest would claim and would be accorded the highest rank. This is a common, if not a universal, phenomenon, to which the history of Egypt and Israel and the episode of Canossa bear witness. It appears also in the priestess of Delphi, in the Flamen Dialis, and the Vestal Virgins. Next to the priests would come the kings and princes of the State, with their retinue of military officers and the rank and file of the army. Below them, again, would be reckoned the common people, whose trade was either mercantile or agricultural, these being the comprehensive terms which included all that was not priestly or royal or military. This was a modification of the Avestan Iranian system, which divided the people into Athravas, Rathaestas, Vastriya Fsuyants (cultivators), and Huiti (artisans), and the modification was suggested by the existence of the pre-Aryan population. These people were the Sudras, and they were generally the labourers or other classes who practised a humble or degraded occupation which was considered to be beneath the dignity of the higher castes. It must, however, be made clear that there was no such clear-cut distinction as we are apt to suppose between these castes, except perhaps that the Brahmans, the Levites of India, kept religion as a close preserve, and, secondly, that to the pre-Aryans were assigned these humbler occupations, not necessarily because they were physically degrading or disgusting, but because they were inferior callings. For the pre-Aryan population

## CASTE—THE ABORIGINAL THEORY

was probably superior numerically to the Aryans and the Sudras were admitted to the Aryan system. So long as caste was not based upon occupation and did not follow occupational lines, the Sudra was free to enter upon the domains of the Vaisya, especially when the need for more extensive cultivation arose, and it is not improbable that when the need for soldiers was insistent the Prince would not be too nice in enlisting able-bodied men who were not Kshatriyas. Conversely, the poorer class of Vaisya who had lost his land or had otherwise been unsuccessful might have consented to till the soil for hire, though he would never consent to become a scavenger or to have commerce with dead things. And, again, the test of a calling was not so much its physical uncleanness (which, however, operated upon the degree of estimation in which it was held) as the religious sanction with which the priests invested it. For one cannot too strongly emphasize that in dealing with an ancient custom we must beware of importing material or utilitarian ideas. That such ideas existed can hardly be denied, seeing that some kind of social gradation is universally experienced wherever men congregate; but, speaking generally, and especially of a country like India, where, as has so often been remarked, religion governs every action from sunrise to sunset, we are far more likely to be on the right track if we refer back to religious sanctions, themselves quite possibly the outcome of popular estimation. If, for example, a flayer of cattle or a worker in leather is of low caste, it may be that originally his trade was considered disgusting, and this may have induced the priests to pronounce the ban of pollution; but it is the ban rather than the disgust which determines the estimation of the caste.

Thus, according to this view, caste did not come into being as the invention of the Aryans for their own preservation, nor as the outcome of evolution of occupation, nor as an inherent ingredient of the family system of the Aryans. Neither was it entirely due to the Dravidians or other pre-Aryans. These factors had their influence, but it was the combination of all that produced caste in its final shape. The essential difference lies in the values to be given to each, and perhaps also in the chronology. The customs of the aborigines—the pre-Dravidians—contain the germ out of which the rest grew; they are not of secondary or partial importance, but primary and decisive. The more civilized Dravidians imbibed these embryonic ideas and erected them into some kind of system, with rules for marriage and injunctions of pollution. The Aryans polished and perfected what they found, adopting incidentally and imperceptibly much of the grosser superstition of those amongst whom they had come to live, and importing something from their experience of their original home. And, finally—but not till long afterwards—the communities who were drawn into intimacy by similarity of occupation split up by imitation into separate castes which approximated to, but were not identical with, the worldly calling. The keynote of the whole process was neither pride of race nor convenience of economic relations, nor any of those things which might influence a modern man, but simply religion. So potent is the force of religion that one turns with reluctance to an explanation of detail which seems to be based on purely material considerations, and one is conscious that while in every society, however primitive, there must be some sort of order and that no society is formed out of a fortuitous collection of unrelated individuals, yet where the religious sanction is wanting the argument is at once weakened. It is this want of the religious sanction, or at any rate of the evidence of strong religious influence, which vitiates the argument from racial purity as well as that from occupation. It is true that when the scientific material is incomplete one must to some extent wander in the realm of conjecture; that conjecture comes nearest to the truth which most closely fits the ascertained data.

# V

# Caste—The Vitality of the System

BUT it is not enough to trace caste to its origins and to declare that it arose in this way or that. We have to account not only for the peculiar phenomenon and its birth but for its strange persistence through so many centuries and through so many historical vicissitudes. Arabs and Scythians, Tartars and Huns, Afghans and Persians, and Englishmen have flowed over the face of India and yet the Hindu religion has maintained itself with caste as its principal social bulwark. It has withstood the powerful schism of Buddha, the violent persecutions of Islam, the fiery onslaught of the early Christian missionaries and the persistent attacks of later ones, and yet caste among the masses of the people remains as firmly rooted as ever, and even among the more educated it has only yielded up the unimportant outworks of the citadel. Nowhere in the world has such an institution been maintained for so long on purely temporal bases. The New Zealander, when he has finished his sketch of the ruins of St. Paul's, may perhaps betake himself to a history of British institutions. He will describe the decline of the privileges, which made of the nobles and the knights a special caste; he will go on to show that the guilds which divided the people into castes on occupational lines gradually disappeared until they became meaningless and survived only in stately halls now crumbled, like St. Paul's, into ruins. He will pursue his theme into the twentieth and succeeding centuries during which the levelling of society has obliterated the distinctions of aristocracy, middle class, and the *tiers état*, and he will find that amidst all these social evolutionary changes the Roman Catholic religion stands where it always stood, because religion is one of the deepest instincts of mankind and because it is only those institutions which are founded in religion that are able to withstand the attacks of time, working through evolution. This, of course, does not mean that the rigid maintenance of a custom which refuses to adapt itself to surrounding circumstances or to listen to the researches of scholars and the progress of knowledge is to be commended. The conservatism of Churches is well known: beliefs die hard and religious customs, the remnants of an outworn creed, still survive when secular ones have long disappeared.

It is not, then, because a custom is good but because it is persistent that we must look for its roots in religion. It is very difficult to conceive that an institution like caste could have survived if it was simply based on the desire of the conquerors (if they were conquerors) to keep their own race free from admixture with the inhabitants. There is, in fact, no such distinction now. If it pleases anyone to call himself an Aryan, let him do so, for nobody cares. If a community claims to be Aryan, and it is worth anyone's while to investigate the claim, it becomes a matter of controversy. When an institution is founded upon common sense or instinct or any other secular consideration, one would expect it to die out as the common sense or instinct no longer feels any need for it, especially when it entails various inconveniences, or in the alternative to shed what is external or unessential, keeping only the core of it. It may be said that that is exactly what is happening to-day amongst those who are indoctrinated with more liberal ideas. They are as anxious as ever, not for the purity of Aryan blood, but for the purity of caste blood; but there is a definite trend towards relaxation of the rules of pollution referring to such matters as commensality and overseas travel. It might, of course, be argued that this is evidence that caste, originally meant to preserve the purity of race, has merely shifted its ground to purity of the caste. But this is not so. The movement is very recent; it is by no means universal even among the educated or in all parts of India. It is the outcome partly of economic pressure, partly of Western influences, and partly of the recognition that drastic caste restrictions interfere with social intercourse. Few, if any, Indians would admit that they are consciously shedding barbaric and antiquated customs which have their roots in pre-Aryan times.

## CASTE—THE VITALITY OF THE SYSTEM

Elsewhere caste is as strong as ever. A recent experiment in the amalgamation of caste and non-caste schools on grounds of economy and efficiency was met by strong protests of religious scruple from the villagers. No appeal to common sense or to the burden upon the State and therefore upon the tax-payer will ever persuade the villagers to allow non-caste men to use the caste wells, thus making one well do the work of two. Ideas of pollution and magical superstition are still rife amongst rustics who probably never heard of the Aryans. No doubt, as Max Müller has recorded, "universal custom is more powerful than books, however sacred. For books are read but customs are followed."[1] It is the contention here that this universal custom could not have survived and flourished except only by religious tabu. Where two races exist in the same country, intermingle, live their lives together, and gradually acquire the same customs and the same traditions, nothing short of a religious tabu will suffice to keep them apart. Sooner or later and in spite of religious prohibition they will coalesce within a period which is conditioned by the configuration of the country as well as by the kind of race involved. Caste has not prevented the fusion of races; it has only preserved the artificial divisions of society and the ideas of pollution.

Nor is the case mended if caste be supposed to rest upon occupation. Writing of the Maurya period (fourth century B.C.), Dr. Thomas says: "It is to this period, no doubt, that we must ascribe the great complexity of the caste system, and the beginning of the association of caste with craft. It seems not doubtful that a number of castes did arise, according to the Brahman theory, by intermixture of the old four divisions which still formed the basis . . . But it is only in a few cases that we find a particular occupation assigned to a particular caste."[2] Clearly an occupational caste could not exist before the occupation itself emerged and this would only happen as society became more complex and the need arose for specialized crafts. To say that the

---

[1] *Chips from a German Workshop*, vol. ii, p. 315.
[2] Cambridge: *History of India*, vol. i, p. 479.

formation of guilds is a natural expression of the herd instinct and that men of the same guild will group themselves into castes for the purpose of mutual assistance and the preservation of trade secrets is no answer to the question why caste with its rigid and complex rules should have persisted so long; for Mussulmans and others who flowed into India were not ignorant of these crafts, and either kept the secrets without caste or else betrayed them, thereby making caste inoperative. Whatever may be said of the marriage laws, there could have been no valid reason for maintaining the laws of pollution, and all that can be said is that caste became so firmly established that it persisted long after the need for it had disappeared. Had this tradition been of full effect, however, one would have expected that the boy born in an occupational caste would have been excluded from any other calling. By degrees individualism would have asserted itself. Boys, either because they felt no aptitude for their father's trade and were attracted by some other, or because ambition led them into another walk of life, would leave the beaten track and so the original lines of occupational communities would become blurred and eventually obliterated. That is just what is now happening in India. The lines of caste remain, but the lines of occupation cut right across them. There was once a barber who made a living by shaving men on a journey by train. Every day he would walk up and down the carriages carrying his razors and brush, plying the business of his caste. But he was ambitious. He wanted to be a railway clerk, to sit on a stool and write things in books, and one New Year's Day he retired to a little room, sat on a chair, and wished hard. His wish came true. He became a clerk and eventually rose to be a station-master. But he must still marry his son to a barber, and all the rules of pollution would still operate upwards and downwards.

It seems incredible that if caste had its roots in occupation, or, to put it more strongly, that it was born of occupation, as man is born of woman and kittens of a cat, it would not have followed the various modifications of different callings. Surely with the passing of the centuries and the growing complexity of society, means would have been devised—by religious ceremony or by purification—by which a barber having changed his profession could be admitted into the caste of the railwaymen. For there is nothing specially sacred about a profession, unless it be that of a priest, and then it is only by courtesy called sacred because the priests are occupied with things of God or of the gods. It is difficult to explain the persistence of this institution otherwise than by referring it back to the early practices of primitive religious cults, adopted, codified, softened, and civilized by their successors in time and in the inheritance of India. If it be asked why even in this modified form it should still persist, may we not reply that the Jew still keeps the law of Moses, still practises circumcision, still observes the Passover; that the Moslems celebrate once a year the sacrifice of Isaac; that until very recently Christians thought it blasphemy to question the Biblical account of the Flood or of the Creation? There is nothing harder to uproot than a dogma or a tenet of religion; and surely the most notable example in the world of this vitality is the caste system of the Hindus.

# vi

## Caste—Professor Ghose's Suggestion

THE views set out in the preceding pages receive striking confirmation from the studies of Professor Ghose of Dacca University,[1] and this chapter will be devoted to summarizing his arguments. The trail of research into the ancient history of India was blazed by European scholars, and their prestige among Orientalists has perhaps obscured the important work which is being and has recently been done by Indian scholars themselves. The modern tendency to scepticism and rationalism has caused such scholars to take an objective view of the literature and to lay what might once have been called sacrilegious hands upon the revealed scriptures, a result natural enough when we consider the growth of the scientific spirit in India. Professor Ghose has put forward his opinions after a great deal of intensive study of the Indo-Aryan literature. The conclusions at which he has arrived are certainly surprising and, to judge by a hint or two he has let drop, they have surprised himself. For Professor Ghose is certainly a Hindu, and his natural predilection would be to support the Aryan theory and to uphold the Brahmanical view of life. One has a preconceived idea, born perhaps of a slight snobbishness to which most of us are, however unconsciously, prone, that the Hindu is proud of his Aryan ancestry and his Aryan culture, and would resent being told convincingly or otherwise that his real ancestors were not this blue-blooded folk but the black-skinned inhabitants whom they dispossessed. And here we have a learned scholar who not only asserts that the Indian culture was three parts or more due to the primeval inhabitants, but rarely misses an opportunity of pouring scorn on Brahmanical wiles and Brahmanical pretensions. One cannot, however, forget that whatever else he may be he is a Bengali, and that his

[1] Nagendranath Ghose: *Indo-Aryan Literature and Culture (Origins)*.

## CASTE—PROFESSOR GHOSE'S SUGGESTION

whole argument centres round the idea that the whole culture was founded or at least profoundly modified by an Eastern Empire which consisted of Magadha, Videha, Panchala, and Anga, that is, all that part of the Ganges valley which lies between Allahabad and Calcutta. This Eastern Empire was non-Aryan or Vratya, that is to say, to use the words of Professor Washburn Hopkins, "entirely outcast persons with whom one may not even have intercourse unless they perform special rites." Professor Ghose is, moreover, a convert, and he approaches his subject with all the notorious enthusiasm of a convert. He shows a certain impatience with those who still cling to the "Aryan" theory with all its incongruities, and far from admitting that the Aryans were superior in civilization, he contends that the boot is on the other foot, that it was the Eastern, i.e. Bengali, Kingdom or Empire which showed all the signs of development and organization while the Aryans were still undeveloped and unorganized. It may be unfair to attribute such prejudice to a work which is professedly scientific and which shows continually every desire to approach the problem objectively; it is, however, only natural that a certain bias should appear which would claim for Bengal the honour of having called the Indian tune and which does to some extent also exhibit the impatience of the convert towards orthodoxy. For all that Professor Ghose's argument deserves serious study and cannot be brushed aside as the mere vapourings of prejudice. His book is evidently written for the initiated; it is full of Sanskrit words and extracts printed in the Nagari character and left untranslated without even a hint of what interpretation he would put upon them, and he assumes a certain familiarity with abstruse Hindu terms of which only students of ancient India have ever heard.

It is admitted that if the Vratyas are outcast (or, more properly, excommunicate) they can be received into the Aryan community by the performance of certain rites. Professor Washburn Hopkins speaks of "admission into the Brahmanical fold," thereby suggesting that by these rites they became full participants of the system, complete with caste, sacrifice, doctrine, and ceremonies. Professor Ghose does not endorse this view. In the Atharva Veda is described the ceremony of Vratyastoma, by which the non-Aryan was "converted" into the Aryan, and this, Professor Ghose holds, was really a ceremony of mass conversion, in principle, though not in detail, not unlike the mass conversion of the Saxons in A.D. 777. The Anupadesa, the non-Aryan Vratya country, was a very long way from the Punjab, the home of the first Aryan settlers, and it is reasonable to suppose that the "conquest" of the country was made rather by peaceful penetration than by direct invasion. Either because of internecine feuds or from the love of adventure and enterprise, some of the Aryans found their way into the non-Aryan country in the Ganges valley, and discovered there a people, religiously less advanced than themselves since the popular religion was largely a hocus-pocus of magic, spells, and incantations, but politically far more developed. Whereas the Aryan settlements were at best only a loose confederation, in which Brahman and Kshatriya contended for domination (on the basis of class, not of caste), the Vratya-land was a well-knit empire under an autocratic ruler who held it together by his own authority. It was peopled by a somewhat heterogeneous collection of tribes and castes, which, whatever may have been their religion and their customs, owned the sway of the Vratya Emperor and were thus in some sense a political unit. The castes are more or less formed on the basis of occupation; the customs and even the gods may differ, but the Brahmans, who are in the main court poets and household priests, differ greatly from the Aryan Brahmans, and the priests of the popular religion are concerned with spells and incantations and exorcisms. The Emperor and his nobles, however, take very little interest in popular religion and belong rather to the school of philosophic speculation which they treat as a close preserve. It is out of these speculations that the Upanishads spring, though doubtless after the penetration of Aryan influence they gradually become moulded to the Aryan pattern. The Rajanyas (or Kshatriyas) were originally foreigners who imposed themselves

## CASTE—PROFESSOR GHOSE'S SUGGESTION

upon the land by conquest and stood to the rest of the people in much the same relation as the Normans did to the Saxons soon after the Conquest of England.

The immigrant Brahmans obtain access to the King or Emperor, who holds conversation with them on the subject of politics and religion. The political side of the question appeals to these Brahmans; they appreciate the law and order which they see around them, as well as the general prosperity of the country, and this is ascribed to the single sway of the autocratic Emperor. If the disjointed Aryan confederacy could be induced to accept the suzerainty of the Emperor, it would be an advantage to everyone concerned. But there was the religious difficulty. The Vratyas did not set much store by their religion, whether of the popular or of the more abstruse kind, but the Aryans did, and they would not accept the rule of an unbeliever with any better grace than a Mussulman of the earlier centuries accepted the rule of a Kafir. If, however, the Aryan religion was accepted with such modifications as would not shock the susceptibilities of the people, there was every chance that the empire might be extended so as to include the Aryan settlements. The idea was attractive—to the Emperor, the Great Vratya, who would thereby obtain a great accession of power and influence—to the Brahmans, who saw themselves rising to great positions in the new State. And so "the bargain is struck; the concordat is agreed to." There must, however, be a great conversion ceremony, and this took shape as the Vratyastoma of the Atharva Veda. It must also include a Rajasuya rite, to consecrate the first monarch of the land, Aryan and Vratya alike. The conversion ceremony, it must be repeated, was not for individuals; that is where Professor Ghose joins issue with European scholars. Caste among the Aryans, at any rate, had not yet made its appearance. The Brahmans and Kshatriyas were still classes which contended for the mastery as kings and popes contended in Europe. Bloomfield, in the opinion of the author of this "romance," is therefore wrong when he speaks of "one who has entered the Brahmanical community after having been converted from an Aryan but non-

Brahmanical tribe." Bloomfield has no doubt that the connection between the Vratya book and the Vratya stoma is not to be questioned; he has no doubt that in Book xv of the Atharva Veda as well as elsewhere the conversion of the Vratya is referred to. But by this conversion the Vratyas did not "become Brahmans." They were simply admitted into the Aryan fold and very probably became Vaisyas, which etymologically only means "members of the vis or clan." It is in this etymological sense and not in the later caste sense that this term must be understood, for it is part of the argument of the author of this "romance" that the advantage to the Aryans in this supposed "concordat" was the acquisition of man-power, however obtained, to the Aryan vis. The author does not believe that the pure-blooded Aryans were in such numbers or were so unified that they could have conquered the country unaided, nor that they were particularly squeamish as to who was admitted to the Aryan community. The whole argument is, one may say, based on the theory that the Aryans were politically far inferior to the men of the Eastern Empire.

And so when the great Vratya stoma ceremony had been performed and the Eastern Empire had become, as the Roman Empire became Christian, Aryan in name, if not in fact, the Western Brahmans, the Aryan missionaries, gradually rose to power in the State and while they introduced the Aryan rites, modified to suit the popular taste, they and the king were engaged in abstruse metaphysical discussions out of which grew the doctrines of the Upanishads.

Such is the "romance" in which Professor Ghose has given the rein to his imagination. Yet it is not wholly a romance, for it is supported in many details by discussion of the various authorities and by the disentangling of much that is, it is claimed, otherwise inexplicable. Leaving the main body of the argument for the present, we may here touch on one of the most important points. What, if the romance is wholly romance, is the meaning of the Atharva Veda in general and of the xvth book in particular? The bulk of the Veda is taken up with spells and incantations and is quite different

## CASTE—PROFESSOR GHOSE'S SUGGESTION

in character, as in time, from the Trayi, the other three canonical Vedas. The Aryans were probably not free from these superstitions, but, if they had been so important a part of religion as they appear to be in the Atharva Veda, they would surely have been prominent in other writings admittedly Aryan. It seems incredible that these spells and this magic should not have their origin in the beliefs of the non-Aryan population. How, then, came they to be incorporated in the Hindu canon? It is difficult to accept the statement of Professor Dutt of the Hooghly College, Calcutta, that "tribal and cultural divisions of society could not be shaken off by the natives even after their conquest by the Aryans, and, under the changed circumstances, they became hardened into caste divisions." To this he ascribes "the curious fact that the caste rules are more rigid among the Dravidians of the South." But we may endorse his opinion that "the practice of the conquered aborigines contributed as much to the development of caste as the racial and class prejudices of the Aryan conquerors" with the reservation that it was the practice of the aborigines, whether "conquered" or not, which was the real basis of the caste system. Professor Dutt, therefore, adopts the rather lame conclusion that for the time being we shall have to remain satisfied with the view that the *varna* division of society was mainly Aryan in character though accentuated by the peculiar conditions of the Aryan conquerors in India "because we have no data about the pre-Dravidian influence upon the Aryans." But that is surely to ignore the inferential value of customs and practices which we know do exist even now. In the absence of direct evidence we have to fall back upon inference from known facts, if that method is likely to lead us nearer the truth. We cannot rely entirely upon the literature written either by Brahmans or under Brahman influence. We need not be satisfied, even for the time being, with a theory that does not fit the facts and is so manifestly defective at so many points, any more than our ancestors were obliged to be satisfied that an eclipse of the moon was due to a dragon, or that the world would come to an end on a given date. No doubt, whatever theory may now be advanced may have to be modified in the light of fuller knowledge, especially as disclosed by archaeological efforts, but that need not prevent us from accepting a theory "for the time being" which does fit the facts; and it has all along been the contention that such a theory is to be found in the aboriginal basis of caste which was modified by Aryan influence and not the other way about.

The Atharva Veda was not, in the view we have been considering, an Aryan compilation at all. It was a Vratya collection, put together for the edification and guidance of the priestly class which had come into existence through the medium of the proselytizing Aryan Brahmans and is therefore founded upon the superstitions current in the land, duly leavened with an admixture of the Vedic religion. Among minor indications which support this view mention may be made of the place given to the tiger. It is remarkable that in early Indian literature—in the Panchatantra, for example, which is a collection of fables of unknown date but which seem to have been current long before they were so collected—it is the lion, not the tiger, as we might have expected, who is the king of the jungle, and Professor Berriedale Keith remarks that "the tiger, a native of the swampy jungles of Bengal, is not mentioned in the Rig-Veda, which gives the place of honour among wild beasts to the lion, then doubtless common in the vast deserts to the east of the lower Sutlej and the Indus." In the Atharva Veda, on the other hand, not only does "the tiger [the most distinctive inhabitant of the Anupadesa] . . . compete with the lion and even prevail over him as a familiar literary figure but it is on his skin . . . and on it only that the consecration of the king can take place. (A. V. iv. 8. 2.)." When, therefore, this rite of Rajasuya is adopted with due "rishification" by the Brahman priesthood, they do it, tiger's skin and all. We may be tempted to ignore such indications as this of the true home of the Atharva Veda, but in discussing the very vexed question of the original home of the Aryans, Dr. Giles lays considerable stress on the question of the fauna and flora mentioned in the older

## CASTE—PROFESSOR GHOSE'S SUGGESTION

literature, and he specially mentions the tiger. "The wolf and the bear were known, but not the lion or the tiger." If to-day we should find an ancient document in which a prominent place was given to the kangaroo, we should certainly not be inclined to assign it to Europe or Asia.

We are not bound to accept every detail of this romance, even if we are led to accept its main conclusions. It is extremely probable that the Aryan invasion of Vratya land was in fact accomplished through the peaceful penetration of Aryan immigrants, and it is quite unlikely that the Vratyas were regarded as outcasts in the sense in which Professor Keith uses the word. According to the same authority "the description of the Vratyas well suits nomadic tribes; they are declared not to practise agriculture, to go about in rough wagons, to wear turbans, to carry goads and a peculiar king of bow, while their garments are of a special kind." It is not easy to see why, with one exception, this description suits nomadic tribes in particular, for the use of rough wagons and particular kinds of weapons and dress need show nothing more than the observation of strangers who had come across unaccustomed things. That they did not practise agriculture does, however, suggest that they had not passed the nomadic or pastoral stage, if we can be quite sure what is meant by practising agriculture. To this day there are in India aboriginal tribes whose idea of agriculture is to burn down patches of jungle, sow grain, and more or less let Nature do the rest, moving on to a second patch when the first is exhausted. In the fertile valley of the Ganges little or no agriculture would be needed to produce some kind of a crop, and in the delta of the Godavari I have seen fields which were sown after they had simply been trodden by bulls or buffaloes when the river silt had been allowed to do its work. Professor Ghose himself seems, however, to admit this lack of agriculture when he says of Vratya-land that it was "the earth of the pṛthi- or pṛthu-Vaniya of both the Puranas and Atharva Veda, he who taught his subjects the art of agriculture [indicating, no doubt, thereby, the staple industry of the Eastern Empire]."

## HINDU CUSTOMS AND THEIR ORIGINS

The chief difficulty here, as elsewhere, is to fix chronology with any approach to accuracy. The description of the Vratyas is taken from the Panchavimsa Brahmana of the Sama-Veda and the Sutras of that Veda and the period ascribed to these is 800–600 B.C. Late as this is, it does not fix at all the period to which the description relates, and the Veda legend to which Professor Ghose pays so much attention and which ascribes to Brahman magic the two sons who became respectively the ancestors of the Nihadas or aboriginal tribes and of the more settled Vratyas, does not help us to any sort of a decision. It seems far more likely, however, that even if the Vratya stoma was a rite of mass conversion of the people, it was not the work of a handful of Aryan immigrants who worked upon the ambitions of the Emperor but that it was brought about only after long preparation and propaganda by a more numerous immigration of Aryans—and especially of Aryan Brahmans—into the East. Though the Emperor and his Court may have been indifferent to the superstitions of the people and have been willing to accept the new ideas in exchange for political advantage, it is not likely that the mass of the people who would have been quite indifferent to politics and who were by hypothesis wholly ignorant, would have abandoned their own faith so easily, especially as they lived in a world "beset all round by demons and evil spirits who have to be constantly kept appeased or outwitted by the necromancer's art." There are limits to autocratic power and even the history of ancient India itself shows that the ruler could not afford to fly in the face of prejudices strongly felt. No doubt the newcomers did their best to soothe the popular susceptibilities by introducing and incorporating charms and spells and even by adopting some of the older non-Aryan gods, but this could hardly have been enough to overcome the opposition of the orthodox, and where men feel strongly about religion there are sure to be many orthodox. The Australian aborigines, for all that their religion may be of a very low order, have certain practices which they esteem sacred and inviolable. There must surely have been a very long period of penetration, during which the new ideas filtered down from the philosophic Court to the more intelligent of the population. It was not a question of conversion at the point of the sword; the whole hypothesis rests on the assumption that the "concordat" was made with the willing consent of an obedient people and was not a hole-and-corner arrangement between the Emperor and a few stranger priests.

We may now return to the details of Professor Ghose's argument. Who were the Suta and the Mágadha? The Suta has been described as a "bard-herald," and his primary occupation seems to have been to sing the praises and to "act as the repository of the annals and chronicles of the imperial house" but that was by no means his only calling. He might also be (and apparently was) a soldier, a driver of horses, elephants, and chariots, and even a sort of doctor. Professor Keith in the list of the Court entourage calls him the "charioteer." Washburn Hopkins notes that while he was a bard he was also a charioteer. "They made a special sub-caste and lived at Court." Professor Ghose, however, maintains that his inviolability did not depend, as Professor Keith suggests, on his character as herald. "The writers of the *Note on Suta* (Keith–Macdonell)," he asserts dogmatically, "have gone wrong in tracing his inviolability to his heraldic functions" because it was not the Suta but the Duta who was the herald in the European sense. He was "inviolable" not because he was bard-herald but bard-priest. In a society such as that of the Vratyas, the man who kept the records, maintained the traditions, and chanted the king's praises was obviously a very important person and was even treated as on an equality with a Brahman. This is borne out by the legend that when Lomaharsana, who was certainly a Suta, was killed by Baladeva, the latter had to do penance for *brahmanhatya* or the killing of a Brahman. The fact was that "when caste entered into the Aryan scheme of things, the Suta started (along with the Mágadha) as a Brahman and standing on exactly the same level as the Aryan Brahmans." They were the bard-priests of Vratya-land and officiated as priests both at the Rajakarmani ceremonies of the king as well as at the domestic rites of the people and would therefore after the conversion of the people when the Aryanized religion became the official faith, take rank as priests with the later importations.

The Mágadha, on the other hand, seems to have been a sort of Court jester or buffoon whose duties, however, were similar to those of the Suta in his capacity of bard-priest. There seems to be some confusion of thought about this person owing to the similarity of the name Mágadha with the country Magadha. Professor Keith speaks of the "man of Magadha who is brought into close connection with the Vratya in a mystical hymn of the Atharva Veda which celebrates the Vratya as a type of the supreme power in the universe." This is significant. For if the Vratya was merely "regarded as an outcast" it is certainly strange that he should also have been celebrated as a type of supreme power in the universe. Professor Ghose suggests an answer to the puzzle. The Mágadha, who may perhaps have got his name from Magadha, was not merely a "man of that country" but a well-defined official at the Court—"the Court buffoon, and ministers perhaps to the vices of the king, the lewd associates of gamblers, singers, and harlots, all the riff-raff parasite crew that is usually to be found in the entourage of an Eastern king or nobleman who happens also to be a man of pleasure." All authorities seem to be agreed that both Mágadhas and Sutas were Vratyas or non-Aryans. The words "man of that country" seem to refer to the description of the Mágadha as *Mágadha desiyaya Brahmabandhu*, which Professor Dutt translates "of the country of Magadha"; but Professor Ghose disputes this. He points out that the word is Mágadha not Magadha, and argues that *desiyaya* cannot therefore refer to country but signifies "like but not completely." The interpretation is intended to confute Weber's conjecture that the expression "is only explicable if we assume that Buddhism with its anti-Brahmanical tendencies was at the time flourishing in Magadha." The term, it is argued, has no reference to country but only to community and is intended to include "the Sutas and the Videhas or such of them at least as were still sticking on to priestly work of sorts." Professor Ghose gives the word in Sanskrit; Professor Dutt prints it in Roman but without any diacritical sign; exactly what difference the long "a" would make must be left to philologists.

But if the empire of the East—in Vratya-land—were at once the most powerful and the best organized that the Aryans had yet encountered, the hymn of the Atharva Veda would be explained. The ruler of Vratya-land would seem to them to be the type of supreme power just as to some people the Roman Empire dominated the world at a time when it really dominated very little beyond the littoral of the Mediterranean. The Mágadha, however, became *brahmabandhu*, an opprobrious term signifying a "spurious or degraded Brahman"; he was, therefore (with the Suta), received into the Brahman (not Brahmanical) fold, though from the description given above he cannot have been regarded as a reputable character, and this accounts for the term *brahmabandhu*. Manu says that the Mágadha is the offspring of a Vaisya by a woman of the Kshatriya or Brahman caste. But Baudhyayana makes the Mágadha the offspring of a Sudra man and a Vaisya woman. This seems to imply a certain fluctuation, as if the status or rather the composition of the Mágadha was not exactly defined. "The mixture of castes is produced by adultery on the part of the pure castes and by marrying those who ought not to be married and by men deserting their respective occupations," and among those of mixed origin we find the Mágadha. Manu, however, is obviously no guide in this case, for the compilation which we have is ascribed to a date some centuries after Christ, reckoned by Dr. Burnell at not earlier than A.D. 500. Clearly, then, between the time of which we are now speaking and this date of Manu there elapsed some thirteen centuries, which in British history would take us back to very early Saxon times; many changes would have taken place and the Vratya Empire would have become completely Aryanized. For chronology is all-important in these discussions and it is much to be deplored that our knowledge of the accurate chronology is so imperfect. We are dealing throughout with movements which advance almost imperceptibly—movements in which for a century, perhaps, there is no appreciable progress. The importance of chronology is not always recognized. The "rise" of caste, the "emergence" of untouchability, the introduction of this custom or that are sometimes spoken of as one might speak of M. Blériot's flight across the Channel, or the early experiments with railway trains. It is far more likely that such things grew insensibly and that those who lived in such times would not have noticed the growth. It is a truism to say that by looking back we can obtain a truer perspective than by looking around us; it is equally true that when we look back we are apt to telescope the movements of centuries into the course of a few years. It cannot be too often repeated that the growth of caste from the first germs to its full stature was a matter of centuries, perhaps of ten, perhaps of more, and it is difficult for anyone to grasp what ten centuries may mean in the course of progress.

The conclusion reached is that both the Suta and the Mágadha were officers of the Court to whom were to some extent entrusted the functions of priests and that, as the country became Brahmanized, they were received into the Brahman caste, though regarded as "spurious" or at least degraded types of Brahmans. The important points in this view of the case are (1) that the Suta and Mágadha were in no sense Aryan; they were not "degraded" because they were the offspring of mixed marriages, but were true Vratyas absorbed into the Aryan communion by virtue of the Vratya stoma, (2) that these were not individual conversions but conversions of well-recognized communities, and (3) that they were communities of some importance and influence in Court affairs and therefore with the Vratya Emperor. I do not subscribe to Professor Ghose's view that it was the Aryan Kshatriyas who were absorbed in the Eastern Rajanyas and that the Suta and the Mágadha Brahmans absorbed the Brahman immigrants, for that would have retarded and possibly even prevented the eventual Aryanization of the country. His view is, however, possible, though the point is of no very great importance.

But what is to be said of the *varna-ashrama-dharma*, the core

## CASTE—PROFESSOR GHOSE'S SUGGESTION

and the distinctive tenet of Hinduism which we comprehensively call caste. Professor Ghose claims to have shown that, far from caste having been invented by the Aryans, they found it in full flower in the Eastern Vratya Kingdom. It is remarkable that the Brahmans, to whom have been attributed so much self-glorification and so much pride in the origins of their system, have nothing to say of the origin of this cardinal tenet. In the very early stages of the history of a people struggling for existence and competing with others in like case, it is natural that they should have regarded the warrior as their leader and that the military caste should have been predominant. When they settled down to a more corporate tribal life and began to consider the unseen forces which—at any rate to their imagination—peopled the air, the priest became the more important, as the mediator between man and the Invisible, whether god or devil. This has been the almost invariable rule; it is evident in the history of mediaeval Europe and it is conspicuous in the history of Israel. All the leaders—from Joshua, if not from Moses, to Eli—were warriors who had no pretensions to any priestly functions and the appearance of Eli may be said to mark a change in the attitude of the people. Nor did the warrior caste yield its supremacy without a struggle. In Europe the Empire contended with the Papacy; in Israel the king was rebuked for daring to sacrifice because the priest was late. That, it would seem, is exactly what happened in the Eastern Vratya Empire. The rulers were of the Rajanya, i.e. the Kshatriya caste, though no doubt at first it was little more than a class and only gradually gave way to the priests. And in Aryanland too the warriors contended for the supremacy with the priests. All this, however, proves nothing. It is based upon the hypothesis necessary to the theory under discussion that the Eastern Vratya Empire had advanced beyond the stage of a loose tribal confederation and was, by comparison with the Aryan organization, a well-knit, coherent whole. It had, in fact, reached the stage at which the king's word was law and could not be overruled by priestly privileges or pretensions.

## HINDU CUSTOMS AND THEIR ORIGINS

*Varna* in this view was a non-Aryan conception but what was *asrama*? In its complete Brahmanized form the life of man consisted of four *asramas*—the *bramhachari*, the *grihasta* the *vanaprasta*, and the *sannyasi*. But we must be careful to note that this structure grew up gradually. It is entirely inconsistent with what we may reasonably assume to have been the state of Aryan culture. There is, indeed, something ludicrous in the idea of these Aryans, who, if they were not exactly nomadic, must have been constantly on the move in their march eastwards, retiring from the world to the solitude of the forests to meditate as hermits living on what Nature could provide and afterwards begging their bread, as we must suppose, from the despised conquered tribes. Professor Ghose, who frankly admits a bias in favour of a Brahman origin of the *varna-asrama-dharma*, is driven to the conclusion that neither *varna* nor *asrama* was of Brahman origin, but were non-Aryan and Eastern Vratya institutions. The *brahmachari* was in this view only the period of pupilage which should fit the youth for the status of *grihasta*, the stage of householder and family man, beyond which few ever went. For the *grihasta* never did; he "passed over" to an existence in the *pitrloka* where he was dependent on others for his sustenance, conceived in terms of this world, so that it became incumbent on him to beget a son, not merely for the sake of having male offspring but also and chiefly for the oblations which male descendants were alone competent to offer. The *vanaprasta* and the *sannyasi* had no place in such a scheme, for, by hypothesis, they renounced the world and with it all that appertained to it, including sons. The *asrama* was a resting-place or a stepping-stone from one state to the next, the final goal being the attainment of Brahman, and this final goal could in the subsequent Upanishadic teaching only be attained by passing through the allotted stages. "The whole *asrama* idea," it is argued, "is foreign, indeed antagonistic, to all Vedic notions." It is Upanishadic and the Upanishads were the outcome of the non-Aryan culture of the East.

This view certainly seems to explain certain contradictions in the Hindu system. It is one thing to obtain salvation

## CASTE—PROFESSOR GHOSE'S SUGGESTION

by reaching the *loka* of Indra or some other heavenly abode where individuality remains intact, and quite another to obtain the same salvation by absorption into the Brahman or Para-Atman of the Upanishads. Or, again, it is said that marriage is a sacrament which can never be dissolved, not only in this world but in others. It is binding for all time and beyond it, so that a woman who is once the wife of a man can never be the wife of any other man. This explains what seems to our material mind the barbarous custom of becoming *sati* or pure, for the wife, having merged her identity in the male, the more important partner, could only be certain of remaining pure by joining the man in the world beyond. There was thus a deeper meaning in the practice than is apparent on the surface, and horrible as is the idea of self-sacrifice of the body in this manner, cruel as may have been the means of enforcing it, there would not unnaturally be a repugnance to abandon it amongst those to whom the body meant very little, while the unity of the man and wife was paramount. For the same reason we may see in the repugnance to the remarriage of widows the principle that a woman being already married by an indissoluble tie cannot marry again without loss of chastity. But neither of these things is compatible with a belief in the absorption into the Universal Soul by which individuality is extinguished. It may please subtle brains to argue that the drop of water merged in an ocean (a favourite image) remains, nevertheless, an individual drop of water, though not perceptible to human senses, but that is a refinement which satisfies no one. Nor can it be said that the true belief in Upanishadic doctrine can justify the intense desire for a son as the offerer of oblations to the ancestor, unless it be on the principle of rebirth, which itself hardly fits in with any excessive reverence for the ancestor, since it is only those not fit for absorption that are reborn, and as no one seems to know when the rebirth has taken place, and consequently when the oblations can safely be discontinued, they must be continued indefinitely. It is apparently because the idea of *loka* or Heaven cannot be reconciled with the doctrine of the Para-Atman that Professor Ghose declares that the whole notion of Karma and of the *asramas* is non-Aryan and comes from Vratya-land.

But these contradictions, or at least these irreconcilable doctrines, suggest something more. They suggest that two different systems were blended with great ingenuity, no doubt, but not so perfectly that the original elements cannot be detected. And it is in just these fundamental doctrines that the difference would naturally appear. For though it might be possible to rewrite, or at any rate to refurbish, the ancient doctrine in such a way as to make it more in conformity with Brahman ideas, it would be very difficult, if not impossible, so to rewrite it as to substitute an entirely new system of belief while apparently upholding the existing system. If anyone tried to reconstruct the Christian system it might be possible to disguise or even repudiate apostolical succession; it would not be so easy to repudiate the doctrine of immortality or the Fatherhood of God. Now it will be observed that the heaven of Indra and similar conceptions are entirely Vedic, that is beyond doubt. But the idea of absorption into the Para-Atman is Upanishadic. It is difficult to conceive how a homogeneous system could have a place for both these conceptions and how the one could have grown out of the other. Upon this reasoning the abhorrence of widow remarriage and the ancestor worship would have to be referred to that part of the system which remains individualistic, for it would hardly be reasonable to bind a mortal woman for all eternity to a spark which had become indistinguishable from the Eternal Fire, nor would there be any point in offering food to a spirit who had become one with the Universal Spirit. The doctrine of Karma would, however, remain unaffected by such considerations. A man is what he is by virtue of his conduct in a previous existence. But Karma ceases to operate when he reaches the stage of immortal bliss. As long, therefore, as transmigration continues, that is, until the man has reached perfection, the question of individuality does not arise. For the man has simply become another mortal, has taken upon himself some other mortal and phenomenal shape, and as long as this process lasts (though it is not, as some seem to think,

## CASTE—PROFESSOR GHOSE'S SUGGESTION

endless) it does not matter whether the soul is individual or absorbed. These refinements are too difficult for the common folk, who are certainly influenced by the doctrine of Karma, nor are they ordinarily worked out to their logical conclusion by the more educated, because, man being by nature imperfect, it may be assumed by any one generation that the ancestors have not yet attained salvation and the consequence is that oblations must be offered upon that supposition. The argument, therefore, amounts to this. The Hindu system contains elements which are incompatible and must be incompatible because they are fundamental. An attempt was made to blend these warring elements but not so successfully that the differences cannot be seen. One of these elements was the old Vedic Aryan religion which can easily be identified by reference to the Vedas, especially the Rig. The other main stream cannot therefore be traced to this Aryan source, and it is reasonable, therefore, to trace it to a non-Aryan one. The burning of widows, the institution of child-marriage, the dislike of widow remarriage, and similar developments came much later on when the two streams had coalesced and flowed on without regard of the votaries to possible discrepancies.

Professor Ghose's main argument is that both caste and the Upanishadic doctrine have their roots in the Eastern Vratyaland and that neither the one nor the other can be ascribed to the Aryans. Caste, he contends, was already there when the Aryans penetrated into the basin of the Ganges; they did not explain origins because there was nothing to explain. But this, of course, only puts the problem a step further back. If caste was already there, we are still not enlightened as to how it got there. But if it was a non-Aryan institution, adopted and adapted to Aryan usages, there is at least a great probability that it began amongst those primitive peoples who preceded the Eastern Vratyas and practised it in a manner not, indeed, coincident with but similar to totemism, with all its tabus and ideas of pollution, and especially with its notions of endogamy and exogamy.

# vii

## Untouchability

OF all Indian institutions, since the practice of becoming Sati was made illegal, none has attracted more attention or is more repugnant to the Western mind than that which condemns human beings to social ostracism, so that they cannot even be touched, and in parts (too often confounded with the whole) that their very shadow pollutes and they are forced to declare themselves unclean, like lepers. Nor are those disabilities confined to sentiment alone, to the degradation of mind and spirit which brings these unfortunates to acquiesce in a total loss of self-respect. They have distinct economic disadvantages. In a country which lives in villages and where Government is expected to supply the usual social facilities, they entail the digging of two wells for drinking water, where one would suffice, and the establishment of two schools, one of which may be, and probably is, poorly attended, to the evident loss of man power. The practice in Madras of segregating the pariahs in outlying hamlets, perhaps half a mile from the main village, causes inconvenience to those who want to call up labour, yet may not approach nearer than the outskirts, and the reluctance of caste Indian officials to enter these hamlets for purposes of inspection leads to all sorts of sanitary abomination which may end in a widespread epidemic of disease. It is not necessary to enlarge further on a topic which has been the subject of denunciation not only by missionaries but by the more advanced section of Indians. There are only two things which can be said in favour of the custom, and neither can be said to be anything more than a pale shadow of controversial argument. The institution rests upon tradition and authority, and orthodox Indians revere tradition and authority to a degree that recalls the intolerance of the Scotch Covenanters.

## UNTOUCHABILITY

One great difference (says Sir Sivaswami Aiyar) between Greek and modern thought on the one hand and Hindu thought on the other is that the Hindu is satisfied with tracing the origin of rules to some text of Scripture or some authoritative tradition, and does not press home the question as to rational basis of the rule. He is satisfied with an appeal to authority, and does not believe that mere unfettered intellectual reasoning can furnish guidance in matters of morality.

That, no doubt, might be said of other countries, including England. We do certain things because they are customary; we cling to certain beliefs because they are traditional. The difference is perhaps rather of degree than of kind. But in some sense the passage does explain why a custom which seems to have nothing to recommend it, a custom which in cultured eyes is callous, barbarous, and cruel, survives in all its intensity among the unlettered folk and is still frequently found among even the educated. For the modern European mind which has only recently shaken off the superstition that it was little short of blasphemy to doubt the literal truth of such legends as Adam and Eve in the Garden and of Noah's Flood, finds it now difficult to be patient with a simple blind appeal to authority in the face of all that reason and humanity and generosity can say against it. In this fundamental difference lies to a large extent the difficulty of a mutual understanding; in this fundamental difference too lies many an undiscerning accusation on the one side and on the other many an injured susceptibility.

If this argument can be counted less as a defence than an excuse, the second affords some slight palliation of the lot of the pariahs. Though they are untouchable they do not—until the recent agitation of Gandhi and others brought to them more clearly a sense of their own degradation—appear to feel any humiliation in so regarding themselves. As a French Catholic missionary has put it in a recent book, "Il est Paria; il le sait . . . Ils se considèrent comme soumis fatalement à une irrévocable destinée."[1] Untouchability is to them simply a social convention, no more to be disputed than the man who touches his hat to you disputes your right

[1] Pierre Lhande: *L'Inde Sacrée*, p. 6.

to his respect. Does that sound a startling proposition? Yet the pariah would be as surprised if a Brahman were to take him by the arm as would the waiter be if you asked him to sit down and share the dish he was handing. Moreover, the very fact that they are thus segregated is to some extent a defence against oppression. They are left to themselves for the simple reason that no one wishes to interfere; the pains of pollution are too high a price to pay. This, however, does not go very far to alleviate their material disabilities, such as obtaining water in a drought when their own wells (if they have any) run dry, nor even, if they so acquiesced in the social convention, are they enabled to rise above the settled sense of hopeless inferiority and to claim what the West would call the ordinary rights of manhood. If any such attempt is made, there are ways and means—often atrocious—of putting them in their place, and to the bigoted followers of orthodoxy, they, like many other atrocious things done in the name of religion, and not in India alone, are justified by the claim that they are intended to uphold a divinely given ordinance. For all that, the pariah in the field sings at his work; you would not think to listen to him that his lot is an unhappy one, and as the French author just quoted says "he is not at all envious of the lot of other castes."

The origin of the custom is obscure. Most European writers are inclined to record the custom with varying degrees of disapprobation and to leave it at that. Others who have attempted an explanation conjecture that it arose from a natural disinclination of the better classes to mix with those who were engaged in disgusting pursuits and who thereby acquired insanitary habits. Thus Dr. Slater says:

> Untouchability in some cases is a natural result of occupation; thus the sanctity of the cow causes the flaying of cattle, and even working up of leather, to be regarded as occupations of a somewhat sinful character; hence the Chandalas and Chakiliyans, leather-working castes, are untouchable. It is not so easy to see why the great rice-cultivating castes of Paraiyans, Pallans, and Cherumas are also untouchable; but it may be noted that it is only where the geographical conditions make it possible

## UNTOUCHABILITY

to impose all or nearly all strenuous labour on a depressed caste, and at the same time intensify the desire to escape such labour, that agricultural labourers are untouchable. Untouchability, once established, tends to justify itself; the Paraiyan, being untouchable, does not scruple to eat mutton and drink toddy, and neglects various niceties of behaviour regarded as essential in higher castes.[1]

This theory is manifestly open to many objections. In so far as it rests upon the sanctity of the cow, we have first to show that this sanctity preceded the practice of untouchability, for until the cow became sacred there could have been no sin attaching to the occupation of leather making. There is no evidence of this precedence; on the contrary, as I shall try to show, the sanctity of the cow, as a universal practice, was of slow growth and was not fully established until comparatively late. There do not seem to be any data for assigning the practice of untouchability to any given period, but it is probable that it was established much earlier. Assuming, however, that the veneration of the cow came first, we are still no nearer an explanation why the flayers of cattle and the workers in leather should be visited with so dire a penalty as untouchability, because it is only the living animal that is sacred; the cow may not be killed by violence, but a cow that dies in the ordinary course of nature is treated like any other dead animal. It is left to rot in the sun, to be devoured by kites and vultures, or to become the food of hyaenas. Had the carcase been still sacred, one would suppose that it would have been reverently buried or otherwise disposed of; it would have become a pious duty to see that the sacred animal was not thus left to be torn in pieces by birds or beasts of prey. It may be retorted that the caste Indian shuns the use of leather and looks with some disgust upon the trade of leather tanning, which involves the flaying of cattle. This, however, is to put the cart before the horse. Leather tanning and the flaying of animals—not only of cattle—are somewhat unpleasant trades which, having been left to the outcastes, have become identified with them.

[1] Slater: *The Dravidian Element in Indian Culture*, pp. 156–7.

Leather has, therefore, become polluted because it has been handled by polluting men and not because it is in itself polluting nor because it is in any way sinful to work in it. The water which a pariah hands to a Brahman, the food which a pariah cooks—these things are not polluting in themselves but only by reason of the pariah's touch, for the same food cooked by a Brahman and the same water handed by a Brahman would be accepted without demur. Leather, by hypothesis and in the absence of evidence to the contrary, must have passed through the pariah's hands; it is his polluting qualities that make it polluting. The flaying of cattle and of animals generally is the necessary process for obtaining the raw material out of which leather is made; obviously, the men who want the raw material will take steps to get it, and, leather making being relegated to this mean estimation, no one is likely to undertake the supply of the raw material, except those who propose to work it up or those who are even lower in the social scale.

Next, it is argued that untouchability is the natural result of some occupations. The only instance given is that of the flayers and leather workers and it is difficult to see why any other occupation should make a man untouchable. There are, no doubt, certain occupations—a butcher, for example, a fishmonger, a chimney-sweep, or a coal-heaver—which entail at times some physical pollution; one does not want to shake hands with a butcher when his hands are covered with blood, but no one minds tapping him on the shoulder. The toddy drawer who usually caters for the very lowly, and whose occupation has a certain stigma, is not untouchable; neither is the fisherman whose job entails the handling of dead fish. It is a far cry from becoming untouchable at a time when you are physically dirty to being untouchable at all times and everywhere. For to the orthodox a pariah remains untouchable not only when he is pursuing his daily avocations but even when by reason of education or otherwise he has left one calling for another. No doubt in such cases some laxity has been allowed in these later days; a pariah pleader may sit in court with his caste fellows, because the English Government will not tolerate nice distinctions in its courts, but the orthodox would no doubt prefer that he should at least be given a seat apart. A certain man of the untouchable community was educated at the cost of Baroda State, which has a system of such education on condition of service. It was commonly said that he was forced to resign his post because his position became intolerable by reason of his caste. The heterogeneous collection of people who travel by train must put up with some proximity to an untouchable; Mrs. Sharpe, who evidently knows Gujerat and at least a part of Rajputana, tells how on one occasion a Sadhu friend travelled in company with a sweeper alone in a third class carriage because no one else would get in; and again, how her own sweeper had to miss three trains before he could find an empty compartment.[1]

We then come to what is perhaps the most formidable criticism of all. A very large number of these outcastes are "ploughmen, formerly *ascripti glebae*." "Strictly speaking," says the *Encyclopaedia Britannica*, "the Paraiyans are the agricultural labourer caste of the Tamil country in Madras and are by no means the lowest of the low," and in Tanjore, the home of Brahman orthodoxy, these labourers are called *pirakudi—kudi* being a general suffix and *pira* meaning to be born: in other words, the children of the soil. Why should such folk, following a highly respectable and honourable calling, be regarded as untouchable? Dr. Slater is puzzled; he solves his difficulty by suggesting that the natural desire to escape strenuous labour in a hot climate has relegated the field work to the outcastes, who, being outcastes, infect one another with nasty habits and with customs abhorrent to higher castes. The explanation will not serve. It is not by any means every agricultural labourer who is an outcaste; thousands of others cultivate their own lands and yet preserve their caste. Many others "eat mutton and drink toddy" without sacrificing caste, and it can hardly be said that some of the lowest castes "preserve" the niceties of behaviour regarded as essential in higher castes. If it be argued that those who are now agricultural labourers

[1] Thorpe: *The India that is India*, p. 94.

## HINDU CUSTOMS AND THEIR ORIGINS

were in the distant past engaged in unpleasant callings, and that caste is a fixed, immutable thing, so that once an outcaste a man can never be anything else, that is surely to make an unwarrantable assumption, for there is nothing to show that these outcastes never practised any but the most degraded occupations. The argument, therefore, amounts only to this. Some occupations are degraded or disgusting —notably, in Hindu eyes, working in leather and flaying of cattle; contact with those engaged in them is therefore prohibited. Some others are not, but as some—only some —who are engaged in them have become identified with the others and have sunk to their level, they have incurred the same disabilities. And this result was the direct consequence of their own self-degradation.

Nor can we safely attribute this custom to our old friends, the Aryans. For even upon the accepted hypothesis that the Aryans, having established caste for the preservation of the superior stock, reserved the three highest orders— the twice born castes—to themselves and relegated the despised and conquered "aborigines" contemptuously to the Sudra caste, there is still no place for the casteless. Why should this lordly people who had already attained their object by sifting the grain from the chaff take the trouble to go further and sift the chaff itself into higher and lower kinds, and why should they have gone further still and decreed that as between these higher and lower kinds there should exist such a drastic bar as untouchability? If it be said that this was not the doing of the Aryans but of the Sudras themselves, inasmuch as the Aryans only introduced the four main castes which have since split up into innumerable sub-castes, to become full-fledged ones in their turn— if it be said that in so splitting up the castes the peoples of India, Aryan and aboriginal alike, were only following the normal lines of evolution and that the lower ones imitated their betters, why did these lower ones introduce something quite alien to the letter as well as the spirit of caste by establishing this very definite line of cleavage? The outcastes, it is true, have established castes among themselves, so that in the West the Dhed considers himself the superior

## UNTOUCHABILITY

of the Bhangi, and in the Telugu country the Mala is of higher social rank than the Madiga. This shows an imitation that might have been expected, but it serves rather to emphasize than to explain the anomaly of untouchability. There was, in short, left in India a certain class which for no apparent reason was not only not admitted into the caste system but was definitely excluded from it. The word "outcaste" is misleading; it suggests something that has been thrust out of a system in which they once held a place. But these people are casteless; they never had a caste, even though some may for dignity's sake call themselves Panchamas, the fifth caste, and, as just now remarked, they may have chosen to make social distinctions among themselves.

The existence of these no-caste people forms, therefore, one of the strongest arguments against the theory that the Aryans were the authors of caste for their own purposes, and it is strange that in the discussions on the subject the no-caste man is rarely, if ever, mentioned. For if the case be strong that the origins of caste must be looked for in India itself, it is stronger still that there must be found the beginnings of the no-caste. The two are intimately connected; a discussion of the one is not complete without a discussion of the other. A scientific theory must stand or fall by its own completeness and the story of caste is not complete if the no-caste is not taken into account. It is plain that the explanation is not to be found in the Aryan writings. Nor is there anything which suggests that it might have been imported from abroad. And yet so widespread and so deeply rooted a custom cannot have sprung up in a day, nor could it have lasted so long if its origins were not to be sought in the dim centuries of long ago. "Outcastes," says Sir Sivaswami Aiyar, "seem to have always existed in society and to have been regarded as untouchable. . . . The Chinese traveller Hieun-Tsang," who, however, does not carry us back beyond the seventh century A.D., "noticed the segregation of the outcastes outside towns and villages," so that by that time the custom appears to have been well established. If, then, an ancient custom was not introduced by the Aryans, and if it was not imported, it is more than probable that the origin of it is to be sought in pre-Aryan India.

As in the case of caste, the custom is more strictly observed in the South than in the North, and it is on the Malabar coast that it reaches its extreme limit. Missionaries and other writers are fond of dwelling upon the pollution of an outcaste's shadow and on the rigid degrees by which he is enjoined to keep his distance, but these extreme regulations are not observed everywhere. It is, however, true that in the South the *paracheri* or hamlet assigned to the no-caste people is usually entirely separated from the village proper, while in Bombay, the Dheds' quarter, though inhabited only by Dheds, is a part of the village itself, and it is some commentary on the idea of physical pollution that these quarters are sometimes admitted to be the best kept and the cleanest in the village. Ceremonial is allowed even by Indian writers to be a leading part of everyday Hinduism, and has been described as crushing the life out of the religion by its excessive observance. We must, therefore, accept the position that since the custom was not derived from the Aryans it probably arose in the South among the Dravidians or aboriginal population.

Now the word "pariah," which has been adopted by the English language as the generic name for an outcaste and has been given the meaning of a man who has no place in society, is usually derived from the Tamil word *parai*, a drum. It is certainly the case that drums are beaten outside the temples and more especially at the head of wedding processions by these outcastes or no-caste people. And Kalhana, the twelfth-century bard-chronicler of Kashmir, mentions drums as the peculiar property of the outcastes of his day. Whatever else these people may do, whether they cultivate the fields or work in leather, this occupation of beating drums on ceremonial occasions may fairly be called hereditary. The very name, then, of Paraiyan suggests that when caste became occupational these people took, or were given, the distinctive title of their hereditary occupation. They were the class who performed the most humble ministrations to the gods, and the connection of drum-beating with evil spirits (for it is supposed that those maddening sounds, incessantly repeated, will drown inauspicious noises) suggests further that their original functions were connected with magic. But how did they acquire those functions? Now the helots of ancient Sparta were "probably the aborigines of Laconia who had been enslaved by the Achaeans before the Dorian conquest." They were "State slaves bound to the soil—*ascripti glebae*—and assigned to individual Spartiates to till their holdings." And again in ancient Rome we find that the slaves were employed in various artisan services, or as cooks or ploughmen, or even as petty traders, such occupations being thought to be beneath the dignity of a Roman. Bearing these analogies in mind—for of course the evidential value of societies far removed from India in time and place is very slight—there is a strong probability that the outcastes were the survivors of the conquered peoples, who, as caste tended to coincide with occupation, became the drum-beating, leather-working, and farm-labouring classes to which as serfs they had been relegated from early times. They were not the races conquered by the Aryans; the Paraiyans belonged to the aborigines who were conquered by the Dravidians and being of a different race they were not admitted to the totem or similar clans with which marriage is always intimately connected, since that would have led to free intercourse and the gradual degradation of the race. But this prohibition cannot have been absolute; there are always exceptions. In the course of the centuries—some forty or more—the inevitable miscegenation may very well have obliterated the racial distinctions between aboriginal and early Dravidian. These people have been admitted to a sort of lowly participation in the Hindu system in the atmosphere of which they have lived for so long, for Hinduism is at once the most tolerant and intolerant of creeds. It does not proselytize; you cannot become a Hindu as you can become a Mussulman, and those within the fold are liable to the most rigid restrictions. But it has always been ready to embrace aboriginal tribes who are willing to submit to its laws, though it may assign to them a very lowly place and they have always been kept at a distance and have been excluded from the temples. It would seem, therefore, that anthropological arguments are in any case not conclusive when we consider these factors which must have profoundly modified the original racial characteristics and must have changed their outlook.

Thus the Dravidians applied to the Paraiyans the same test which the Aryans are assumed to have applied to the conquered inhabitants. They reduced them to the position of serfs and assigned to them those duties which it was thought beneath their own dignity to perform. Nor was marriage the only consideration. The disabilities of the Paraiyans were due also—and to an even greater degree—to the mystical qualities inherent in Tabu. To admit such a man to the totem family was not only contrary to the social order; it would bring upon the clan the anger of their particular god. But to admit him to the worship of the god within the sacred precincts of a temple was to call down authentic fire from Heaven, whereby they would be consumed. It would be a sacrilege of the same kind as the offering of unconsecrated or unorthodox fire by Korah, Dathan, and Abiram. But though debarred from taking an active part in worship, the Paraiyans might yet do the menial services connected with it, provided that they did not entail the pollution of the sacred building. In Christian terminology, the Paraiyan, although he could neither officiate at the altar, nor preach a sermon, nor even be one of the congregation, might still ring the bell—on one condition. He could not regard himself as of the communion; he was, in fact, excommunicate. And, as such, he was ceremonially unclean. No washing with water, no cleansing ceremony, could remove that stain which was indelibly fixed by the operation of tabu. To touch him, to have any dealings with him, save, as it were, at arm's length, was by a sort of contagious magic a defilement. You could employ him to till your fields because that entailed no contact of any kind; beyond giving an order, you need have no further communication with him. The seal of pollution was set in his forehead; it was inherent in him as surely as the blood in his veins.

## UNTOUCHABILITY

And so from being the vile, degraded fellow which Indian opinion had made him, he became viler and more degraded from the kinds of occupation left open to him. As the mediaeval knights of Europe disdained the calling of a trader, as indeed down to our own day to keep a shop is not the occupation of a gentleman, so Hindu society disdained certain occupations. And since caste was determined by birth, that meant that by the accident of birth you were excluded from certain callings and were in effect restricted to only a few. The casteless man was of no account. Nobody cared what became of him; no one was interested in teaching him to live better; and his acute and constant poverty, combined with a sort of fatalistic acquiescence in things as they are, prevented him from rising above the squalor in which he was accustomed to live. To that extent the lot of the casteless man has been determined by environment and occupation, but it is difficult to believe that the custom of untouchability had its origin in them.

The impurity which thus debarred him from intercourse with those above him in the social scale and which denied to him any real participation in the external worship of the gods—at any rate, of any communion with the castes—did not extend to spiritual things. A holy life raised the pariah, as it raised others, above his fellows. A pariah might be physically untouchable; he might be excluded from visible worship but by a virtuous and holy life, he might attain to sainthood. The ethical system of the Hindus no more excluded him from beatification than the teaching of Christ excluded the publicans and sinners. It was, no doubt, difficult for a people so greatly debarred from self-expression to attain to such rarefied heights, but, though difficult, it was not impossible. The law of Karma works both upwards and downwards; upon the theory of transmigration the pariah might hope to be born into a higher state or in cases of intense virtue might hope with his betters to achieve immediate salvation (*Moskha*) without that interminable succession of rebirths which is the lot of the less endowed, and which has given to Hinduism its character for pessimism.

Upon this theory we get a rational explanation of the

existence of these people all over the country and of their preponderance in the South. For if the Aryans found a civilized people with civilized customs, as our later knowledge leads us to believe, it would surely be natural for them to continue those customs or such of them as were suitable; and it is not unreasonable to suppose that the custom remained most vigorous amongst those people with whom it originated, and especially with those who were least exposed to modifications due to the irruptions of foreigners. Nor need we suppose the custom to have been either barbarous or cruel in the eyes of those who invented it or found it established, for ceremonial purity frequently involves the avoidance of contact with the unhallowed; ceremonial defilement is frequently conveyed by food and water. It is true that the levitical defilements were only temporary and for a specific reason, but it is not difficult to imagine a society in which a whole class was looked upon as permanently without the pale, especially in the conditions, as far as we know them, of ancient India.

# viii

## The Brahmans

ACCORDING to Hindu tradition, there were originally four castes—the Brahman, the Kshatriya, the Vaisya, and the Sudra—representing respectively the priests, the warriors, the artisans, and cultivators, and (according to the usually accepted theory) the remaining inhabitants conquered by the Aryan invaders. These four correspond to the Iranian divisions of ancient Persia, where they appear as "priests, warriors, cultivators, and artisans," the Sudra class being unrepresented because there were no conquered aborigines in Persia. There is a great temptation to assume that the caste system—or something like it—was part of the stock-in-trade of the Aryan race before they split up into their various divisions. It has, however, been pointed out that, if that had been the case, we should certainly have had some more obvious references to castes other than the Purusha-Sukta of the tenth book of the Rig-Veda, and the conjecture that the invaders had forgotten the old Iranian ideas and then recalled them later on has been scouted as too absurd and fanciful for serious criticism. If, however, we assume that caste was inherent in the Aryan scheme of life, it is not altogether so absurd. For the Aryan folk, when they arrived in India and under the conditions of the invasion, might well have discarded these divisions, and have revived them as the conquest proceeded and society began to develop. After all, the division is not unnatural and, indeed, is just what might have been expected in such a society. But the more important criticism is that there is nothing to show how or why the main features of caste arose—the endogamous and exogamous divisions, the tabus on eating and drinking, the idea of untouchability. If the germ of the idea did come from Persia, why did it develop upon such very peculiar lines?

But given the idea of a classification upon the lines of

caste, there is nothing remarkable in the orders represented. When an invading host is still engaged in the conquest of a country, it is natural that special honour should be paid to the warriors and the military leaders. This pre-eminence will continue until the country has settled down and become amenable to the common law. Then when the warrior class is no longer required, at any rate to the same extent, the learned men become more prominent as lawgivers, as priests, as the repositories of the sacred Law. Meanwhile, the ordinary business of life goes on; the common people engaged in trades and crafts, or, in early times, more particularly in agriculture, are classed together because they follow callings which may be called similar or which at least admit of a single classification. They are dependent on the soldier class for their protection and upon the priestly class for religious instruction, including regulations for marriage, for death and burial, and for birth, as well as for the laws that govern their lives. This classification of the orders is well known in many countries; it is not peculiar either to India or to Persia. The High Priest was specially honoured in Sumeria, as he was in England and France and Germany, and the pretensions of the popes to dispose of empires and to give commands to kings and emperors are a commonplace of European history. This being so, it is surely superfluous to speculate upon the origin of the Brahman caste as the offspring of the bringers of the heliolithic cult who "mingled their blood with the Dravidians." This is the surmise of Dr. Slater supported by Professor Elliot Smith.[1] His main reasons for his contention, which he does not claim to have proved but only to have harmonized with the facts, are:

(1) that the Brahmans have a tradition of descent from an ancestry different from that of the commonalty. "In the South of India they interpret this tradition as indicating that they are of Aryan descent and other castes of Dravidian descent." It is not clear what weight Dr. Slater attaches to this tradition, for he entirely rejects the interpreted claim to Aryan descent.

[1] Slater: *The Dravidian Element in Indian Culture*, p. 157 sq.

## THE BRAHMANS

(2) The carrier of the heliolithic culture claimed divinity, and it is the traditional theory that every Brahman is a god. This is hardly correct. It may be that every Brahman is looked upon as the representative of divinity and even as contåining more than his proportionate share of the divine spark, but it is hardly true to say that he *is* a god. Moreover, it is not stated how and when this tradition of divinity arose and there is nothing to show that he was so treated when caste first began or first developed into a regular system.

These two reasons need mean no more than that the priestly caste, when they rose to the full height of their power, claimed to be distinguished from the mass of the people by the aristocracy of descent and, having made good the claim by the general acquiescence of the people, laid further claim to divine or semi-divine honours, which they found the people ready to ascribe to them. Inordinate claims by the priesthood are not unknown in the history of Europe down at least to the Middle Ages, and there are clear indications of them in the history of Israel, especially in the career of Samuel, most reactionary of all the priests or prophets of whom we have a record. Once this undisputed supremacy is granted, there seems to be no reason why the priesthood, who in India claimed to be in close communion with the gods through ritual and sacrifice, as in Europe they claimed to be the mediators between God and the people, should not have gone a step further and accepted the divine honours which the people gave them, thereby establishing a tradition that they were demi-gods.

(3) The carriers of the heliolithic culture combined the worship of the Sun and the Serpent. As the Nambudris of Malabar worship cobras in the shrines of Nayar households, their connection with Serpent worship is obvious. And if Brahma is a solar deity (which is not improbable) "the whole Brahman caste" is even more closely associated with Sun worship. But if we start with the postulate that Sun and Serpent worship were closely connected, it is surely a long step from a particular sect of Brahmans, even if it is "the most venerated and most conservative of all Brahman castes" who worship cobras for the special benefit of a

## HINDU CUSTOMS AND THEIR ORIGINS

particular non-Brahman caste in a limited area in India to the generalization of the whole Brahman caste. It is not certain that the word Brahman is directly derived from Brahma. The Brahman of the Upanishads is quite a different conception from the world-creator.

(4) The carriers of the heliolithic culture brought from Egypt a knowledge of the arts of spinning and weaving as well as of agriculture. The sacred thread of the Brahman should be of cotton. "This appears to be a very clear indication that Brahman ascendancy has one of its roots in the descent of Brahmans from foreigners who earned the gratitude and homage of the population of India by teaching them to spin and weave." Dr. Slater wrote before the excavations in the Indus valley had produced any results, and we now know that a people existed there, built houses, wore jewellery, and were adepts in the carving of seals, at least one thousand years before the earliest date assigned to the Aryan incursions. They were roughly contemporary with the people of Ur. And in Ur have been found many examples of textiles which show not only that spinning and weaving were known but also that the arts had already attained a high degree of excellence. Although the sacred thread of a Brahman should be made of cotton, that of a Vaisya should be made of wool (though it seldom is). It would be necessary to show that there was a special connection between wool and the Vaisya before we can safely draw conclusions from the cotton thread of the Brahman. No doubt the Vaisya was originally a cultivator, but cotton cannot be excluded from agriculture, even if we suppose the raw material to have been tree cotton. The connection of the sheep with agriculture, which might well have embraced the keeping of flocks, does not seem close enough to enable us to draw any conclusions of this kind from it.

This certainly seems rather a flimsy foundation on which to build a theory or even to found a serious suggestion. For even if the Brahman caste was evolved in a manner different from the evolution of all other castes, which there seems no sufficient reason for thinking, we are still faced by the fact that while we have records of civilization back to about 3000 B.C., the earliest record we have of caste is certainly not earlier, and is probably later than 1500 B.C. The military class became, in popular language, a caste in all the conquering nations. The profession of the soldier ranked high, because it at least gave the opportunity for power and glory, if not for wealth also. But the power of the priesthood, which was supposed to have special relations with the Deity and which could blast by curses and excommunications, was always prominent, and in most cases became predominant. The institution of caste, as was suggested earlier, was evolved slowly, perhaps very slowly, and if it had its roots in totemism and tabu, it might well have taken on the rigid form which we know. If we combine these two factors, the insistence on ceremonial purity with the power of the priesthood, we need hardly look any further for the beginnings of the Brahman caste.

Professor Dutt of the Hooghly College, Bengal, aptly compares and contrasts the rise of the sacerdotal power in Europe and in India.[1] While on the one hand the celibacy of the European clergy prevented them from having an hereditary vested interest in the position of the Church, on the other the purely sacerdotal function of the Brahman avoided those clashes of temporal interests which were so conspicuous in the struggle between the Empire and the Papacy. The Indian Church (to use a convenient expression) was not hampered by the acquisition of fiefs; it "could build up its spiritual domination unhampered by the necessity of mixing and jostling with the ruling class for everyday existence." There was thus not the same struggle for temporal power, though there seem to have been disputes. "The temporal rulers in ancient India did not differ much in their pride and ambition from their brethren in other parts of the world, and as elsewhere they resented the claims and pretensions of the priesthood, not because of any territorial greed but rather because the priests claimed to be superior by reason of their priesthood, and because such claims did, in fact, clash with the undoubted right of the

[1] Dutt: *Origin and Growth of Caste in India*, vol. i, pp. 50–55.

Kshatriya to govern." We can see that the same thing happened in early Israel in the story of Saul and Samuel. It is quite evident that though Samuel bent before what we should now call "public opinion," he had no intention of allowing Saul a free hand, and he was determined that, if he was to be kept in leading-strings, the hand which held them should be his own. And so, when Saul showed signs of becoming refractory, Samuel promptly intrigued against him and set up a new king in the person of David, a most unlikely choice which he perhaps thought would arouse no suspicions. But Samuel died before Saul and left no successor, so that David, being a strong king, had no particular difficulty with priests. There was, however, in all this no question of territorial power; it was the spiritual power claiming to interfere with the Government, a claim which was the more insistent because Samuel had himself held despotic power before the elders demanded a revision of the constitution. That, or something like it, must have been the real contest between the Brahmans and Kshatriyas of ancient India. There was, however, no regular opposition such as that of Gregory VII to the Hohenstaufen Emperors, and this was the more difficult to meet, because while Gregory was succeeded by a series of nonentities, the Brahman priesthood, being a loose confederacy without an acknowledged head, carried on their claims as a corporate body.

If, then, it be admitted that the Brahmans, at least in the earlier stages, became the superior caste by reason of their priestly office and all that is thereby implied, it is not unnatural that they should have made use of their position to glorify themselves, as the priesthood has shown itself apt to do in other countries. That they did this in extravagant fashion, claiming privileges unheard of elsewhere and even arrogating to themselves the position of divinities, may be admitted. But it may be said, as a general proposition, that men can only go as far as they are allowed to go, either by law or by popular opinion, and the Brahman was no exception to the rule. It is, however, certainly indisputable that they were allowed to go much further in India than in any other country, and that this was so was due to a variety of causes. First, by the time the Brahman pretensions reached their height, the caste system had been fully developed and the prestige of it was such that the priesthood, now firmly established at the head, had no difficulty in making good their extravagant claims. Secondly, there had been a stage when the ritual sacrifices counted for more than the gods themselves, and the efficacy of these was made to depend on the exact observance of minute detail. The least deviation was apt to make them of no effect. These minute details were known only to the Brahman priests; the sacrifices were supposed to compel the deities to all sorts of benefits to the worshipper. It was therefore obvious that those who held the secrets of the ritual held the material prosperity of the people in their hands. But the most important cause of Brahman supremacy was the fact that they held the monopoly of learning. Not only were they learned in the rituals and in the Vedas, but they were able to put their own interpretations upon the texts and this they very naturally did in their own favour. They were able to do even more. For, as the literature grew, they were also able to lay down laws for the main castes, and, since there was no one to say them nay, the laws were in practically every instance favourable to the Brahman caste. These laws, by similar manipulation, were eventually invested with the character of sacred books, so that the prerogative of the Brahmans became in the end a part of the religious dogma. Many of these things were, no doubt, trivial and, to our thinking, puerile; but some—and amongst them those that related to the criminal law—were of the highest importance. A Brahman, for example, was exempt from capital punishment, and in almost all cases was subject to a lighter penalty, because of his caste, than were the other castes. Conversely, wrong done to a Brahman was more severely punished than wrong done to other men; the murder of a Brahman was the worst crime it was possible to commit. When, therefore, we read of "Brahman redactions," "Brahman manipulations of text," "Brahman pretensions," and so forth, it is only fair to remember that with the enormous power they wielded and the enormous temptation to which they were exposed, it would have been almost superhuman if they had acted otherwise. In all probability Gregory or Innocent or any other of those popes who sought so strenuously to exalt the sacerdotal order at the expense even of the kingly would have done much the same thing, stopping only at a claim to divinity, which would not have been in conformity with Christian doctrine.

The Brahmans did not, however, attain this position of superiority without a struggle, especially with the Kshatriyas, or, at least, without arousing a jealousy of their privileges which has remained more or less ever since. During the course of their history, moreover, they largely abandoned the priestly functions and took to many other occupations. We hear of them as soldiers, physicians, cultivators, tradesmen, shepherds, carpenters, hunters, and many other things. No doubt this multiplicity of occupation, though at first it may have been held as a degradation of the priestly caste, ended by a general levelling up. The Brahman carpenter would still receive respect as a Brahman, but as a carpenter he would to some extent—to the extent, that is, that there was growing competition—find the competitive level and by degrees it would come to be seen that a Brahman carpenter was no better than any other carpenter, and certainly not by reason of his birth. It must be remembered, however, that this attitude towards the caste did not take shape till after the pretensions of the caste, as a caste, had been admitted. The Brahman, therefore, always carried with him a kind of halo, nor has he ever quite lost it—at any rate in the eyes of the people. Though in these days the sacerdotal functions are for the most part confined to men of little learning—men who know enough to recite mantras at wedding and other festivals, without knowing or even caring to inquire what the inner significance is of what they do—and the bulk of the Brahman caste or the educated part of it is engaged in modern pursuits—in the service of Government, in the law, in journalism, in education—it still remains true that the Brahmans have, not indeed the monopoly, but at least the lion's share of what modern education has to give. Bishop Whitehead has committed himself to the statement that in a certain school there was hardly any difference as regards ability and intellectual development between Brahmans and outcaste Christians, so far as was revealed by the results of a scholastic examination. This may very well be true within the limits laid down, for the passing of examinations may depend on little more than application, perseverance, and a fair share of brains, and no one will claim that the Brahman has a monopoly of these. But if it be extended into the wider sphere of the affairs of life, it is certainly not true. Blood tells; the centuries which have left their mark upon the Brahman features have developed an intellectual ability generally unequalled by other castes. That is why the Brahman has so largely monopolized the service of Government and why Government is, in accordance with modern ideas, so anxious to hold the scales even that they will even promote inferior men, rather than give too great weight to the caste.

There is, however, another class of Brahman which trades upon its prerogatives, is entirely ignorant equally of spiritual as of mundane affairs, and battens upon the generosity or credulity of the people. They are the worst kind of parasite, which will even go to the length of protesting violently, if what in their arrogance or their greed they consider to be their due is taken from them. In a certain Indian State where the Maharaja had set his face against useless extravagance of this kind and had determined that charities must be discriminate and deserved by the recipients, these parasite Brahmans had the impudence to appeal to the British Resident, from whom, of course, they got short shrift. But these so-called charities were a religious obligation in the eyes of some of the people as well as in those of the ladies of the Palace, and the Maharaja's task was not easy. Of such people little good can be said; their outlook is very narrow and seldom extends beyond their own stomachs or at least their own self-interest. Happily they do not represent the majority nor any large minority. *Non ragionam di lor, ma guarda e passa.* But there are also many Brahmans

## HINDU CUSTOMS AND THEIR ORIGINS

who use their ability to overreach others, to insinuate harsh things of other castes, to grasp at places for their own fellows or relatives. That is not to be denied; it must, however, be remembered that the ethics of the East differ from our own. For good or ill, the individualism of the West has not yet taken firm root, though the idea seems to be growing. The East has not yet assimilated the conception of the State as a corporate entity which demands service from each man and woman. The unit is the family and the larger unit is the clan or caste. This conception is cardinal; to lose sight of it is to misunderstand much that seems to be mere intrigue and self-seeking. If it is not so obvious in India as it is in China, that is probably because for 150 years India has had a Government to which Western ideas are second nature. There are to-day many Indians to whom the idea of public service to the State comes first, and to whom anything that savours of intrigue or corruption is abhorrent. But there are also many others, born and bred in the Hindu atmosphere, whatever college or school may have done for them, to whom caste and family are the predominant considerations. They may pay lip service to individualism and selection by merit, which latter is by no means always observed in the West, but they are still Indian at heart, and to them the primary duty is to the family not constituted as we know it but embracing all kinds of agnatic and cognatic relationships. It is thus not a question of nepotism in the European sense but rather of the discharge of an obligatory duty, as important as was to us the rally to the colours in 1914. It is very difficult to appraise this attitude of mind. We ourselves have been accustomed all our lives to the principle that the call of public duty or of the country's needs outweighs considerations of family, and rather than incur the suspicion of jobbing a son or a nephew into a place a man in authority will deliberately choose the inferior. This principle has been stretched so far on the continent of Europe that in certain countries—notably in Germany and Russia—the individual hardly counts. The people belong to the State; they are there for the good of the State and for no other purpose. India goes to the opposite extreme and in so doing she has—perhaps naturally—incurred the condemnation of European observers.

It is, moreover, the Brahman who is looked upon as the chief opponent of British rule. That is an accident. It is an accident because by reason of his birth which has given him such unparalleled advantages he is better fitted than others to compete with the able men who compose the Government of India. For it is truer to say that the opponents of British rule belong rather to classes than to castes, and these classes are, of course, those who have most profited by British education. It is the lawyer, the journalist, the schoolmaster—all of whom are products of our own system and who before our advent were either unimportant or did not exist at all—who form the nucleus of the malcontent party. Mr. Gandhi is the most notable, but not the only, non-Brahman opponent of British rule. And these classes are, of course, for the reason given, mainly Brahman. It is sometimes said that when India has put into practice her new constitution, the Brahmans will seize the opportunity for the oppression of lower castes. That is not at all likely. What oppression, if any, there is, is in the villages and among the peasantry. It is there that caste reigns in all its rigidity; it is there that the low-caste man is jockeyed out of his land and that the lot of the no-caste man may become intolerable. Educated India has greatly changed its attitude; if the principles of the West have not yet grown to full stature, they have at least struck roots and are growing rapidly. The movements of the present day are nearly all in the direction of social service. The emancipation of women, the care of children, maternity problems, village improvement, are ideas which have no doubt been inspired by European conceptions, but are being enthusiastically adopted by Indians. This means that while the equality of man is not recognized (which is not to be wondered at, since it palpably does not exist) it is more and more coming to be seen that there are certain rights common to humanity and that respect for these makes in the end for national prosperity and welfare.

The Brahmans, in fact, like the Pharisees, have suffered

from an inordinate emphasis upon their shortcomings and a certain indifference to, if we may not call it ignorance of, their origins or at least of the environment in which they have been brought up. The Pharisee, held up unfairly to everlasting scorn as hypocrite and viper, has become the very type of the sanctimonious ritualist whose utter contempt for humanity and his duty to his neighbour is only equalled by his punctilious observance of "the washing of cups and pots, brazen vessels, and of tables." The popular conception of the Brahman is largely due to the influence of the missionaries, to whom he is the embodiment of arrogance and oppression. He has presumed to lay claim by reason of birth alone to a superiority which morally is spurious, because in fact there are many righteous men of inferior caste and even of no caste at all, since a high morality is the monopoly of nobody, and intellectually is only maintained and justified by the oppression of others and especially of the outcastes. That is, of course, true; but truer of the past than of the present. For the awakening of the lower-castes and of the outcastes is such that the Brahman can never again attain to that point of discrimination—to say nothing of divinity—which he once claimed and which was granted to him by the acquiescence of the people. No doubt he has much to gain in the new order of things —not merely what are called the loaves and fishes of administration, but also in the respect and reverence (and therefore also in power) with which, in spite of much hostility, too often deserved by his traditional arrogance, he is still regarded by the mass of the people; but that respect and that reverence tend now and will tend more and more, as education advances and men become more awake to their rights as men, to diminish. Nevertheless, the prestige will remain as long as the caste system endures. For as the Pharisees were the guardians and interpreters of the Mosaic Law to the people, and as the written law was the most precious possession of the Jews, since it contained the revelations of the Most High, so the Brahmans are the guardians and interpreters of the scriptures which to the Hindu are equally the revelations of God. And it is characteristic of the Hindu that he pays

## THE BRAHMANS

special reverence to tradition and the written word. Of course, in these days the scriptures which can be read in English and other tongues are no longer the close preserves they once were, but even so it requires a subtle and an educated brain to follow the reasonings of the commentators, and though the Brahmans have not now the monopoly of learning, custom, heredity, and tradition combine to leave such matters largely in their hands. The regular priests—the Brahmans who still follow the caste calling—are generally quite unlearned in all that pertains to the secular life and even in those things which to us make up religion. But occasions will arise when a man would ask: "What ought I to do in such and such circumstances?" and he may go to his priest for advice. In matters of ethics he is more likely to trust to his own conscience and his sense of right and wrong. All those points of ritual which seem of such vital importance seem to us unspeakably trivial. It might well be said of the Brahman, as it has been said of the Jew: "The Gentile would at once notice that the Jew did many special acts as a religious duty; that he made a point of doing things, in themselves apparently trivial, in a particular way and that he refrained from doing other things which to the Gentile seemed harmless or indifferent."

The Brahman has, it seems to me, received less than justice from the majority of European writers. There is more than one reason for this. It is (somewhat grudgingly) allowed that the brains of the country reside for the most part in the Brahman caste, but that, it is said, is because for centuries the Brahman made a close preserve of learning, so that his own ability is made a cause of offence. On the other hand, by his arrogance and pretensions he has certainly earned a great deal of dislike from the less favoured, though here again one may suppose that there is a trace of envy of the privileges which society has given him. To the European he is the embodiment of arrogance and oppression and this, with the Anglo-Saxon sympathy with the underdog, is enough to condemn him, especially in the eyes of the missionaries, who, if they have better opportunities to observe the inner workings of Hindu social conditions, are at the same time presented with *ex-parte* statements by their own clients. But perhaps the chief offence is that, alone as a class among Indians, he has the brains to stand up to and to criticize the Englishman. The popular notion is that all Indians, of whatever caste or education, must by reason of their colour, or their birth as Asiatics, necessarily be inferior to the white man. This is, of course, the outcome of the European penetration into Asia, equipped with military weapons and discipline, as well as with the wealth and the organization of the West, which have established the superiority of the white man both in the military and the economic field, and that superiority has not been questioned, much less challenged, until very recently. The European had hitherto enjoyed the comfortable feeling of a kind of paternal patronage. To go into the villages as some Lord Bountiful, to be treated everywhere as the Ma-Bap, the Mother and Father, whose children the villagers are, gives a pleasant sense of power and even of integrity which flatters the national pride.[1] Criticism, on the other hand, is not so pleasant; when it is just, it disturbs the complacent sense of superiority, and when it is unjust, it exasperates.

The Brahman, then, for all his faults is not so black as he is painted. In a country where religion was everything and where it still counts for so much and where to the onlooking Gentile "the only side which he can observe is that where his religion found its most characteristic expression in action," it was natural that the Brahman should still be regarded as the lord of creation, which by reason of his knowledge of the ceremonies and sacrifices and of the magical properties inherent in them he actually was in primitive times. It was equally natural that since others so regarded him, he was not loath so to regard himself. If in later times he may justly be accused of intrigue or of playing for his own hand, that is partly because of his environment and partly because of the belief in the all-importance of the family unit. When English education was introduced, he was quick to see where his advantage lay and no one profited more than he by the

[1] I am told that this attitude of the villages is passing away, if it has not already passed.

new system. As his star waned in the sacerdotal, so it rose in the political firmament. And those who attain power in politics are seldom free from the suspicion and the accusation of intrigue.

It is the combination of these factors—the arrogance and pretensions, the occasional (but not universal) oppression and contempt of others, the power of criticism, and perhaps a certain faculty for intrigue—which has led to the popular belief that the Brahman caste as a whole is the sworn enemy of British rule and all that it stands for in India. Yet, on the whole, the Brahmans have gained more, and stand to lose more, than anyone else by the discontinuance of it. It is they who, as we have seen, chiefly profited by the introduction of English education; it is they who obtained thereby, if not a monopoly, at any rate a very large share of Government posts; it is they who have swelled the ranks of the lawyers. If this be so, why, it may be asked, have Brahmans so often been found as uncompromising critics or even open enemies of British rule? The answer is simple. Every thinking man knows quite well that India has travelled upon her present road too far to turn back. She has the example of Japan before her eyes and ever since the Russo-Japanese War there has been the latent feeling that what one Asiatic people can do, another can do. But Japan is what she is because she has abandoned the old seclusionist ideas and has adapted herself to the tendencies of the modern age. By her own effort she has become one of the foremost military powers of the world and is fast becoming one of the foremost economic powers also. It is quite apparent that unless India wishes to abandon herself to the state of the Middle Ages, she must keep pace with the modern world. She cannot now dispense with the material comforts of the age; she is too closely wedded to the legal system to want to scrap it for another; she professes unbounded enthusiasm for education, and that not of the old type which confined itself to the Sanskrit writings and to learning religious mysteries by rote, but more and more of the type which will give general knowledge and will fit boys and girls to become good citizens. If, therefore, the British power were to disappear—as of course it cannot in a single year—if the British power were to disappear gradually, it is certain that these cardinal institutions would remain and the Brahman would have the same predominance in them as he has had all along. If, on the other hand, there should be a swing back to the older ideas, if the cry of "Back to the Vedas" should turn out to have more substance in it than is at all probable, the Brahman would still be the gainer; for he would recover that semi-divinity with which he was invested in olden times. But though these alternatives are probable they are not certain. It may be that the character of the administration will gradually change through the newly awakened consciousness of the inferior castes, who will become more insistent on obtaining their full share, or again it may be that in the altered circumstances of the modern world the Brahman can never recover his old ascendancy and that the lower castes will tend to assert themselves more rather than less. In any case, however, it is difficult to see how the Brahman can be a loser, even if he gains nothing, but it is mere cynicism to suggest that he has been actuated all along by nothing but self-interest, that the criticism and agitation in which he has so often been prominent have in them no traces of the natural desire to be of more importance in his country than he now is. In other words he is exhibiting the same sort of patriotism which we ourselves would clamorously approve if the positions were reversed, or which we should politely support if the struggle were between two nations and we ourselves were only interested spectators.

## ix

## The Cult of the Cow

YEAR after year takes its toll of human victims in riots between Hindus and Mussulmans. On the Mussulman side these generally arise out of some real or imaginary insult to a mosque; on the Hindu side out of the killing of cattle. It is difficult to apportion blame, for both sides are often quite unreasonable in their demands: Mussulmans requiring Hindus to cease playing music when passing a mosque on all days and at all hours of the day, whether there is any one in the building or not and however urgent may be the Hindu necessity; Hindus, again, suddenly objecting to the slaughter of cattle which has been peacefully done by a Mussulman butcher for months together. With the Hindu music we are not here concerned, but may remark in passing that it is clearly a survival of a pre-Aryan cult, relating to demons and other evil spirits. But what is the origin of the extraordinary veneration of the cow, in which term is of course included the bull and the calf? It is quite unlike the affection which Anglo-Saxons have for the dog and the horse; the dog is valued for its fidelity, its companionship, and its intelligence; the horse largely for its utility, but also, no doubt, for its noble appearance and its endearing qualities. We may grieve over the death of a horse or a dog, we may deplore the necessity which compels us to destroy the animal, but we do not regard either with a veneration akin to (though not identical with) worship. There is in this veneration nothing of that humanist feeling which convinces us that it is better to put an animal out of pain than to let it linger on useless and in suffering. For though there is very little intentional cruelty, not perhaps more than in most other countries, compassion for the beast extends only to the taking of life. Not long ago a carter was driving his oxen to market across a river bed. Cart and bulls became engulfed in loose sand and could not be extricated. Eventually the man got the cart free but not the bulls and they were left to their lingering fate while crows and kites pecked at their living eyes. This is an extreme instance, partly to be excused by the urge to reach the market on which the man's own subsistence depended. But it is unlikely, to put it no higher, that the man would have solved the problem by deliberately killing the animals. In lesser ways we can observe the same sort of ignorant callousness to animal suffering. Fowls are carried head downwards, donkeys are overloaded to the permanent injury of their legs, bulls are driven with sore necks and with no attempt to save them from the chafing of the yoke. I once had occasion to plead the cause of veterinary science, not only in the interests of the animals but also in those of the peasantry, but a colleague argued that "they are only animals" and the economic plea was brushed aside.

Yet in spite of what seems to us callousness to the suffering and indifference to the welfare of the animal creation, the very idea of killing a bull or cow is to the Hindu almost as repulsive as is infanticide to us. It is hardly an exaggeration to say that to commit this sacrilege is to him the mark of an inferior civilization. It is true that *ahimsa*, one form of which is an extreme reluctance to take any animal life, is a marked feature of Hinduism. Certain Jains, as is generally known, will cover their mouths, lest they should harm some small insect inadvertently, and will sleep in bug-infested beds to give the creatures a chance of a full meal. But while Hindus are averse from taking animal life, it is only in the case of cattle that we find a shuddering repugnance. To kill a cow is a crime, and what is worse, a sacrilege.

What is the explanation? It has been suggested that the cow, as the giver of milk and its products, and the bull, which is used as a pack or draught or plough animal, were so predominantly useful to ancient India that they were invested with almost divine qualities. Some expositors have gone even further and conjectured that, while the buffalo was well enough known, the bull was an imported beast and was therefore rare. *Omne ignotum pro magnifico*. It was looked upon with the awe of the primitive people as a novelty;

## THE CULT OF THE COW

its obvious advantages were quickly recognized, and so it became invested with a divine halo. To kill it was a thing that was not done. There was something uncanny about its rarity, and it was far too valuable as the staff of existence. Religion then stepped in. What had been a custom for utilitarian reasons became a religious tenet. To kill a bull or cow was declared to be only one degree more venial than to kill a man; indeed, it was worse than killing most men, for homicide was at most murder, whereas bovicide was both murder and sacrilege. Tradition persisted, as it has a habit of doing, until the killing of kine was regarded with the same kind of horror with which a bishop of the Church of England would regard the insolent misuse of the consecrated elements.

This explanation fails to satisfy. Generally speaking, it is unsafe to refer ancient customs of this kind to utilitarian conceptions which savour too much of the European and the modern not to be regarded without suspicion. For even if we add the religious sanction there was nothing to be gained by it. We, to whom the horse was (until the age of mechanism) so invaluable, do not kill horses unless they have become too old for life to be more than a burden, or have been so crippled or diseased that, according to our notions, it is more merciful to destroy them. No one wants to destroy valuable property so long as it is valuable, but if that was the origin of the veneration and the immunity of kine in India, the religious sanction went far beyond it. Miserable cows with staring coats and bones sticking out, useless for any purposes of milk-giving—bulls too weak to draw a plough or a cart, perhaps with only three legs, are to be seen anywhere in India and at any time. Yet they are as sacred as the others. It seems incredible that, making such allowances as we will for the strength of tradition, and admitting as we may that kine were pre-eminently useful, the custom should have gone to such lengths or that religious feeling should have expressed itself so strongly. For the goat is also a useful animal; it has been called the "poor man's cow." Yet goats are often sacrificed. Moreover, the rustic Hindu, who would shudder at the thought of killing a bull or a cow, has no great reluctance to sacrifice a buffalo on occasion, and Bishop Whitehead in his study of religious customs in Telugu villages frequently mentions rites in which the sacrificial buffalo plays a prominent part. And a buffalo, which is also a bovine animal, can be used for draught or the plough and for milk, and many a household has its buffaloes for these very purposes.

Who invented this custom? Sacrifice is, of course, known to almost all ancient peoples and the Rig-Veda mentions it frequently; it is perhaps significant that the offerings of milk and ghee and grain, and of the intoxicating liquor which the Aryans deified under the name of soma, take equal rank with the sacrifice of animal life. It suggests that in very early times there was dedicated to the gods all the best of what man had to offer; but, as time went on, the idea gained ground that a blood sacrifice was the worthiest, probably because it was more costly, just as in the book of Leviticus a turtle-dove was substituted for the prescribed lamb, if the woman could not afford the latter. And so, it would seem, greater stress is laid upon animal sacrifice in the Yajur Veda, which prescribes formulas for the priest and is conceived in the spirit of Leviticus. So important did the sacrifice become that in time it transcended the gods themselves and the old hymns of praise became the formulas of ritual. What was it that brought about the change? It is, of course, possible to argue that such a transition was simply the result of evolution. The change of climate and of habits, the influence of a more settled life, and the tendency of religion to develop into a system combined to give the priests a more dominant status and their sacrificial functions a certain factitious importance, just as in modern times the severity of certain forms of Christian worship is based upon the fear lest the accompaniments of ritual should obscure the deeper meaning of religion. It is, however, far more probable that the earlier Aryan religion in which there is very little trace of a dominant priesthood or of any settled system, beyond that of a general reverence for Nature personified in or presided over by the gods, not only became modified by contact with indi-

## THE CULT OF THE COW

genous cults, but also adopted the organization of the priesthood with its elaborate system of ritual which it found already established. Thus, after the Yajur Veda, we have the Atharva, which is linked up with the Rig by embodying some of its hymns of praise but is mainly composed of incantations and charms and spells which are very far removed from the simple, if lofty, Nature worship of the Rig, and which must have been the results of a cult or cults to us inferior but to them attractive. There is nothing fanciful in this, especially if the Aryans were not, except in the West, the insolent conquering hordes they are generally represented to be, but only a tribe of warriors who, when they had firmly established themselves in the lands they wanted, sent out feelers into other lands, conquering them too, not by force of arms, but by peaceful penetration, by a greater religious zeal, and by a more flaming enthusiasm. In like manner did the Israelites debase the purer monotheism of Jahveh by adopting the cults of the tribes by whom they were surrounded, a practice which is so constantly denounced by the Hebrew prophets.

But though to-day blood flows freely in the sacrifices, the cow and her kind are notable exceptions. How came it that this extraordinary reverence for bull and cow arose and became so deeply rooted in Hinduism? Professor Berriedale Keith, after recording that the Aryans slaughtered oxen as "in some degree a sacrificial act" and in any case as an act of hospitality, is driven to point out that there is no inconsistency between the eating of flesh and the growing sanctity of the cow which bears already in the Rig-Veda the epithet *aghnya*, "not to be killed." But he adds significantly "if this interpretation of the term is correct," implying that there is some doubt about it. And he draws the conclusion that "it is merely a proof of the high value attached to that useful animal, the source of the milk which meant so much both for secular and sacred use to the Vedic Indian." That seems a very flimsy and casual explanation. Why, if the Aryans slaughtered oxen both for sacrificial and for hospitable purposes, should there be any "growing sanctity of the cow," whose qualities must have been long known and

## HINDU CUSTOMS AND THEIR ORIGINS

appreciated? What caused them thus to realize, if slowly, that the cow must be venerated almost to the point of deification?

Now the date of the Aryan irruption into India is conjectured by scholars to be about 2500 B.C., and the date of the Rig-Veda (which is a miscellaneous collection of hymns) to be between 1200 and 1000 B.C. It is not unlikely that these conjectural dates will have to be revised in the light of Egyptian and Chaldean discoveries, as well as of those in the Indus valley, for the state of Sumerian civilization, as disclosed, for example, by the excavations at Ur, has revolutionized ideas of the conditions of life of thirty centuries ago. Be this as it may, authorities are agreed that a very long period, which may have been 1000 years or more, elapsed between the first Aryan invasion and the earliest hymns of the Rig-Veda, and the Rig-Veda itself is spread over some two centuries. It is, therefore, quite possible that the word *aghnya*, which, doubtful though it be, seems to be the only authority for the immunity of the kine, occurred long—anything from ten to twelve centuries—after the invasion, and at a time when the Aryans had become familiar with and had been influenced by the indigenous or pre-Aryan cults which they found in the country. It seems to be quite certain that the Aryans did not bring with them or indeed adopt for centuries this idea of the sacredness of kine. That it grew very slowly with the Aryan tradition may be admitted, for Professor Washburn Hopkins says that later on, in the period of the Sutras and Epics, it is "an old rite of hospitality to kill a cow for a guest," an offer which it was etiquette to refuse. It was, nevertheless, killed if the owner wished to kill it; the offer to the guest seems to have been a piece of formality, to be refused as formally, much as swords are offered and returned in India as a knightly and graceful ceremony to-day.

The argument is thus tending towards a solution of the problem in India itself. But as Max Müller has reminded us,[1] we must exclude the possibility of the custom having been brought from outside either by the Aryans, who for

[1] *Chips from a German Workshop*, vol. ii, p. 219.

reasons of their own allowed it to lie dormant, or by others who found their way into India. The sacred bull Apis will naturally occur to everyone. Apis and Mnevis were two bulls who became sacred at the request of Isis, who "besought the priests to dedicate one of the animals of their country, whichever they chose, and to honour it in life as they had formerly honoured Osiris, and when it died to grant it obsequies like his." It was therefore ordained "that they should be worshipped as gods in common by all the Egyptians, since these animals above all others had helped the discoverers of corn in sowing the seed and procuring the universal benefits of agriculture." The priests therefore had a free hand and they chose the bull for a certain definite reason. But the bull thus chosen seems to have been an individual, for "although he was worshipped as a god" (and became identified with Osiris) ". . . he was not supposed to live beyond a certain length of time which was prescribed by the sacred books and on the expiry of which he was drowned in a holy spring."[1] If, then, the Indian custom is in any way dependent on the Egyptian, it must have been radically altered in three respects. All cattle were not sacred in Egypt but only those which were dedicated to Osiris. Secondly, there was not only no objection to the killing of an animal but it was definitely prescribed, while in India the prohibition is absolute right up to the time of natural decease. Thirdly, though cattle in India are regarded as sacred animals and treated with veneration, they are not actually worshipped and the veneration stops short of deification. Except, therefore, for the fact that the Egyptian animals were bulls and were sacred, there is no analogy between the two cases, unless we are prepared to do violence to probability and to make unjustifiable assumptions.

The ceremonial connection of the ox with agriculture and especially with the harvest is a widespread custom and it seems to be prevalent in Northern Europe. Frazer gives instances from France, Germany, Switzerland, and Hungary. Here we apparently have the embodiment of the

[1] Frazer: *Golden Bough*, p. 476.

Corn-Spirit as a cow or bull and it might be suggested that it was an Aryan custom which took this form in the West, while in the East it became a veneration of kine as personifying that Spirit in each individual. Max Müller, however, drawing a distinction between traditional customs which spring from an instinct common to mankind and those which are merely national, deriving their origin from the original ancestral stock, warns us that unless we observe this distinction we may go very far astray. If it could be shown that this consecration of the bull as a corn-spirit was only found in the races derived from the Aryan stock, that might be a point in its favour, though there are other objections. Unfortunately, however, this same custom, bull and all, has been found in Guinea and also in China, and since similar customs are connected with other animals all over the world, it would seem to be one of those referable to a primitive human instinct rather than to a national or racial institution. Moreover, in some of these cases the bull is killed and in some others it is represented by a man or an effigy, so that there seems to be very little in common with the sanctity of the cow in India.

But that is not all. If the custom of venerating animals had been one of the features of the early Aryan cult, we should have expected the choice to have fallen upon the horse rather than the bull, for the horse would have been more useful to a nomadic conquering people both for war and for hunting. And this apparently was so, for we find that the gods "drive through the air in cars drawn chiefly by horses but sometimes by other animals."[1] The horse was therefore cast for the highest part that an animal can be supposed to play, to draw the divine chariots. And later on it is the horse sacrifice, the *Aswamedha*, which is the emblem of Imperial claim and therefore to be performed very rarely and only by kings. This, of course, does not mean that the horse was worshipped or even treated with special veneration for its own sake; there is no hint of that in the Rig-Veda. It does, however, suggest that the Aryans appre-

[1] Macdonell: *Hymns from the Rig-Veda*, p. 11 (Heritage of India Series).

## THE CULT OF THE COW

ciated the horse and thought it worthy of the highest honour. Yet the horse in these days is not paid any special respect, neither does it enjoy any special immunities or privileges. It is prized for its market value, as we may prize an animal for what it will fetch, but no more. If, therefore, oxen took the place of horses on utilitarian grounds it must have been after agriculture and trade were more highly developed, when the bull and the cow were looked upon as prime necessities for a pastoral life. It might be fairly claimed that kine became sacred at a later period when the Aryans had settled down to a more peaceful life; there is no inconsistency in this supposition, and it would also explain the word *aghnya* on which so much depends. On the other hand there is equally no inconsistency in supposing that during the long interval between the first invasions and the collection of the Rig-Vedic hymns the Aryans must have come into contact with the earlier inhabitants, whether we call them aborigines or Dravidians, and absorbed certain of their customs and beliefs. It is on the contrary the most natural thing in the world. If, as Max Müller has remarked, the existence of similar folk tales may in certain circumstances be evidence of the historical contact of races, it is obvious that when the two races are fused they cannot but have an influence upon one another.

In the Rig-Veda cattle are almost always spoken of as valuable property; "actual direct worship of animals is hardly found there," as we might have expected, had ancient Egypt been our source. A typical hymn to Indra says:

> Who slew the serpent, freed the seven rivers,
> Who drove the cattle out of Vala's cavern,
> A conqueror in fights; he, men, is Indra.[1]

Here no doubt the allusion is allegorical. Indra is the god of the rain; the clouds that hold the precious water back are "Vala's cavern," where the "cows," that is, that which is most profitable to man in a thirsty land, are held prisoners by a demon. Indra has therefore released the cows; the land is refreshed and yields her harvests. Anyone who

[1] Rig-Veda, ii. 12.

has watched for the rain in India, or who has seen the crops withering and blighted for want of it, can appreciate the Aryans' worship of Indra and his pre-eminence among the gods. But the "cattle" even in the metaphor are not sacred; they are the most valuable of the gods' gifts to men, or in modern parlance "they are worth their weight in gold."

Or again more clearly in a hymn to Usas, the Dawn:

> Mete out to us, O Dawn, largesses; offspring,
> Brave men, conspicuous wealth in cows and horses.[1]

As the dawn drives away the darkness, brings the light by which men can work, and discloses the treasures of the earth, she is characteristically bountiful. She not only brings the worshipper wealth and children, but bestows protection and long life, fame and glory, on the benefactors. Here, as is usual in the Veda, cows, which it will be noted are classed with horses, simply mean wealth. Wherever there is any mention of kine it is either allegorical or simply indicative of wealth. There is no pre-eminence given to them nor is there any allusion to their sanctity. The comparison of gods to bulls of course proves nothing; Eastern literature is full of imagery and even we describe a man as "bold as a lion" or "sly as a fox."

If, then, the Aryan literature shows no trace of this custom of venerating the cow, if the Aryans ate beef and sacrificed bulls freely, and if such traces of bovine sanctity as we can find elsewhere are so dissimilar that we are not justified in linking up the two, we must look for the practice in India itself, but we cannot ascribe it to the Aryans, for it has already been shown that the mere fact that kine are specially useful is not enough to explain this excessive reverence. Dr. Slater, on the watch as usual for the economic origin, says:

"As remarked above the Indian domestic ox is pretty certainly derived from some non-Indian species of wild ox; and it is therefore natural to suppose that it was introduced by some invading pastoral tribes, by the Aryans in fact."[2]

[1] Rig-Veda, i. 92.
[2] Slater: *The Dravidian Element in Indian Culture*, p. 107.

## THE CULT OF THE COW

This is, however, at best, only a reasoned guess and it is demonstrably unfortunate. The excavations at Mohenjo-Daro and Harappa take us back to 2800 B.C., or at least one thousand years before the date assigned to the Aryan irruptions. The excavations have not yet proceeded very far and admittedly have not told us very much about the social life of the people, but one of the things they have shown is that the bull was quite well known even to those early inhabitants, since it appears not infrequently on seals, as do other animals. There is, however, as yet no evidence that it was held in any particular veneration, though Sir John Marshall says that the bull was worshipped. But while the worship of the bull is not good evidence of the general sanctity of cattle, it shows that an animal that had risen to the height of deification must have been known and appreciated. Dr. Slater proceeds to argue that his supposition explains very naturally the prohibition of beef-eating, and especially of cow-killing which is so important a factor in Indian religion. "The newcomers, in order to protect their cattle, would naturally make the killing of them, and especially the killing of cows, a crime and a sin; and in order that the tabu might be effective they would make the prohibition apply to their own people as well as to the natives. Vishnu, as well as Siva, is associated with the bull, one of the names of Krishna being Rajagopal, the king-cowherd. Putting these indications together we reach the hypothetical conclusion that though the Dravidians in prehistoric times kept buffaloes and used them in the cultivation of their paddy fields and therefore associated them with the Goddess of Fertility, they did not in the proper sense breed them and never learned from them the biology of the birth of calves, but this knowledge came to them first by the observation of the more valued bull and cow." This explanation, which follows closely the utilitarian theory, is open to serious, if not fatal, objections. It suggests that the Aryans when they arrived about 2500 B.C. brought with them these valuable cattle, which were placed under tabu, either then or not long afterwards, for a tabu could hardly have been effective otherwise. But the Rig-Veda is at least one thousand years later, according to accepted chronology, and as we have seen, the Aryans even then and for a long time afterwards freely ate beef and sacrificed oxen. Again Dr. Slater assumes that it was the Aryans who domesticated and introduced the bull, the Dravidians having been content with the buffalo, but there seems to be no ground whatever for this assumption, unless it be the very slender ground that buffaloes are freely used in South India to-day. The reference to the biology of birth is obscure; if it has any bearing on the subject, it must be remarked that there is no adequate reason for supposing that the Dravidians learned it from the bull and not from the buffalo; if they had no bulls or cows, the buffalo was to them as valuable as the cow afterwards became. The only explanation that fits in with the theory is that the Aryans, whether they introduced the bull or not, found as time went on that the supply of oxen was not equal to the demand, and in order to preserve them they invented the religious tabu, much as we in our modern way preserve game in districts which have been overshot. But an undiscriminating tabu would be a very drastic method of preserving the species; it would entail, as it does now, the finding of pasturage for useless beasts. The problem of adequate grazing grounds has long been acute owing to this very tabu. Strict preservation soon leads to a glut of animals and in the case of domestic animals, at any rate, to a degeneration of the species. Elephants in the Nilgiri Hills became at one time a positive nuisance and even the famous lions in the Gir Forests of Kathiawar showed signs of becoming a menace to surrounding villages. The Aryans would soon have found out the inconvenience of an absolute prohibition, if they are to be credited with so much economic sense. Nor is it easy to induce a whole people to give up a long-established practice, while the opposition of the priests to the discontinuance of the sacrifice would probably have been strenuous. Such reasoning is too like groping in the dark, a catching at straws to bolster up a preconceived theory.

The cow is every bit as sacred in the South as in the North, the more so perhaps because the South is pre-eminently the home of the Saiva cult and, as everyone knows, the bull is sacred to Siva. If, as Professor Rapson says, the Dravidians retain their own customs, it is difficult to see why they should have adopted this reverence for the cow unless in obedience to a law which became universal. But why was such a law made, if, as we have seen, the utilitarian argument fails to convince? Just as caste is more strictly observed in the South than in the North, so one might have expected that an Aryan custom would have been observed in the North with enthusiasm, in the South with indifference. If on this hypothesis the law or custom had been imposed upon an unwilling or indifferent people, it would naturally have fallen into disuse when the practical results were found to be inconvenient and Aryan pressure, never very great in the Peninsula, became relaxed with the gradual fusion of the race. One must not overlook the immense power of tradition, expecially when it has arisen from a religious prohibition; the same tradition, however, exists in the case of caste, yet now the restrictions of caste are being relaxed in certain respects, and among certain classes who would still think it a sin to kill even a maimed and suffering cow and to whom the very thought of eating beef is horrible.

It is admitted that the Dravidian civilization, whatever it may have been worth, preceded the Aryan in North India, and it is in accordance with all theories and known facts of primitive races that after the nomadic and hunting stages were passed, the pastoral stage followed. It requires no great straining of argument to assume that the Dravidians followed the usual law, and, having driven the aborigines into the jungle where they still are, had settled down in the fertile plains of India when the Aryan invasion took place. Now pastoral peoples are inclined to worship deities of fertility, for it is a tendency of all early races to suppose some supernatural power to be in charge of the various departments of human welfare. The incarnation of the fertility spirit is found also in various parts of Europe and in other parts of the world in which it sometimes takes the form of the bull but also of many other animals. And we know that the aboriginal tribes, whether we call them proto-Dravidian or by some other name, did, until quite recently, practise human sacrifice in order to ensure a good harvest, the best-known instance being the Meriah sacrifice of the Khonds of Orissa, where the poles to which the victims were bound were still to be seen forty years ago. A more civilized people would naturally object to human sacrifice.

There is more to commend this hypothesis than the more usually accepted utilitarian theory, especially because it relates a primitive sanction to a definitely religious idea. There are, however, two objections to it. First, these fertility ceremonies generally ended in the shedding of blood, either of the human being or of the animal. And secondly, the divine victim was usually a selected individual, not a whole species. I do not think, however, that it is possible to explain variations of custom in every detail, why certain savages abstain from women when going to war or on a hunting expedition, or why others practise different magical tabus or customs. It must be confessed that such an argument is not of itself a sufficient reply to the Utilitarian theory which obviously fits in with the protection of the whole species. We must, however, remember that other animals besides the bovines are also sacred and ought not to be killed, and that here no possible question of the preservation of the breed can arise, at any rate in countries and at periods when close times for game in the interests of the species were unknown or were disregarded. No one can by human device other than that of game laws preserve the breed of the wild monkey, the peacock, or the cobra. The monkeys are often a pest and some shooting would in parts conduce to human comfort, but no game laws would ever be required to protect them, unless indeed the European market demanded skins to satisfy a prevailing fashion. The cobra is a dangerous snake and snakes cause more loss of human life than all the dangerous beasts put together. The close connection of the monkey with the worship of Hanuman and of the cobra with that of Vishnu might perhaps account for the sanctity of these creatures, but there does not seem to be anything which relates the peacock to religion, except that according to Frazer "the Mori clan of the Bhils in Central India worship the peacock as their totem and make offerings of grain to it." It might, therefore, be that the peacock and the monkey were originally totems of savage tribes, and that together with the bull their special sanctity has survived because the eponymous tribe was more powerful or crushed others out of existence. The monkey, as we have seen, was probably the totem which suggested the fable of the monkey auxiliaries of Rama on the expedition to Ceylon, and the cobra, being at once sacred to Vishnu and also a dangerous reptile to be propitiated as such, would have an additional reason for keeping its sanctity.

We may, therefore, be not far astray if we ascribe the beginnings of the sanctity of animals to totemistic ideas. We have, however, made the assumption that the tribes to which these totems belonged had generally suppressed the others, and, of course, there is no evidence of this. Nevertheless, it is quite probable that a custom of this lasting and widespread influence did not follow a single line of development from a simple source but emerged from the blending of more than one idea. The bull, whatever rank it took as a totem, is obviously a beast of fertility, inasmuch as it ploughs the land and fertilizes it by its droppings, while the cow supplies the milk, butter, and ghi which are, besides the corn, all that are needed for sustenance. But that is not enough to class it as a divine Spirit of Fertility. Now the bull is sacred to Siva, who does not appear at all in the Vedic theocracy; he is identified with, and is still sometimes called by the name of Rudra, who is a minor Vedic deity. Rudra, however, had nothing to do with fertility or with kine in the literal sense; he was a Storm-god and was associated with the Maruts, the deities of wind and storm. Consequently, he was a terrible god, a god whose anger it was well to propitiate, though he had also milder qualities. Thus a hymn of the Rig-Veda says:

> When mountains bow before your march,
> And rivers, too, before your rule,
> Before your mighty roaring blast.[1]

[1] Rig-Veda, viii. 7.

And again:
>From heaven Maruts bring to us
>Abundant wealth, distilling joy
>With plenteous food all nourishing.[1]

But though Rudra is "implored not to stay or injure in his anger his worshippers and their belongings" he is also invoked as the "best of physicians":

>Where is that gracious hand of thine, O Rudra,
>That is so full of remedies and coolness?[2]

There is no trace of a Fertility-god here nor any connection with cattle. Vishnu too, who appears under his own name as a minor Vedic deity, was clearly a Sun-god at that time; he makes his three strides over earth, air, and heaven. Later on, no doubt, in his transformed capacity of Preserver and Reproducer, in which one can still detect a trace of the Sun-god, there seems to be a more obvious connection with vegetation, but the only outward symbol that connects him with reproduction is the *namam*, or trident, which is said to represent the union of the sexes. His animal companions are the kite and the cobra, and neither of them suggests reproduction in any form.

Siva, on the other hand, is usually called the Destroyer, and as such he retains something of his Rudraic character as Storm god. Otherwise his character seems to have changed completely. There is nothing left of the Good Physician "full of remedies and coolness," nor does he, except as Rudra, inspire only fear. Mahadeva and the many variants of Iswara may equally inspire awe, or reverence, or even love. He has, therefore, become the destroyer of things evil, the purifier of the world, and the regenerator. This transformation, the disappearance of one side of his Vedic character, and the substitution of another, together with the change of name to Siva, the Auspicious (reminding us of the Eumenides), as well as the symbols which surround him, suggest that the Vedic god came into contact with some other god already established who possessed similar

[1] Rig-Veda, viii. 7. [2] Ibid., ii. 33.

attributes, and was, according to the custom of primitive peoples, a deity of fertility. The fusion of one god with another is not unknown and the case of Apis and Osiris may be mentioned; though the Egyptian culture may have been one and undivided, it is quite likely that the Vedic Aryans, after they had settled in the country, combined with Dravidians to form a distinct civilization. The fact that the original Vedic nature gods gradually vanished suggests that the Aryans had come into contact with new ideas which profoundly modified their metaphysical conceptions. This view of the transformed character of Siva as the destroyer of evil and the purifier and therefore the beneficent guardian of the human race is borne out by the legends, in one of which Siva, as Nilakanta, swallows the poison intended for the injury of mankind, and in the other, as Rudra, he quenches Kama, the personification of lust, with his fiery eye. No great stretch of imagination is needed to see how the attributes of Siva were gradually transferred from the physical to the moral sphere, from the destruction and regeneration of nature to the purification of the soul.

The principal emblem of the transformed Siva is the lingam and no words are needed to prove that this is a symbol of reproduction. His constant attendant is the bull, known as Nandi. But this bull is something more than the vehicle on which he rides. In South Indian villages the god Aiyanar, who may be called the Village Constable, has a number of rude clay horses arranged near the shrine, so that he can take his pick of the stables when he goes on his rounds. That is what they are there for, and they do not seem to be the symbol of anything. At Conjivaram during the Garuda festival the gods ride round the town on various steeds which are changed from day to day, but they are taken from the store-room of the temple, where during the rest of the year they are kept. Garuda, the kite-steed of Vishnu, may possibly have some connection with the avatar of Vamana, the dwarf who compassed heaven, the earth, and the underworld in three strides and who is reminiscent of the mighty striding Vishnu of the Veda. We may perhaps recall the eagle of Zeus as the royal bird which seems to

## HINDU CUSTOMS AND THEIR ORIGINS

dominate the sky and to search out the earth but there seems to be no other symbolism involved. Garuda is not found in conjunction with Vishnu in statues and reliefs nearly so often as the cobra who guards the god with outspread hood and who may, again as a mere conjecture and if Vishnu can be regarded as a god of vegetation, be analogous to the Greek dragon who guarded the apples of the Hesperides.

But the bull of Siva stands in a different category. It would be unsafe to generalize, to say that Siva is never represented in statues and sculptures with his bull; it is, however, true to say that in many, if not in most, such representations the bull is not to be found. On the other hand, the bull Nandi is generally to be found in Saiva temples, and in the same position. He stands outside the shrine facing it and in a recumbent posture. He is usually fashioned with much care and often with considerable artistic taste; the material used is hard stone. Unlike the clay horses of Aiyanar and the flimsy vahanams, which are easily replaced, and are merely the trappings and accompaniments of the god and his processions, this bull is evidently meant to last. He is part and parcel of the temple and his position and posture suggest that he is not considered as a mere riding animal, ready and alert if the god should choose to mount him, but the custodian and obedient servant of the god. Together with the lingam he becomes the symbol of Saiva worship, as in Christian churches the plain cross, which is nothing in itself, becomes the symbol of the deepest mysteries of the Christian faith. It is difficult to see how these symbols can represent anything but the worship of the principle of Fertility embodied in Siva the Destroyer and Reproducer.

In the development of this custom of venerating cattle to the point of refusing to kill them under any circumstances, it is not unlikely that the rise of Buddhism and Jainism played a considerable part. Gautama Buddha was born in 563 B.C.; the date of Mahavira, the reputed founder of the Jain sect, is not exactly known, but scholars are inclined to accept 468 B.C. The age of the Sutras is calculated to be 600–200 B.C., and it thus covers the rise of both sects. But the well-known doctrine of *ahimsa*, which, in the case of

## THE CULT OF THE COW

the Jains at any rate, extended to a prohibition against the taking of any animal life, could not have been the origin of the excessive veneration of cattle in particular, though it may well have consolidated a feeling that was growing up amongst the now mixed population. That the Aryans, as reflected in the sacred books, had not yet got so far but had in some measure accepted the idea seems to be clear. We are told that "it is an old rite of hospitality to kill a cow for a guest; and as a matter of form each honoured guest is actually offered a cow. The host says to the guest, holding the knife ready to slay the cow, that he has the cow for him, but the guest is then directed to say 'Mother of Rudras, daughter of the Vasus, sister of the Adityas, navel of immortality (is she). Do not kill the guiltless cow; she is (Earth herself) Aditi the goddess. I speak to them that understand.' He adds, 'My sin has been killed and that of so-and-so; let her go and eat grass.' But if he really wants to have her eaten, he says, 'I kill my sin and the sin of so-and-so' (in killing her) . . ."[1] Evidently, then, cow killing was not absolutely forbidden, but it had become so distasteful that the guest's refusal was couched in the set language of a religious formula. The allusions to Rudra, to Aditi, and the Adityas are significant.

Agriculture is practically universal in India, but it is comparatively rare to find places where the breeding of cattle is carried on systematically. The cow (or the bull) would therefore be valued not as we value them, for their intrinsic or their pedigree value, but because they—every cow and every bull—embodied the Spirit of Fertility. To destroy either and therefore the embodied spirit would be to jeopardise the produce of the fields and perhaps the results of a whole season's labour. There is nothing in nature perhaps more sacred in India than the rivers. It is not the Ganges alone which has this character; the Godavari, the Krishna, the Kaveri, all share this attribute of divinity, though the Ganges may be pre-eminent among them. And this deification of rivers is presumably testimony, if any were needed, to the value of water as personified in

[1] *Cambridge History of India*, vol. i, p. 232.

the rivers. In other words, the rivers embody the Water-Spirit and to do reverence to them is to propitiate the Spirit by which alone the fields can yield their produce. I suggest that in very similar fashion the Fertility-Spirit was embodied in the cattle and that the epithet *aghnya* arose when the Aryan civilization, impinging upon the older cults and embodying some of the practices which they found already existing, took on the idea of the sanctity of cattle, just as it took on and absorbed the idea of exogamy in connection with caste. In this way we can account for the universality of the tabu. We cannot be content with any specialized spirit which would be inherent only in a given consecrated animal, for that would not explain why all cattle are sacred, neither would it satisfy the millions of acres, scattered about in thousands of villages, which might be injuriously affected by the death of the sacred bull either by accident or deliberately of which they might and would know nothing. Thus the slaughter of any individual cow would have a purely local effect; and this idea would be in entire conformity with that of Immanence which may well have been in operation before it was erected into a principle. Indeed, it is hard to account for the practice in any other way; for, as I have said, the extreme value put upon bovine life could, on the hypothesis of utility, hardly have been extended to animals which are manifestly useless.

We may now gather up the threads of the argument. The utilitarian theory is not satisfactory: (1) because it is too modern in conception, (2) because it would have caused a glut of animals in the then state of pasture and the inconvenience would soon have become glaringly apparent, and (3) because it does not account for the preservation of beasts which are clearly useless for any purpose whatsoever. The custom is not Aryan, since the Aryans not only sacrificed oxen but ate beef until a comparatively late period. We must also reject any idea that the practice was due to importation from foreign lands, because we have no evidence that there was any such general sanctification of the bovines and where bulls were considered sacred they were in the end slaughtered or otherwise done away with. The suggestion

## THE CULT OF THE COW

that the bull was imported by the Aryans and was made sacred partly because it was novel and partly because it was valuable is refuted by the occurrence of bulls in the finds of Mohenjo-Daro and Harappa.

On the other hand, the idea of totems was very widespread amongst the pre-Aryans and the totem is sacred to the extent of immunity from destruction. And as the tribes advanced from the earlier to the pastoral stage, they would follow the very usual custom of worshipping or at least venerating deities of fertility. One of these deities was Siva, a non-Vedic god, though identified in certain aspects with the minor Vedic deity called Rudra; and the bull is related to Siva in a very special sense, more closely than is any other animal with any other god. But as agriculture advanced, those two things which most contributed to the production of crops, water, and cattle, tended to be credited with divine attributes, so that the rivers which embodied the Water-Spirit and the cattle which embodied the Fertility-Spirit were looked upon as sacred. No one of course can injure the rivers but the Fertility-Spirit is inherent in every individual bull or cow, so that to kill these animals is to kill the spirit which they embody and hence to anger the Universal Spirit, a part of whose essence is to be found in each of them. The anger of this spirit may well lead to the ruin of the harvest, either by drought or by locusts or by disease or even by floods. The peculiar sanctity of the bull and cow would thus be related to primitive ideas in which the spirits of good and evil played, and still play, so important a part.

# X

## Some Maratha Customs

INDIA has advanced and is still advancing in many ways along the lines of Western civilization. Western thought and Western ideas permeate much of her political, industrial, and even social life in a way and to an extent that makes any return to mediaevalism practically impossible. The cry of "Back to the Vedas" can never, in any practical sense, be more than a slogan; for, as an American has put it: "Ascetics like Gandhi and Tagore can no more wean their people from Western comforts than Mrs. Partington could sweep back the incoming ocean with her broom." But Western influence goes deeper than mere material comforts. The emancipation of women, the attitude towards widows and the depressed classes, the gradual abandonment of the more irksome of caste restrictions, the rise of journalism and even the format of newspapers, the predominance of the legal profession—all these and many others are indications of the power of European influence; the growth may be slow and progress may seem to be almost imperceptible; the impulse comes mainly from above, but it is working all the time, and if its effects are most clearly seen among the educated, it is none the less to be found among the masses also. Those who can look back fifty years upon India, cannot but acknowledge how different are not only the material conditions, expressed by the oft-quoted railways and posts and telegraphs and by the later introduction of electric light in the towns and of mechanized transport, but also the general outlook and the attitude of mind to social questions. A cynic may label these things as veneer, something that is laid on and will rub off, if only you rub hard enough. Such a view is neither fair nor true; European influence is rather an organic growth, sometimes struggling to exist against adverse conditions, sometimes striking roots that

## SOME MARATHA CUSTOMS

are neither deep nor lasting, but on the whole making headway in the country.

Yet behind all this much remains that is essentially Indian. England has wisely refused to interfere with religion and all that religion connotes; she has refused to force the pace in social legislation and has even been content to tolerate what she cannot approve rather than offend the susceptibilities of a highly sensitive people. Consequently, we find among the customs still prevailing some that are not only reminiscent of magic and tabu, but are the authentic expressions of them as contained in the sacred books, and especially in the Atharva Veda. In many cases they are no doubt simply survivals; they remain because they are ordained. The priests do not understand them and the people cannot explain them. If you ask "Why do you do so and so? What is the object of this or that? Why do you use such and such materials in your rites and no others?" the answer is invariably "I do not know. It is our custom."

There are various theories about the origin of the Marathas, the inhabitants of Maharashtra, which is defined as the region around the upper waters of the Godavari and the lands between it and the Krishna. Dr. Barnett considers that the population was of "more or less Dravidian blood upon which were superimposed successive strata of Aryan immigrants entering apparently from Vidarbha (Berar)." Ranade, who in some sort is the panegyrist of the Marathas, claims that the Aryan and Dravidian elements have been mixed "in due proportion" (whatever that vague term may mean) modified to some extent by the Scythian invaders from Bactria; but Professor Rapson thinks that the Scythians had had little or no influence on the make-up of the race, and he leaves us to gather that there was not very much of the Aryan to be found in Maharashtra. Edwardes, on the other hand, flouts the idea that the Marathas were of Scythi-Dravidian origin. On the strength of a Note by Mr. R. E. Enthoven, at the time in charge of the ethnographical survey of Bombay, he concludes that "the Marathas, whether of high or low status, are descended without any appreciable foreign admixture from the primeval tribes of the Deccan and the Southern Maratha country." From these varying theories we may perhaps take it that the main stream of Maratha blood is aboriginal, modified by Dravidian admixture and possibly by Scythian but with very little Aryan influence. Like the rest of India, however, they have adopted Aryan customs and religious ideas.

Now when we are dealing with a mixed race whose elements are chiefly Dravidian and aboriginal, it is natural to suppose that the cults of these peoples survived to some, if not to a large, extent. It may be objected that in Christian lands, Christianity has obliterated other forms of religion; that Druidism, for example, exists only in the ruins of Stonehenge and such places and in the Welsh Eisteddfod in name, if not in essence; and that Paganism has vanished from Europe. But in the first place it is common knowledge that Christianity has adopted and adapted some of the customs and ideas of Paganism. The very name of Lent, though now associated with fasting and mortification of the flesh, denotes a spring festival, and the form of the marriage service has traces of the old Roman civilization. In the second place, while Christianity has always been an intolerant religion, never allowing other cults to survive if they could be suppressed, Hinduism has always been a tolerant religion, ready to receive and incorporate other cults within itself and to make them part of itself. "From the Rishis of the Upanishads," says Professor Radhakrishnan, "down to Tagore and Gandhi, the Hindu has acknowledged that truth bears vestures of many colours and speaks in strange tongues. . . . Hinduism developed an attitude of comprehensive clarity instead of a fanatical faith in an inflexible creed. It accepted the multiplicity of aboriginal gods and others which originated, most of them, outside the Aryan tradition and justified them all. . . . Many sects professing many different beliefs live within the Hindu fold."

Hinduism has thus worked not by obliteration or suppression, but rather by absorption and assimilation. This flexibility, while it is largely responsible for the unregulated state of the system, which has thus been made to include at once the grossest superstition and the most subtle metaphysical speculation, suggesting on the one hand "the heathen" who "in his blindness bows down to wood and stone," and on the other intellect, keen enough to compete with, if not to surpass, anything that Europe can show, is also the main reason why Hinduism has been able to withstand the onslaughts of the various militant and proselytizing religions.

This being so, it is not astonishing to find much in the present-day rituals which is reminiscent of, and is clearly founded upon, ancient magic and aboriginal belief. Still less need we be surprised when the case is one of a people largely descended from aboriginal stock, even though it has been overlaid with some thin coating of Aryan veneer or been otherwise influenced by further admixture. We may add to this the quite exceptional value which the Hindu attaches to tradition and authority. That is why in the bustle and hurry of the modern world these things are done simply because they have to be done and very few pause to ask the reason why. European observers have noticed that even during the most solemn ceremonies such as marriage or the investiture with the sacred thread (corresponding in some sort with the Christian rite of confirmation) the assembly chatters and laughs together as if nothing unusual were happening and the priest's voice droning or chanting the sacred verses is drowned in the babel that is going on all round. It has often been said that the religion of the Hindu pervades his every action from the cradle to the grave, but one may go even further than this, for religious ceremonies begin before the child is born. The first of these is the *garbha-dhana* (the gift of the womb) and is intended to facilitate conception. The wife is dressed in new clothes and ornaments and is seated with her face to the east. The husband anoints himself with fragrant oils and after a bath takes his seat beside his wife. He then sips water and prays for purity in all that concerns the conception, and the couple then bow to the sun. In the evening they put on white clothes and enter the bedchamber. Everything is laid down in detail which might shock the modern—especially the European—mind but which is really intended to leave nothing undone to secure a child healthy in mind and body.

It must be remarked that the Hindu has not the same qualms that we have in speaking about or even in representing the natural functions of the body, so that what appears to us indecent or prurient seems to them only the natural expression of the great mysteries of Nature.

There seems to be more of symbolism than of magic in this ceremony, which, however, is falling into disuse. No doubt since every detail is carefully laid down, each has its meaning. The new clothes may perhaps suggest that the woman is entering upon a new phase of life with the conception of a child, or—more probably, perhaps—it may be that the new clothes, like the sipping of water and the evening garments of white as well as the man's bath, are symbolic of the purity of mind and body which are always considered so necessary to a solemn undertaking. It is a means of directing the mind to concentration on which here as in all ceremonies the greatest stress is laid. The only suggestion of magic is in the position of the wife with her face to the east. We shall have to return to this point later.

There are clearer indications of magic in the next ceremony called *Punsavana*, which takes place in the third month of the pregnancy for the purpose of ensuring that the child shall be of the right sex. As everyone knows the Hindu is specially anxious for male children who alone can ensure the repose of his soul. For all that daughters are not always unwelcome and in the South the birth of a first-born daughter was called *Lakshmi*, opening the womb. "The right sex" is, however, more often the male. In the first fortnight of this month and with due regard to the auspices of the stars and of the time, in other words, under the direction of the astrologers, the man gives his wife a barley grain in her right hand, and places two mustard seeds or two beans on either side of the barley. He then pours a drop of curd upon them and calls upon her to eat. This done, she takes a sip of water, which she probably needs after the dry mouthful, and the man touches her upon the womb with the words "With my ten fingers I touch thee, that thou mayest give birth to a child after ten months." He then

## SOME MARATHA CUSTOMS

pounds the last shoot of a certain tree, mixes the powder with ghee or a silkworm and with pap made of *panick* seeds (there seems to be no English equivalent) or a splinter of a sacrificial post which is taken from the north-easterly part of it and exposed to the fire; or he takes the ashes of a fire that has been kindled by attrition and inserts them into the right nostril of the woman, whose head rests upon the widespread root of an Udambara tree (*Ficus Glomerata*).

All this is a mass of symbolism with which is mingled some magic, though it is hardly possible to assign a meaning to every detail. It is quite inconsistent with Aryan ideas as set forth in the Rig-Veda, and it points unmistakably to the survival of an aboriginal custom among the Marathas. It is conceived in the spirit of the Atharva Veda, which, as we have seen, is a mixture of sublime hymns and of magical spells and incantations, and is, therefore, in all probability, the product of two intermingling civilizations. The symbolism of touching the womb with the ten fingers is obvious, even though the period of gestation has been conveniently stretched; it has been conjectured that the beans represent the male half of the principle of fertility; some evidence of this is to be found in three hymns of the Atharva Veda in which the throwing of beans accompanies charms to win a man's love. These are clearly sexual hymns and, if the conjecture is right, the use of the beans would suggest that the offspring desired is a son. It is more than probable that the mustard seed and the curd are allied to, or are symbolic of, the same principle of fertility; the mustard seed being pungent may have been regarded as a stimulant. We must not forget, however, that Jesus used the same figure in one of his well-known parables. The grain of mustard seed is there the small beginning, destined to spread and to grow into a great tree. And as Jesus was wont to use homely metaphors which could be easily grasped by the uneducated, we may suppose that mustard would be recognized as an example of prolific nature. It is but a short step from that to its symbolism of conception in the human womb. As for the curd, there is, as we have seen, good ground for thinking that the cow embodied the Spirit of Fertility.

The curd, therefore, as a product of the cow would partake of the same essential quality. It must be noted, however, that the beans, the mustard seed, the barley, and the curd are to be eaten by the woman, and this suggests that magical qualities were attributed to them. In swallowing them the woman would take into her body some portion of the universal spirit of fertility. That primitive tribes see an intimate connection between the fertility of the earth and the reproduction of the human race is proved by the examples collected by Frazer from Africa and America, of the orgies of men and women practised at the time of sowing the seed, and he adds that "it would be unjust to treat these orgies as a mere outburst of unbridled passion; no doubt they are deliberately and solemnly organized as essential to the fertility of the earth and the welfare of man." Even more to our purpose, because it is a custom of an aboriginal tribe in India, is the festival of the marriage of the Earth to the Sun-god, celebrated by the Oraons of Bengal. "After the ceremony all eat and drink and make merry; they dance and sing obscene songs and finally indulge in the vilest orgies. The object is to move the mother earth to become fruitful . . . . On the principle of homoeopathic magic, the people indulge in a licentious orgy." No doubt these examples prove the exact opposite of what we are now discussing; the union of the human sexes is supposed to increase the fertility of the earth, but there seems no good reason why, on the same principle, the opposite should not hold good and the fertility of nature be held to induce fertility in the woman. The use of ashes of a fire kindled by attrition may have some obscure reference to Agni and the Vedic worship of the Fire-god. For Frazer says that "in the ancient Vedic hymns of India the Fire-god Agni is spoken of as born in wood."[1] Fire produced by friction or attrition seems to have something supernatural in it, as other tribes seem to have thought; the god, the divine spark, is in the wood itself. Fire produced by igniting phosphorus and applying a lighted match would not seem divine to anyone, however little they may understand the reason why.

[1] *Golden Bough*, p. 708.

## SOME MARATHA CUSTOMS

Lastly the barley. If it be accepted that Demeter is the Corn-Mother and that "of the two species of corn associated with her in Greek religion, namely barley and wheat, the barley has perhaps the better claim to be her original element,"[1] the connection between the barley grain and the spirit of fertility would seem to be established. We must note, too, that "there are grounds for believing that it is one of the oldest, if not the very oldest, cereal cultivated by the Aryan race." It may well be that barley was cultivated in India before the Aryans were heard of, but in any case the use of barley in such a ceremony suggests that the custom is a very ancient one. It cannot be pretended that these explanations rest upon any firmer foundation than plausible or probable conjecture; those who described the facts of the ceremony had no explanation to offer. If, however, they are anywhere near the truth, they do suggest an intermingling of Vedic ideas, as exemplified by the fire, with the older aboriginal cults.

Yet another ceremony takes place in the fourth month of the pregnancy. After the ceremonial bath and the donning of white clothes by the pair, the husband performs regular sacrificial rites which include a hymn to Varuna. He then seats his wife on the west of the fire, and standing in front of her, so as to face west, he parts her hair from the forehead backwards with a porcupine quill that has three white spots, at the same time holding a bunch of unripe fruit, and recites certain mantras for the protection of the womb. Here we have the three elements combined, of Vedic worship, of sacrifice as contained in the fire and the oblations, and of magic as seen in the mystic symbolism and the incantations. It looks as if there had been a deliberate attempt to fuse the old aboriginal worship with the more refined ideas of the Vedic Aryans. The parting of the hair with a porcupine quill seems to be analogous to similar parting with a thorn which is considered to be symbolical of ploughing and hence of reproduction. There seems also to be some special virtue in the quill of a porcupine but neither research nor ingenuity has availed to explain what it is. Fruit is

[1] *Golden Bough*, p. 399.

sometimes used as a substitute for a child; and a child placed in the lap of a bride is supposed to communicate fertility. The fruit is to be unripe and no doubt symbolizes the foetus in the womb which it will take another five months to bring to perfection and in the fourth month may well be regarded as unripe.

The first two of these ceremonies—the *Garbhadana* and the *punsavana*—have, however, fallen into disuse, probably because as society became more complex and there were greater demands on the working hours, most people have neither the time nor the inclination for any ceremonies save the really important ones, perhaps also because the Hindu world has grown more sceptical of the efficacy of such rituals. We may pass now to the first of the important ceremonies, that which celebrates the birth of the child. These ceremonies are divided into three parts, called *Jatakarma* or the physical birth, *Medhajanana* or the birth of intelligence, and *Ayusha Vardhana* or the boon of long life.

When the child is born, the father lays an axe on a stone and a piece of gold on the axe. He then turns these things upside down and holds the boy over them, at the same time repeating the mantra:

Be a stone, be an axe, be invincible gold. Thou art indeed the Veda called son; so live a hundred autumns. From limb by limb thou art produced; out of the heart thou art born. Thou art indeed the Self called Son; so live a hundred autumns.

The special interest of this prayer, beside the sympathetic magic implied in the materials used, is that it is taken from the Atharva Veda. The thirteenth hymn of the Second Book is described as a prayer for the welfare and long life of an infant:

Thou hast put about thee this garment in order to well being; thou hast become a protector of the people against imprecation; both do thou live a hundred numerous autumns and do thou gather about thee abundance of wealth. You stand on the stone; let thy body become a stone; let all the gods make thy lifetime a hundred autumns.

The actual words or something very closely akin to them are used on a later occasion, at the ceremony of the Upanayana, the investiture with the sacred thread which denotes the spiritual rebirth of the child. It would seem that the formula was transferred from the one ceremony to the other, or that much the same formula was used for both, since the two are so closely connected.

The Sutikagni, or Birth-fire, is then kindled and the father fumigates the new-born child with grain mixed with mustard seed. He throws them eleven times into the fire, praying for the protection of the child from demons and other evil spirits. It is difficult to explain the recurrence of the mustard seed; perhaps on the analogy suggested it may represent a charm designed to perpetuate the race by ensuring that the child will have offspring with the fecundity of the mustard. Fire, of course, is a common feature in all sacrificial rites, but in the thirty-second hymn of the Sixth Book of the Atharva Veda it is used as a special charm against demons, and having regard to the prayer and to the solemnity of the occasion that seems to be the special object here. The number eleven, too, has a tinge of magic or at least of symbolism, for it represents the Matas or Mothers to whom the child is committed. The man then washes his hand and touches the ground repeating these verses:

O thou whose hair is well parted! (that is to say, thou in whom the seed successfully sown has brought forth fruit). Thy heart dwells in heaven, in the Moon; of that immortality impart to us a portion! May I never have to weep for the distress caused to me by my sons.

I know thy heart, O Earth, that dwells in heaven, in the Moon. Thus may I, the Lord of immortality, never weep for the distress caused to me by my sons.

This is clearly an invocation to the Earth-goddess and it strengthens the suggestion that the parting of the hair is connected with the ploughing of the furrow. The verses with the typical refrain are in the style of the Atharva Veda though there does not seem to be any extant hymn which exactly corresponds.

## HINDU CUSTOMS AND THEIR ORIGINS

Upon this ceremony there follows the rite of the Medhajanana. The father gives the child some ghee with a golden spoon to which he has tied a piece of *darbha* grass. The child is held towards the east and the father, as it were, "baptizes" it in the names of the Rig-Veda, the Yajur, the Saman, the Atharvan, and the Angiras. The child is then bathed in lukewarm water with prayers for freedom from disease and for earthly bliss. The father then places the child in the mother's lap and addresses her thus:

May no demon do harm to thy son, no cow that rushes upon him. Mayst thou become the friend of treasures; mayst thou live in prosperity in thine own way.

Then he washes first the right and then the left breast with appropriate formulas and finally touches both the breasts, placing a water-pot near her head and asking the waters "to watch over his wife, the mother of a good son."

I cannot pretend to explain the details of this ceremony. No doubt some mystic meaning was attached to the golden spoon, and *darbha* grass often figures in sacred rites. We may, however, notice two points—the position of the child to the east and the use of the water-pot. In many of these ceremonies the position is most carefully described. Attention has already been invited to the "north-easterly" chip to be taken from the sacrificial pillar; then again the man must face west, the woman east, and so on. The east is of course the direction of the rising sun and if the woman, who is the more important participant in ceremonies of childbirth, faces east the man who faces her must turn towards the west. On the other hand, the south is always carefully avoided. The south is the abode of Death and the kingdom of Yama, and so there is a custom that a man should not lie down with his head to the north because he would then be facing south, with his feet ready to start on their last journey. But a corpse is laid out with its face to the south because that is the way the soul must go. The north, on the other hand, is an auspicious quarter. Wherever you are in India the Himalaya is to the north of you and the Himalaya is the abode of the gods; obviously if you want to propitiate them, you must do so in an attitude of adoration, for they, like Jahveh, are jealous gods.

Water plays a considerable part in these ceremonies, and it is not confined to cleansing properties. The placing of a water-pot near the mother is evidently symbolical. It may well be that just as the sacrificial fire was, in some sense at any rate, an offering to Agni, the god of fire, so the water pot was meant to propitiate the water deities, especially Indra, though we need not suppose that the Aryan deities of the rain were the first of their kind. In a country like India, where after a long, hot drought a single shower will carpet the earth with green, and where so many things were thought to be obtainable by the exercise of charms and incantations, the primitive tribes could hardly have overlooked the value of water, which has been recognized in so many uncivilized parts of the earth. We are thus led once more to the cult of fertility in which so many of these ancient customs seem to have had their roots.

These ceremonies, though still practised, do not seem to be obligatory. Now, however, we come to a rite as universal as is the rite of baptism in Christian countries—the *Namakarana* or naming of the child. It takes place on the 12th day after birth, when the mother is reckoned to be able to leave her bed, and being now ceremonially pure, is free to move about the house. The father lights the sacrificial fire called *Aupasana* and the *Sutikagni* is taken away. He offers twelve or thirteen oblations—the reason for the number is not apparent—and prays for health and wealth. He then gives the child a secret name—of an even number of syllables if it be a boy, of an uneven number if a girl, and this name is known only to the father and the mother. Another name is given to the child for common use, and it is by this latter name that the child is known to the world. It has been suggested that the possession of two names was in ancient days supposed to ensure success, but it is more likely that it is a species of tabu and is connected with magic. Thus Frazer says:

Amongst the tribes of Central Australia every man, woman, and child has, besides a personal name which is in common use, a secret or sacred name which is bestowed by the older men upon him or her soon after birth, and which is known to none but the fully initiated members of the group. This secret name is never mentioned except upon the most solemn occasions; to utter it in the hearing of women or men of another group would be a most serious breach of tribal custom, as serious as the most flagrant case of sacrilege amongst ourselves. . . . The native thinks that a stranger knowing the secret name would have power to work him ill by means of magic.[1]

Nor is the custom to be found only in Australia. Illustrations are given from ancient Egypt, the island of Nias in the Malay archipelago, The North American Indians, the upper Congo, and this particular instance of the Brahman is also mentioned. The custom has variations; in some cases a man's name may be communicated to strangers; in others the reply to the question "What is your name?" is given by a slave. It is said that "the superstition is current all over the East Indies without exception," and that if in the course of administrative or judicial business a native is asked his name, instead of replying he will look at his comrade to indicate that he is to answer for him, or he will say straight out "Ask him." I can only say that in the course of trying several hundred cases in Court and after many years' administrative experience in India, I never found any difficulty in getting a man to give his name. That may perhaps be because he is not afraid of speaking his common—or false—name and is only reluctant to give the true or secret one.

The penalties of revealing the name are as varied as the custom itself; they are all agreed on one point, that they are the work of demons or evil spirits or of the malice of ill-wishers. The young Maratha Brahman, however, who gave me most of the information regarding the customs of his people, did not seem to be greatly troubled by the fear of demons, for he told me what his secret name was. He did this in a somewhat shamefaced manner, as if he knew he was doing wrong, and in something of an undertone, as if he hoped the spirits might not hear. It is, of course, possible that there was little harm in telling the name to a foreigner, and that

[1] *Golden Bough*, p. 245.

## SOME MARATHA CUSTOMS

the low tone was to avoid being heard by prying Indian ears. It is more probable that in this more sophisticated age, he who had received a good education of the European type, looked upon the whole thing as so much hocus-pocus, and that he would have had no scruple in telling the name to anyone but was a little afraid of offending the orthodox if there should be any such about. The name, at any rate, was quite safe with me, for I forgot it by the next day and the only object I had in asking for it was for the purposes of this inquiry.

On the sixth night after the birth of a child the worship of the goddess Sashti (Sashti = sixth) is performed, for the removal of calamities, the attainment of long life and health for the new-born baby, its mother, and father. The father first worships Ganpati who is not a Vedic god and whose special function it is to remove obstacles. Ganpati seems to be a favourite god with the Marathas; in Baroda State, where the ruling house and many of the leading officials are Marathas, there is a special procession in his honour with elephants, horses, and troops, and to the drowning of the god, which takes place at the end of it, the Gaekwar family contribute a special image of their own. We are not here concerned with the meaning of this rite, but it may be remarked in passing that it is connected with agriculture. To return to the Sashti worship; the father then scatters mustard seed with the prayer:

Fly away, ye evil spirits and goblins that dwell on earth. May all the evil spirits that obstruct our life be destroyed at Shiva's command.

Then he takes a jar of water, an emblem, as we have seen, of fertility, and worships Varuna. As Varuna is the kindly god of the sky, we may not be far wrong in supposing that the water-jar is also intended as an oblation. Next he sets up the image of the goddess and does obeisance to her. After that the goddess Durga is invoked with the "Sixteen Mothers" for the protection of the child; then the six Kritikas, Brahma, Siva, and Narayan (Vishnu), and Kartikeya, the son of Siva. We may pause here to note the extraordinary jumble of different cults which indicate that the whole ceremony has grown, as it were, by accretion, and is in effect an example of the intermingling of the races and their religious ideas. Varuna is a purely Vedic god whose worship in the temples has completely disappeared and who is no more to the Hindu of to-day than Apollo or Athene to ourselves. Brahma, Siva, and Vishnu make up, of course, the post-Vedic Trimurti, and though Siva exists in Vedic literature as Rudra the Storm-god, and Vishnu also appears as a minor deity, not distinguished by avatars, the Trimurti as such is a conception of Upanishadic times, of those times when religious speculation and philosophy had taken the place of the earlier and simpler Nature worship of the Aryans. Finally, both Ganpati and Durga (Kali) appear to be importations from aboriginal cults grafted upon the Hindu system with that easy adaptability which is so characteristic of it. Nor, as far as one can judge, is there any discrimination or order of precedence; the worship of all is necessary to the ceremony; no one deity is honoured more than another. The intermingling of these cults in so solemn a rite as the "baptism" and naming of the child shows how difficult it is to separate the one from the other in the mosaic called Hinduism, how difficult it is to say with any certainty that the aboriginal cults have had only a secondary influence on the religion, and leads us a step nearer the conviction that the roots of Hinduism are to be found in those aboriginal cults rather than in the Nature worship of the Aryan invaders.

We next arrive at what appears to be pure symbolism. A sword, a bamboo mace, a conch shell, a churning stick, Vishnu, and a plough are invoked. These articles with the exception of Vishnu, who seems to be out of place in the collection, appear to indicate a choice of professions open to a boy to whom these elaborate ceremonies mainly apply. The first three indicate the profession of arms, for the conch shell was used as a trumpet in battle and may be the appropriate accompaniment of sword and mace. Alternatively, it may be that the conch which is used in temples is meant to symbolize the profession of a priest. The plough, of course, is for agriculture. The meaning of a churning stick is more

## SOME MARATHA CUSTOMS

obscure. It may have some dim reference to the churning of the Ocean to discover the amrita (Greek ἄμ-βροτος) of immortality and may thus signify long life. This would, however, seem to be out of keeping with the rest, were it not that Vishnu seems to be worshipped in his character of protector and preserver rather than in his more general character of the second Person of the Trimurti. It might perhaps be symbolical of cattle, and cattle in early days meant wealth. The only other explanation seems to be that the boy may belong to no particular profession and is destined for a life of domesticity; but this is hardly likely. We have to bear in mind that these rites are ancient and were invented at a time when there was not much scope for a boy's ambition but when every able-bodied male was expected to contribute something to the social community. War was the most honourable of all professions, hardly excepting the priesthood, and though war was the special prerogative of the Kshatriya caste, it is generally agreed that enlistment for the army was not, and could not be, confined to that caste. Wealth, especially wealth in cattle, was greatly desired and there are many prayers for this particular boon. And there always remained agriculture, then as now the most important of all Indian industries.

After a long prayer to the goddess Sashti for the protection of the baby, couched in the usual form of repetition, the child is "baptized"—that is to say, the father touches his eyes with water and another long prayer to each of many gods in turn is recited. Then the father takes eleven threads and makes eleven knots in them and the nurse or mother puts this composite cord round the child's neck. The lying-in chamber is fumigated with mustard seed, salt, and the leaves of the nim tree (*Melia Indica*), which is thought to have special disinfectant properties. Further worship of numerous gods follows. The Brahmans are entertained as usual and finally the *tilak* or so-called caste mark is put upon the baby to symbolize his reception into the community.

It is a long and elaborate ceremony, full, no doubt, of symbolism and magic. The eleven knots are for the eleven Mothers already mentioned. The knots are clearly magical.

The idea seems to be one of entanglement and the use of knots as a charm or amulet has been noted in various parts of the world. They may be used either to injure or to benefit the patient. You may either entangle your victim so as to make him an easy prey to the evil spirits or you may entangle the spirits themselves. Frazer gives many examples of both kinds, taken from ancient Rome, from the East Indies, where knots are thought to tie up a woman in childbirth, from England and Scotland, as well as from less civilized parts. "A net, from its affluence of knots, has always been considered in Russia very efficacious against sorcerers," and again, "often a Russian amulet is merely a knotted thread. A skein of wool wound about the arms and legs is thought to ward off agues and fevers." We may perhaps allude in passing to the belief that a bracelet of grass or straw will serve—at least temporarily—as an antidote to snake-bite, as I have myself seen in South India. In this type of the ceremony the knots are evidently of the beneficent type and are intended to ward off or entangle the evil spirits who have thus to contend not only with the knots, but also with the eleven Mothers.

In the sixth month occurs the rite called *Annaprashana*, which celebrates the first feeding of the child with solid food. It is a Vedic ceremony, since oblations are offered to Varuna, and in Vedic times it seems that not only was flesh offered to the baby but that different kinds of food had different virtues—goat for physical prowess, partridge for saintliness, boiled rice and ghee for splendour, fish for swiftness. The natural repugnance of the Hindu to the taking of animal life which received such great stimulus from the Jain and Buddhist doctrine of *ahimsa* seems to have resulted in the substitution of vegetable foods, so that the food now offered is curds, ghee, and honey, As, however, the ceremony is a religious one, prayers are offered that water and plants will be kind to the boy and do him no harm.

The last of the ceremonies which concerns the infant is the shaving of the head. At the age of one year, or, according to some authorities, two, the head of the child, whether

## SOME MARATHA CUSTOMS

boy or girl, is shaved, and in the case of the boy a mantra is recited:

The razor with which Savitri the knowing one has shaven the head (or beard) of King Soma and Varuna, with that, ye Brahmans, shave his head; cause vigour, wealth, and glory to be united in him. The razor with which Pushan has shaven the beard of Brihaspati, of Agni, of Indra, for the sake of long life with that I shave thy head.

This mantra, allowing for differences in translation, is almost identical with a hymn in the Atharva Veda (vi. 68):

Savitar (the Sun) hath come with razor; come, O Vayu (the Wind) with hot water; let the Adityas, the Rudras, the Vasus wet him in accordance; do ye forethoughtful shave (the Head of) King Soma. With what razor the knowing Savitar shaved the head of King Soma, of Varuna, therewith ye priests shave it now of this man; be he rich in kine, in horses, in progeny.

So far the rite appears to be purely Vedic. All the gods invoked are Vedic gods and the mention of Soma is specially significant. There seems to be nothing which in principle might not find a place in Christian worship. That is to say, there is nothing beyond invocation and prayer, nothing that suggests either magic or superstition or is in any way referable to aboriginal beliefs. But then follows something that takes it outside the circle of the Aryan system. Someone of a kindly nature gathers the hair and buries it—in a cow stable, or near an Udambara tree *(Ficus glomerata)*—or in a clump of the sacred *darbha* grass, commending it to the care of the Vedic gods.

This is a clear instance of the belief in witchcraft, for "the notion that a man may be bewitched by means of the clipping of his hair, the paring of his nails, or any other severed portion of his person is almost world-wide and attested by evidence too ample, too familiar, and too tedious in its uniformity to be analysed at length." Even the selection of places where the hair is to be concealed has its counterpart in other parts of the world, where, as here, there is generally some religious idea connected with the place chosen—a temple or a cemetery or a lucky (i.e. auspicious) tree. One might have expected that the Indian tree would have been the pipal (*Ficus religiosa*) but the *Ficus glomerata* has evidently some religious significance to the Marathas, since, as we have already seen, the pregnant woman lies with her head on a root of it during one of the earlier ceremonies. It is possible that, since it is not always easy to find a tree of this kind or a clump of *darbha* grass, the cow stable became sacred, for almost every house in a village will have some kind of stable for cattle, at any rate amongst the large class who own land, however minute the holding. That there is some special sanctity attaching to hair is also seen in the top-knot or *kudimi*, which is carefully preserved in the South, when the head is otherwise shaved. The practice seems to have arisen from the idea that the soul must have some outlet, the idea which caused the Egyptians to paint an eye on the corner of a sarcophagus. Or it may be that strength and therefore virility resides in the hair, as in the Samson legend, and the power of begetting a son is all-important to the Hindu.

The great ceremony of initiation with the sacred thread which takes place on the eve of manhood may be compared with the rite of confirmation in Christian lands, but it also suggests some affinity with those rites which are so common, and are held so sacred, among savage tribes. It was the rite which introduced the initiate into the first period of a Brahman's life. The status of *bramhachari*, which lasted for at least twelve years, was to be followed by that of *grihasta*, or householder, of *vanaprasta* when the mature man, having passsed middle age, should return to meditation in the forest, subsisting there by what Nature provided, and lastly of Ascetic or Sannyasi when, having renounced the world, he was required to subsist on charity alone. There was in this a gradual relaxation of worldly ties; it was admitted that the man, having first acquired knowledge, should have the opportunity of procuring a son, both to carry on the family name and also to ensure a safe passage for the soul of his father to the other world. But after that the conception that this world was only Maya, a transitory illusion, was fully borne out by the injunction to separate

## SOME MARATHA CUSTOMS

himself from the world and gradually to prepare himself for the next, the only real life. It was an attempt to live up to an ideal and like most such attempts it was only partially realized, for it was never strictly carried out, and in the fourth century B.C. at the time of the Maurya Empire it had practically been discarded under the pressure of worldly affairs.

Whatever may have been the composition of the rite in very early times, it was evidently modified as caste developed, for it is laid down in the Grihiya Sutras that initiation should take place in the case of a Brahman in the eighth year, of a Kshatriya in the eleventh, of a Vaisya in the twelfth. The time may, however, be extended to the sixteenth, twentieth, and twenty-fourth respectively, but if the youth has not even then been initiated, he incurs the terrible penalty of excommunication and to be free again must perform expiatory sacrifices. It has been suggested that these ages were laid down on the assumption of varying degrees of precocity but, having regard to the practice of primitive peoples, it is more likely that they have some mystic significance, and Apastamba, who lived in the age of the Sutras, ascribed to 600–200 B.C., lays down that the age of eight is connected with long life, of eleven with splendour, and of twelve with prosperity. This is appropriate enough if we consider the callings allotted to the three castes, but we cannot resist the impression that Apastamba was arguing on *a posteriori* lines and that he associated with the castes those temporal benefits that seemed most appropriate. And this sort of differentiation persists in other respects. Thus the Brahman should be initiated in spring, the Kshatriya in summer, and the Vaisya in autumn. It is difficult to explain these seasons except on a somewhat fantastic hypothesis. The spring is the season of early vigour and might on that account be thought appropriate to the Brahman, who was obliged to bring to the study of metaphysics all the freshness and physical capacity of youth. The Kshatriya, the kingly and warrior caste, might well be represented by summer when the sun is most powerful, and autumn is the season of the garnering of the harvest, which is pre-eminently the wealth and therefore the prosperity of an agricultural country and particularly of the Vaisya caste, whose original occupation was agriculture. On the other hand, the early Hindu mind has a noticeable predilection for categories; it is fond of arranging its ideas in sets of three or five or whatever number may seem convenient and this attribution of the seasons may be nothing more than a fanciful arrangement beginning with the highest caste and the earliest season. This, like the ages, seems to be a forced attempt at symmetry. For at the age of eight there can have been no serious study, nor could it have made much difference whether it was begun at eight or at eleven and a bright boy of eight would soon overtake a dull boy of eleven. But in order to obtain the requisite number—neither more nor less—the old sages seem at times to do violence to their own sense of logic, to introduce an unnecessary factor or to omit a necessary one.

If we are seeking a utilitarian explanation, and dislike the rather vague suggestion of a mysticism, the meaning of which we do not know, there seems to be some force in the suggestion that the ages correspond to the knowledge which each caste was expected to acquire. The Brahman, concerned with metaphysics and the non-phenomenal world, must begin his studies early; the Kshatriya, who had the difficult task of learning to rule and to lead armies, yet had what was accounted a less difficult task than the Brahman and could begin his education later, while the Vaisya, concerned mainly with agriculture and his private property, could put it off till even later. For education began with the initiation. Until a comparatively late time it was the custom "to consult the forest dwellers," that is, the Brahmans who had entered the third stage of life, "upon high political matters; and in the Law Courts the sacred law was stated by Brahman assessors," so that in this sense the Kshatriya relied upon the Brahman even in his own domain.

On the appointed day, which is determined by the astrologer, a social gathering is held and the initiate is feasted. His head is then shaved and he is bathed and clothed in a garment which has been spun and woven in a single day to the accompaniment of a mantra:

The goddesses who spun, who wove, who spread out and who drew out the skirts on both sides, may those goddesses clothe thee with long life. Blessed with life put on this garment. Dress him, through this garment prolong his life to a hundred years; Brihaspati has given this garment to King Soma to put on. Mayst thou live to old age; put on the garment; be a protector of humanity against imprecation. Live a hundred years full of vigour; clothe thyself in the increase of wealth.

This part of the ceremony appears to have been transferred from a rite of babyhood and the verses are those of the Atharva Veda to which reference has already been made. There follows the investiture with the girdle which, following the differentiation principle, should be of *kusa* grass for a Brahman, a bowstring for a Kshatriya, and a woollen thread for a Vaisya. The choice of these materials is here obvious, for *kusa* grass is commonly used in religious rites and the other two explain themselves. The girdle is wound thrice round the boy to signify that he must study the Samhitas, the Brahmanas, and the Upanishads. The teacher chants:

Here she has come to us who drives away sin, purifying our guard and our protection: bringing us strength by the power of the indrawing and expelling of the breath: the sister of the gods, this blessed girdle.

The novice is then given a skin for an outer garment, antelope for a Brahman, spotted deer for a Kshatriya, and goat for a Vaisya. The antelope is supposed to bestow the gift of memory and it has been suggested that the animal has or is thought to have some special electric power. The other animals probably have some mystic significance, exactly what is not evident. The gift of memory is embodied in the verse recited:

May Aditi gird thy loins, that thou mayst study the Veda for the sake of wisdom and belief, remembering what thou hast learned for the sake of holiness and holy lustre.

## HINDU CUSTOMS AND THEIR ORIGINS

The boy is then committed to the care of the gods with prayers which differ according to caste.

Next the boy is invested with a staff, the wood of which differs as usual with the caste, and it is said to symbolize a long sacrificial period. It should reach the tip of the nose for a Brahman, the forehead for a Kshatriya, and the crown of the head for a Vaisya. It is said that the length of the staff varies with what is supposed to be the stature of the boy, but it seems unlikely that the ancient sages would have assumed a stature in defiance of what was evidently the fact, that the Brahman boy was not always—nor perhaps even more often—the tallest, nor a Vaisya the shortest. If we consider the peculiar sanctity of the staff which is said to represent the control which a student should exercise over thoughts, words, and actions and also during a long sacrificial period, it seems more probable that the length of it was determined by something more mystical than mere physical stature.

Now the Hindu divides up the psychic part of man into three *gunas* or qualities, Sattva, Rajas, and Tamas, or Truth (Reality), Passion, and Darkness (Ignorance), and the Brahman was held to have a larger share of the highest of these. And according to the law of Karma, coupled with the idea of transmigration, your deeds in the present existence will determine what your new existence shall be, whether you will be born again in a lower or a higher sphere. And the highest state you can attain is that of the Brahman, to whom, as we saw, are ascribed almost divine attributes. But since the staff symbolizes a sacrificial or, one may say, a disciplinary period, it is possible that is signifies the relative time which it should ideally take the three castes to attain to that state which will give the best chance of what we may call promotion in the next life. The Brahman being already endowed with a large share of Sattva would require less discipline than the Kshatriya, over whom Rajas holds sway, that is, passion in the larger sense in which St. Paul uses the word when he says "of like passions with ourselves," and the Vaisya would in the philosophical sense be more largely compounded of Tamas. If such an explanation sounds fantastic, one must remember that the ceremony is ancient, that the difference in the states is clearly symbolical, and that primitive man has many curious ways of symbolic representation. It may be objected that we have no right to import esoteric ideas into ancient practices; we have, however, unfortunately no means of dating either the ceremony itself or any modifications of it. It is at any rate clear that caste has taken definite shape and that the order had been determined, so that the outward and visible sign may well express the inward grace that is allotted to the several castes at some period when these ideas had become established.

The boy then receives a new name and is taught the duties of his new life:

Put fuel on the fire. Cleanse with water. Do service. Sleep not in the daytime.

In other words he must prepare himself for discipline during his studenthood by doing the menial duties of the house as a servant.

The next step is to inculcate the path of virtue and right living. The teacher touches the boy's breast with his finger and repeats a prayer which is, in effect, that the boy may become one with himself. There is here more than a hint of primitive practices. We are told that among certain uncivilized or primitive tribes the teacher touches the breast of the novice and thereby transmits to him a portion of his own spirit. The practice seems to be more or less connected with what Frazer calls the doctrine of the "external soul," which conceives that besides the soul which is part of himself a man has another soul which can be parted from him and can enter into another envelope, perhaps a bear or a wolf. The whole idea is not unconnected with totemism. One recalls the story in St. Luke. "Somebody," said Jesus, "hath touched me; for I perceive that virtue is gone out of me."

And so with further prayers to Vedic gods the boy is prepared for the bestowal of the sacred thread which is the symbol of his adoption into the caste. This thread, which is worn over the left shoulder, is a typical example of what I have called a passion for symmetrical classification. It is composed of sets of three: three threads each having three strands and so on. These signify various spiritual conceptions, the triple nature of the spirit, the triple nature of matter, the divine Trimurti (Brahma, Vishnu, and Siva), mind, speech, and body, and the triple control over them. The thread is, in fact, to remind the boy of all those things which concern right living; it is at once the badge of his caste and the guide of his actions. It may be compared to the cross which many Christian priests wear both as a reminder to themselves of their calling and as a profession of their faith to others.

It is at this ceremony that the initiate learns from his father the Gayatri, the most sacred of all mantras, and it is perhaps this part of the ceremony which most lingers in the memory of an eye-witness. The boy is seated upon his father's knee and the two are covered with a cloth while the holy syllables are whispered into the child's right ear, which thereby takes on a sacredness of its own. It is a piece of intimacy between father and son—or if there be no father, then of him who stands *in loco parentis*—which none may hear and none may witness though all the men—and probably all the women too—may know the verses by heart.

In the olden days the novice set out on his journey to Kasi (Benares) for the twelve years of his discipline as a *Bramhachari*. That is now performed symbolically. He goes round the company begging for alms and receiving their blessings, and goes down the street, which is appropriately marked to represent the rivers he will have to cross. The discipline he will have to undergo now is probably that of the High School or other modern institution, but it is expected of him that his whole life shall be lived in the atmosphere of self-discipline and virtue and in communion with the Supreme, which it is the object of the ceremony to inculcate.

I have dealt with this ceremony at some length, not only because it is the most important in a man's life, seeing that it is the one which gives him personality and introduces him to the discipline of life, but also because of the various points of interest contained in it. There is no reason to doubt that the ceremony as we have it now is an Aryan rite. The constant invocation of the Aryan gods would alone be sufficient to show that. But the continual differentiation of the castes shows that it must have been greatly modified at a time when the caste system had taken shape, and whatever may have been the primeval origin of caste, no one, so far as I am aware, disputes that the elaborate classification was in essence an Aryan work, or that the development of caste was largely due to Aryan influence. There are also traces of other factors. The inculcation of virtue and right living, and especially the recognition of the world as a transitory pilgrimage, are Upanishadic in character. No doubt the Upanishads are rather metaphysical than ethical, but the conception of the Universe which they contain leads naturally to the speculation of another world to which this present life is only a preliminary, and that again would suggest the means whereby man can obtain salvation. With all that, however, it is surely startling to find here and there distinct traces of the old aboriginal superstition. Apart from the references to the Atharva Veda, which, as we have seen, is a compound of aboriginal or at least Dravidian magic with the Aryan Nature worship, but which enters more intimately into the lives of the people than either of the other three, there are indications of superstitions which to-day are associated with primitive tribes, but which in times of which we are treating may well be compatible with some degree of material civilization. It is not suggested that the Aryans themselves were very highly civilized. We must get rid of the notion, if any such exists, that they had jumped straight into the developed civilization of, let us say, the Maurya Empire, and it is difficult to discard the idea that they were in much the same relation to the savage inhabitants as were Caesar's Romans to the barbarians of Germany. They were, in fact, little, if at all, superior to the more advanced of the peoples whom they conquered or displaced. There would, therefore, be nothing surprising, if they, coming in contact with barbarian ideas and superstitions, accepted them and incorporated them into the system, and this is what in the case of the Atharva Veda they seem to have done. At the same time, we must remember that while it is not impossible but on the contrary quite probable that they were not unacquainted with magic and superstition, these things occupy little or no place in the system of which we have so much written evidence. And when we are dealing with a people in whose make-up there is so much of the pre-Aryan element, it is far more probable that these magical traces are due to the survival of the older cults than that they formed part of the Aryan ritual. It is hardly possible to trace the evolution of the ritual to its present form, because such matters as historical development did not appeal to Hindu writers. Development, however, there must have been, if only because of the frequent mention of caste, which must have hardened into its well-known form after the introduction of the rite.

What does all this prove? Not very much, perhaps, but in groping after proofs one must not disregard indications. There is first the fact that initiation ceremonies are common among very many, if not most, primitive peoples. Examples are superfluous, since the fact can be verified by so many works on fetishism, magic, totemism, and the like. And these ceremonies are confined to boys and usually take place at the time of puberty. Next we have the not uncommon idea that a man must be "born again": that is to say, he enters upon a phase of life so new and so different that it may be almost described as a physical rebirth. The first birth—the natural one—introduces the baby to the life of the world; the second, with its ceremonies of initiation, "seems to be meant to admit the youth into the life of the clan." Of course, as evolution proceeded some of these customs became sublimated, so that what was originally a crude rite dealing in blood and mutilation, became a symbolic rite in which, while the idea of magic remained, it was only hinted at rather than expressly performed. We have seen an indication of this in the symbolic journey to Kasi, with the intervening rivers represented by chalk lines in the road. We have further the fact that these initiation ceremonies still exist in India, and in their cruder form. "Amongst the Gonds, a non-Aryan race of central India . . . one of the ceremonies at their installation (i.e. of the Rajas) is the 'touching of their

## SOME MARATHA CUSTOMS

foreheads with a drop of blood, drawn from the body of a pure aborigine of the tribe they belong to.'"[1]

Now if we consider the widespread belief in witchcraft and evil spirits which enters so largely into the every-day religion of the masses, surely it must be admitted that aboriginal beliefs have had more influence in building up the structure of popular Hinduism than has been generally allowed. Although it is—and may always be—impossible to prove that the foundations of these ancient customs are to be found in non-Aryan cults, these indications show that there is a very large degree of probability that such is the case. It may be that the Aryans too had their rites connected with infancy and puberty; what is suggested here is that they laid the superstructure upon something that they found there already, and that these initiatory rites, like caste, the sanctity of the cow and untouchability, are evolved from or built upon an archaic foundation peculiar to the country because invented by the aboriginal inhabitants or by their Dravidian successors. In this view the primitive elements are of primary, not of secondary, importance. Much, no doubt, of the original customs has disappeared, especially since the time when metaphysical speculation took the place of the old Nature worship and the ceremonies took on a deeper meaning, but much remained and it is a question whether in the popular view the invocations to Vedic gods and the charms and symbols intended to guard against evil spirits are not more important than the esoteric and philosophical side of the rites. In our own marriage service, though it is adapted to Christian usage, we still retain the Roman idea of the *patria potestas*, so that the woman is expected to "obey the man" and is "given away" by a male relative, thereby indicating that she is in perpetual tutelage and passes from that of her father to that of her husband. The mere fact that she changes her name means that she renounces the family in which she was born to become a member of that into which she marries.

[1] Frazer: *Totemism and Exogamy*, vol. i, p. 43.

## HINDU CUSTOMS AND THEIR ORIGINS

We may now conveniently pass to the marriage ceremony. Much has been heard of the evils of child-marriage in India, which is sometimes carried to extreme lengths and sometimes results in the physical deterioration of both parents. What lies at the root of this child-marriage is the almost excessive respect for female chastity. In India, as everywhere else, much more latitude is allowed to the man than to the woman; what is a mere peccadillo in him becomes in her a social crime. Hence it was very early regarded as sinful for a father to allow his daughter to attain puberty without being betrothed, for to attain to such a state was to expose her to unnecessary temptation. Betrothal is generally regarded as equivalent to marriage, though naturally consummation does not take place till both parties are of a fit age. But marriage itself is a sacrament; husband and wife are united, not "until death them do part" but afterwards also, and in this view we can see why widow remarriage is regarded with abhorrence by the orthodox. Nor is it only the men who object; "In the communities which prohibit widow marriage, widows themselves are unwilling to marry. In the event of their having children any suggestion for remarriage is taken as an insult."[1] For though a man may marry more than one wife (he does not often do so) a woman cannot marry more than one husband, unless she belongs to that very rare class which practises polyandry. The woman is still a wife, married to her dead husband, and he is none the less her husband because they have never lived together. Divorce was, until very recently, unknown, and if the feeling has to any extent broken down, it is under the influence of Western ideas and under the pressure of modern conditions.

The evils of child-marriage are universally recognized by Europe—and more and more by educated Indians. Why then does the custom persist, and why was there such strenuous opposition to the Sarda Act which raised the Age of Consent, an Act which has been described by a learned Mysore Brahman as "striking at the root of Hindu religion and the time-honoured usages."[2] Probably there

[1] Ananta Krishna Iyer: *Mysore Tribes and Castes*, p. 212.
[2] Ibid., p. 241.

## SOME MARATHA CUSTOMS

are four main reasons. In the first place the custom has become so firmly rooted that it is very difficult to eradicate if from the minds of the masses; it is as though polygamy was suddenly to be allowed by English law. It may well be that polygamy is the natural law; never the less, not only would the Church oppose such a measure with all its strength, but there would be very few to take advantage of it, partly, no doubt, for financial reasons, but chiefly because the idea of a legalized plurality of wives would destroy a custom of centuries. Secondly, it is at all times and everywhere, but specially in the East, difficult to grasp the strength of a tradition. That the law was laid down centuries ago for a state of society wholly unlike that of to-day makes no difference; there is the law, divinely given, and it is impious to dispute the authentic Word of God. That is a sentiment which is exemplified again and again in English practice. It is enough that the text is there and that it must be obeyed, and if two texts are contradictory, much ingenuity is spent on trying to reconcile them or to explain away the more inconvenient, instead of following the dictates of common sense and of conscience. Then there is the intense desire of the Hindu for a son; life is short and uncertain. If you marry an immature girl, you cannot hope for issue until at least a year after she has become mature and in that time much may happen. And if the child should be a girl, there is another period of weary waiting. But why not choose a girl who is already mature? If it be answered that mature girls are difficult to find it is also true that suitable boys are often not easily obtainable. And so we are led to our main reason for the practice. Physical considerations took a very subordinate place in the conceptions of early and especially of Upanishadic teaching. The doctrine of Maya, which taught that the whole world may be an illusion, suggested as a corollary that the whole duty of man was to apply himself to things of the spirit. That this phenomenal illusory world was there was not denied; the world was, in fact, very real and men must conduct themselves accordingly. There was, therefore, no inconsistency in praying for long life and material wealth in cattle and sons. The idea of celibacy never appealed to the Hindu mind; it was in fact condemned on religious grounds. It was the plain duty of man to be fruitful and multiply and to replenish the earth, as the book of Genesis puts it. And so three out of the four periods into which human life was divided were given up to the learning of spiritual things or to the application of that knowledge with a view to the Hereafter. The Hindu is far more in accord with St. Paul's teaching than is the ordinary modern Christian. But woman was an inferior creature, as, until recently, she has always been in all countries and in all ages. She was hardly to be placed in the same category as man, and in spite of all that was said and done in the name of chivalry, in spite of such eulogies as we find in the Indian Epics, she was in a completely subordinate position. It did not, therefore, matter what happened to her, so long as she fulfilled her function of ministering to man's spiritual and material needs. The facts that early maternity was calculated to injure her health and that infant mortality was appallingly high were not impressive, for the woman could be used to produce more children, and if children died, that, in the existing state of affairs, was only to be expected.

This is neither to defend the custom nor to apologize for it. It is simply an attempt to explain why it should have become so ingrained a custom that any attempt to alter it meets with strong opposition. It is not unlikely that the practice of becoming Sati is based upon much the same foundations. The woman, being of so little account, had no real existence separate from the man. She was one with him, in a much more intimate sense than the Christian one. Being, as already explained, a wife not for time but for eternity, she unites soul to soul in a manner not contemplated by Western philosophy. This custom of child-marriage, then, has hardened into a tradition which, like many other traditions, has survived when the meaning and origin of them has been lost or forgotten. The epidemic of child marriages which took place after the passing of the Sarda Act and before it came into operation may have been partly due to the influence of the priests and other interested parties who feared to lose their fees and perquisites, but it is a misreading of the Indian character not to attribute it in far larger measure to the break with the past and to what must have seemed an attack upon a long-cherished custom which had or appeared to have a religious sanction. The nearer the bone the sweeter the meat; the respite of six months must have seemed a golden opportunity not to be missed before the blow fell. There is no reason to suppose that the orthodox were not perfectly sincere in their opposition; the laws of Manu, which may be compared with what the Mosaic law means to the Jew, ordain that a man of thirty should marry a girl of twelve and a man of twenty-four a girl of eight. "One should give a girl in marriage according to rule to that (suitor) who is of (good) family, handsome and of like (caste) even though she has not reached (the age of puberty)." Other commentators even say that she should be given to her husband while she still runs about the house naked. But "twelve years seems to be the limit. If unmarried at that age the girl is disgraced and her father has sinned."[1] That is the root of the matter. No appeal to humanity, to physiological cruelty, to the rights of women, to all that appeals to the cultured conscience is likely to make any but very slow headway, as long as it is believed that "her father has sinned."

The words, however, which are quoted from a Note of Dr. Burnell are not accurate. The idea of sin, as understood in Christian countries like the idea of atonement and vicarious redemption, is foreign to Hindu conceptions and is even abhorrent to them. The Christian idea of sin seems to have an element of the personal about it; to sin is to disobey the divine law, but the offence is less against the law than against the personal God who is the author of it. To the Hindu it is rather an offence against authority, which may have been divinely inspired but is not what we should call the authentic Voice of God. The Hindu naturally looks to his own sacred scriptures for guidance as we look to ours, and it is just because European writers on the subject fail to recognize the fact that they show an inability to appreciate the orthodox

[1] Burnell: *The Laws of Manu*, chap. ix, p. 88.

Indian point of view. Thus while Miss Eleanor Rathbone, who went to India for the special purpose of studying this and other social questions, quotes fifty-four authorities in support of her thesis, and though a fair proportion of these is Indian, she makes no reference anywhere to any texts or authorities, nor any attempt to refute them. So that what we really get is a statement of the case from the European standpoint supported by such Indian evidence as accepts it. Yet the whole case for the orthodox lies in these very texts. Do we not read that in the early days of Christianity "certain men came down from Judea" and said "Except ye be circumcised after the manner of Moses, ye cannot be saved"? And this contention was thought so serious that "the apostles and elders came together for to consider of this matter." And there was a stormy meeting in Jerusalem. Can we not hear the modern critic say: "What nonsense! Circumcision has nothing to do with religion. It is simply a painful operation which may be necessary in a few cases but cannot be erected into a principle." Such an argument would not have persuaded James and the others.

From this digression we may now return to the ceremonies. They are elaborate and consist of many parts but two only are essential, the invocation of the gods and the Seven Steps around the sacred fire. The family deities, the Lares and Penates, are solemnly invited; I have seen one of these curious cards of invitation couched in the same language as those directed to mortals—"Such and such gods are requested to attend the wedding of A, son of B, to C, daughter of D." They are then worshipped; the contract is made and the exactly auspicious minute is fixed by the astrologer by an instrument of the same principle as the sandglass. When the ceremony begins the bride and bridegroom face each other on either side of a veil held up by the priests between them. Soon the dramatic moment arrives; the veil is dropped and husband and wife look upon one another for the first time. The bridegroom addresses the bride in terms of supplication, that she will look upon him as her lord, to bring him happiness and, still more important, to bear him sons.

## SOME MARATHA CUSTOMS

Then follows the *Kanyadana*, when the girl is given away by her father or other near male relative. The bridegroom promises to love, comfort, and honour her, and to keep her in sickness and in health. The bride makes no similar promise, probably because as she is simply the property of the bridegroom, made over to his care in place of her father's, and, because she has been taught to look upon her husband as a kind of god, to be borne with in vice as well as in virtue, there is no necessity for such a promise. The pair then exchange garlands and the bridegroom ties the Mangala Sutra, a necklace of gold and glass beads, round the bride's neck. This corresponds to the wedding ring and as long as it is worn proclaims that the man is still alive, for, when he dies, it is removed and the wife by its absence equally proclaims that she is a widow. The Vivah Homa or marital sacrifice comes next. The man prays to Agni, the god of fire, to protect him and his wife from all dangers and to grant them wealth and children, at the same time flinging oblations of fried rice into the fire. He then takes the bride's hand and they walk round it while he says:

O my wife, thou art Rik, I am Saman (alluding to the Vedas); I am the sky and thou the Earth; I am the seed and thou the soil; we shall love each other and have both wealth and children. May we live long!

Near the sacred fire and to the north of it are placed seven heaps of rice and as the woman places her foot upon each heap in turn, the bridegroom chants the appropriate mantras —one for food, two for strength, three for wealth, four for happiness, five for children, six for pleasure. The seventh step is the irrevocable one; they are now man and wife for all time and beyond it. Professor Washburn Hopkins, apparently copying or basing himself upon Oldenberg, gives a rather different version—one for sap, two for juice, three for prosperity, four for comfort, five for cattle, six for the seasons. "Friend, be with seven steps mine." Mrs. Stevenson, however, says that all the pandits whom she consulted reject this and give the version substantially as I have given it.

The wedding proper is now over. But the couple leave the sacrificial fire to observe the constellation of the Sapta Rishis, which we call the Great Bear. There is in this some hint of astrology, in which, of course, most Hindus have implicit faith. There is usually a wedding season, beginning in *Chaitra* or April–May, and it is possible—though I have not been able to verify it—that weddings are fixed at a time of the year when with a practical certainty of a clear sky the constellation is almost certainly visible. But this observation is not an essential part of the marriage. It is presumably only for luck, and those who attach no importance to it are free to ignore it. There follows, or should follow, if the venue has not been changed to the bride's house, the entry into the man's house, where he sacrifices to Agni, evidently as the guardian of the domestic hearth. After this there is a very curious episode. A big basket of cane is placed on the head of the girl's parents, while she sits on their lap. There is evidently some mystic significance in this basket, though what it is it is hard to discover. It is said to be for the long life of the race, but what connection there is between long life and a basket is not obvious. A basket is frequently used for grain, and in a country where the harvest is the chief source of wealth, the receptacle may perhaps symbolize prosperity. Or again, the idea of confining the soul or souls in some kind of vessel is not unknown among savage tribes, and it may be that the basket, a relic of an outworn superstition, is meant to contain the spirit of unborn generations within the compass of the newly married pair, but as the man takes part in the episode and as the basket is placed on the heads of the bride's parents, though by sitting on their knees she may be thought to be within its influence, the suggestion would seem to be too far-fetched, even among others which are well authenticated and yet seem to be obscure. The whole ceremony ends with the renaming of the girl. There is no special significance in this. It only means that henceforward the girl has abandoned her own family and has been received into her husband's.

There is in all this long ceremony a very genuine appreciation of the solemnity of the occasion and a very real devotion

## SOME MARATHA CUSTOMS

to the Deity who watches over the destinies of mankind. There is very little in the ceremonies which can be ascribed to pre-Vedic superstition and the most anxious care is taken, so far as man can, to provide for the future. The object is to secure happiness, and if the result is much what it is in more sophisticated countries at least it can be said that the measure of happiness is neither less nor more than it is elsewhere.

The general word for funeral ceremonies is Shraddha, signifying an act of faith or of veneration in honour of the dead. Although there are strong indications in the Rig-Veda that in those early times the practice was to bury, it is now the universal custom to burn. A verse in the Rig-Veda says:

> Open thy arms, O Earth, receive the dead;
> With gentle pressure and with loving welcome
> Enshroud him tenderly, even as a mother
> Folds her soft vestment round the child she loves.[1]

This change of custom seems to have arisen from a change in the conception of the soul. So long as the soul is conceived as inseparable from the body, an idea which is implicit, if not explicit, in the teaching of St. Paul and in the book of Job, it was natural to think of soul and body lying together in the earth, until that day when both should be called to a resurrection. But as the idea of transmigration gained ground it was clear that there could be no such close affinity with the body. The soul was released by death, to be reborn in a new envelope. It was conceived, however, as an intermediate ethereal body until the time duly arrived for rebirth. The original body was thus like the chrysalis from which the butterfly has emerged, an empty shell which has fulfilled its function and can now be cast away. It can and should be burnt for several practical reasons. It is hardly to be supposed that the modern notion of hygiene entered into the calculations of ancient peoples when they abandoned burial for burning, for it is only of late that Europe has discovered a fact which now appears to be self-evident. But many rivers are held to be sacred in India and it is a

[1] Rig-Veda, x. 18.

common practice to consign the dead to the holy waters. You could not convey a corpse long distances in a country like India, especially in the days of very slow transport, for the very swift decomposition makes it necessary that the funeral should follow the death as soon as possible. Moreover, it is not difficult to convey a handful of ashes over long distances and time is of no consequence. The ashes could be kept for a convenient season when a pilgrimage is made either to Kasi or to some other holy place such as Nasik in the West or Kanchi (Conjivaram) in the South. But there is little doubt that what really brought about the change was the change in religious thought and that practical advantages had but a slight, if any, influence. They were wholly secondary and subordinate—as it were accidental. Theosophists hold that the assumption of the new body varies with the dissolution of the old and that as it is important that the soul should have a local habitation as soon as possible, the sooner the old shell is dissolved the better. And given the theory of transmigration there is something to be said for the logic of this belief. For the soul is a spark of the Infinite—the Atman—and is seeking to attach itself and become absorbed into the Infinite. It ought not, therefore, to be left to wander about in space longer than need be. The idea that the assumption of the new body varies in time with the dissolution of the old recalls the ancient Egyptian notion that the soul co-exists with the body from which arose the practice of mummification and also of painting an eye on the sarcophagus as well as of leaving figurines in the tomb to represent the more corruptible flesh.

But whatever may have been the object of thus substituting burning for burial, the underlying conception of the Hindu funeral rites is ancestor worship which is prevalent all over the world. Every Indian administrator must have experienced the demand for a holiday "to celebrate my father's (or mother's) anniversary." And nothing is more sedulously kept by a pious son than the yearly worship of the ancestral manes. Mr. William Crooke says that the idea of an intermediate body is a later fancy of more subtle intellects (it certainly has the flavour of Upanishadic mysticism) and that the whole funeral rite, especially the offering of Pindas or cakes to the spirit of the departed, was based upon the practice, common among undeveloped peoples, of feeding the dead. "Like the habit of dressing the dead in his best clothes, it probably originated in the selfish but not unkindly desire to induce the perturbed spirit to rest in the grave and not come plaguing the living for food and raiment."[1] Naturally Hinduism in the long course of its evolution has put a more subtle interpretation upon this crude idea but the custom remains not only among the uneducated but among the highest intellects of those who call themselves Hindus and the closeness of relationship to a deceased man is reckoned by his right to offer the *pinda*.

There are three kinds of Shraddhas—immediate, intermediate, and final. The first are intended, as I have said, to furnish a new body for the dead, or, more accurately, to find a new habitation for the soul; the second to raise him from this evil world, the abode of demons and evil spirits, to the ancestral regions where he joins the manes of departed ancestors. When the final stage is reached, the departed spirit, by the intercession and devotion of the survivors, reaches the abode of eternal bliss or is for ever freed from the woes, the misery, or the evils to which human nature is exposed. Considered objectively, there is here a distinct resemblance to the doctrine of the Catholic Church, with this notable difference—that there is no place in the Hindu system for an eternal hell. The soul passes from the present existence to a place of trial or Purgatory and eventually obtains release in Heaven.

Shraddhas may be offered to three ancestors together, in which case they are called Parvana, or to one only, when they go by the name of Ekodishta (in the sight of one). And again they may be Nitya (of obligation), or Naimittik (occasional), or Kamya (desire-accomplishing). The Nitya Shraddha is performed on fixed days—every day or at the new moon—Naimittik is for uncertain times, such as the birth of a son. Kamya is performed with a specific object or to gratify and fulfil a special desire. All these Shraddhas have

[1] Frazer: *Journal Anthropological Institute*, vol. xv, p. 74.

two features in common—the offering of food to the dead and the feeding of living Brahmans. There are elaborate rules laid down for the seasons at which they should be performed and for the kind of Brahmans to be invited and to be avoided. These may be roughly classified as on the one hand the devout, the pious, and those learned in religion, and on the other the physically deformed and the morally reprobate, including the younger brother who is married before his elder, on the ground, we may suppose, of spiritual pride. "To feed one learned Brahman is better than feeding a million men ignorant of the Veda," but to invite those whom the Law prohibits is to divert the sacrifice intended for the manes of the departed to the jaws of demons and evil spirits. A Brahman should never refuse an invitation; if he fails to attend, his punishment is to be reborn as a hog. Great care too must be taken as to the seating of the guests; the place must slope to the South, for that is the abode of Yama, the god of the dead. The spirits are then invoked and food and water are offered, after which they are politely requested to withdraw, and the Brahmans, being fed, depart also.

All these various ceremonies are Vedic or post-Vedic; that much everyone would acknowledge. But they seem to go further back than that and many points are reminiscent of the ancient savage superstition which peopled the world with evil spirits and demons who were ever on the watch for an opportunity to injure the human race. In the course of time, and especially after the great change which converted the early Nature worship into metaphysical speculation, the cruder notions took on a new esoteric meaning, and, as the years went on, this meaning itself grew more and more indistinct, until now there are thousands, perhaps millions, of Indians who do these things and do not know why they do them, just as there are thousands who listen to the Bible every Sunday and have a very limited understanding of it. The blessed word Mesopotamia is not typical of the uninstructed Christian alone. It has been laid as a reproach against Hinduism that it is not ethical. That, as a Hindu has said, may be true in the sense that Hindu writers and thinkers have not discussed ethics in treatises after the manner of the Greeks. But these ceremonies, even if their meaning has been obscured and even if much of it seems to us meaningless mummery, are, rightly considered, the Hindu expression of a belief in the Providence of God and the Hindu method of inculcating right living, and right thinking, according to the faith that is in them.

# xi

## Esoteric Hinduism

IT is a rash adventure to attempt to describe within the limits of an essay the abstruse and complicated system of esoteric Hinduism. The subtle Brahman brain has evolved it after infinite labour and even now it is full of controversial matter. The "Six Systems" alone would require a separate volume to themselves. But Hinduism like most, if not all, religions worthy of the name is based upon certain fundamental dogmata, and if we confine ourselves to these we shall get a picture at least in outline of what it means to the educated Hindu and can see how it differs from other speculations of the kind. There are, of course, many books on the subject, but most of them are too long and too learned for the average reader and too many of them enter into such detail that bewilderment is the chief result. This learned Brahman has expended his life in refuting the arguments of his predecessor and in proving that he and he alone has found the true key to salvation. That missionary, who of English writers has naturally enough the greatest interest in matters of religion, is inclined to take the subjective view and to be influenced by an intelligible bias in favour of his own faith, and as he is writing for others similarly prejudiced he is accepted as a prophet. It is, in fact, very difficult to avoid such a bias, to put away all that one has been brought up to think and to view the subject objectively, both in its social and its religious aspect. If, however, the system is constantly compared with a system in which the writer has been born and bred, which governs his life and in which he ardently believes, it is not really possible to obtain the right perspective. For it is not only the missionary or the minister of another religion who is apt to show prejudice; it peeps out in other writings, either because the writer is making—perhaps unconscious—comparisons between East and West, without making the necessary allowances, or—and more frequently—

because he or she has been content with superficialities and has not had the inclination to look below the surface.

The Hindu system of esoteric belief rests mainly on four or five fundamental conceptions. It postulates a Universal Soul, the Paramatman, corresponding to the Western conception of the Absolute or the Unknowable. The soul of man —the individual Atman—is immortal, and being an emanation from the Universal Self, is also eternal. But during its sojourn in this world, which itself is full of impurity, it takes upon it a portion of, or is sullied by, that impurity. And as long as the individual soul is tainted with that impurity, so long is it unfit to mingle with the absolutely pure. It is, therefore, the aim of every righteous soul to obtain deliverance (Moksha) by release from the cycle of transmigration (Samsara) and so eventually by reabsorption into the Universal Self. But Hinduism abhors as childish and illogical any such ideas as vicarious atonement, whereby salvation is obtained by faith in the original sufferer coupled with repentance for individual sin. It holds a man (which word stands for the human envelope and its Atman) responsible for his own deeds and according to these deeds his next incarnation will be determined. The Atman bears no actual relation to its vehicle beyond the condition just mentioned, that the envelope is predetermined by present conduct. Just as empirical man may be carried one day in a train, the next in a boat, and the day after in a motor-car without any visible effect upon him by the nature of the vehicle, so the soul may be carried in one incarnation by a Kshatriya body, and in the next by a Brahman, if the deeds have been good, or if evil, by a Sudra. The Hindu conception differs from other conceptions in thus dissociating the Atman entirely from the body. It is not a question of the soul being the spiritual half of the body from which it is released at death but rather of the immortal part of a man, seeking to find a new envelope in which to continue its upward striving towards perfection. The Atman may thus inhabit the body of an animal which, though in its phenomenal form it cannot itself attain Moksha, may yet serve as a temporary abode.

## HINDU CUSTOMS AND THEIR ORIGINS

Thus the three main tenets of esoteric Hinduism are very closely related. Karma, or the doctrine that man is master of his fate and that whatsoever he sows that he shall reap, is the determinant factor of Samsara or transmigration, which, after much toil and tribulation, leads eventually to Moksha or Salvation. But this salvation can only be obtained through the purifying of the soul from all those impurities which are too apt to result from sojourn in this world. And this salvation can only be obtained through the operation of Karma. For Karma acts both forwards and backwards, and this is often overlooked by European writers; I am what I am because of my past deeds; and I shall be what I shall be because of my present deeds.

So closely, then, are these two doctrines connected that the one may be said to depend upon the other. As your deeds, thoughts, and general conduct have been in this life so will be determined your next existence. But that next existence is based, not as we might base it, upon class or wealth or material comfort; the dock labourer will not become a duke nor the unemployed pauper a leisured millionaire. The opportunities of virtue and of vice are to be found in caste, for caste is the touchstone of Hindu society. It is, therefore, quite open to the pariah to be born again as a Brahman, just as it is possible for a vicious Brahman to be born again as a pariah. But this doctrine of transmigration is sometimes misunderstood and misrepresented. To those who have been brought up in the belief that "God created Man in his own image" there is something abhorrent in the idea that a man could become so degraded as to be born again as an animal; for the animals are in Western eyes a lower order of creation,[1] and it savours of insult to the idea of God, if not of sacrilege, to suppose that the "image of God" could be so born into a lower order. It is difficult to get rid of the notion that a man is a man, and cannot be anything else; and that if the image of God is to be found in the human shape, it cannot be found in the shape of a lower animal. We are reminded of folk-lore tales in which the Prince

[1] The Hindu does not admit this. To him there are no superior or inferior creatures, but only a vast variety, in which God reveals Himself.

## ESOTERIC HINDUISM

masquerades as a frog or a cat or some other beast, until someone releases the spell. It is, however, very doubtful if a Hindu would look at the matter like that. However shocking it may seem to our ideas, it may well be that the Hindu would rather be born as a cow than as a pariah, for the cow is semi-divine while the pariah is (or was) only half-human. And if you can be born as a cow, the way is open to rebirth as any other animal. And here we get also a side glance at the doctrine of Maya or Illusion; for your incarnation as an animal is not a permanent degradation from the dignity of man. As you behave in the animal form, so will be determined your next incarnation. And that may be, according to your deserts, in the form of a man; if not as a Brahman, at any rate as one of the twice born castes. It is easy to sneer cheaply at the idea, to talk in the language of Malvolio of one's "grandam's soul inhabiting a bird." But in principle it is the same idea as we find in the Christian doctrine of Purgatory—with, of course, essential differences in detail. The Dean of St. Paul's in a broadcast address has defined the meaning of Purgatory and has, perhaps in a qualified manner, declared his own belief in it:

Many Christians (he says) believe in Purgatory. I am afraid there is some confusion in many minds about what the doctrine of Purgatory has meant in Christian history. It is often supposed to be the belief that we have a second chance, that those who have made no spiritual progress in this life may have the opportunity of doing better hereafter. In fact, Purgatory has meant the belief that there is an intermediate state between death and heaven. Only the Saints are pure enough to enter into the presence of God; others who are in the way of salvation need a further purification and have to endure penalties for sin before they can enter the palace of the King. To me the idea of an intermediate state has great attractions. Of how many could we say, "There is no spark of good left in him"? and of how many, "There is no seed of evil"? Do we not feel of almost everyone we have known that he is too good to be cast on the scrap-heap of the Universe, and too far from perfection to be fitted for the full vision of God? So I believe that our opportunities of training and development continue after death, and that many who have little chance of going very far in this life of the spirit here will be given wider experience hereafter.

That is exactly the attitude of esoteric Hinduism. "Only the Saints are pure enough to enter into the Presence of God." It is undoubtedly true that Hinduism has considered the possibility that there are men, however rare they may be, who can attain Moksha, that is, Salvation, without going through the refining influences called transmigration. Of course it would not speak of "entering into the Presence of God" because such a phrase implies the personality of God and the Atman or Universal Spirit has no such personality. The Saint "enters into the Presence of God" as a drop of water enters into the ocean, to be lost in the waters though still retaining some individuality as a drop. It is perhaps difficult for us to seize the idea for we can only think of individuality as something that is separate or can be separated. The Indian mind, which loves subtleties and abstractions, finds no difficulty in the conception; no substance, it would argue, loses its identity by being merged in some other substance or by taking on a different "name and form." The steel which is used in a motor-car is none the less steel because it has been given the form of a vehicle; the oxygen and hydrogen that combine to make water remain oxygen and hydrogen, and by a certain process can once again be separated into the original elements. It is childish to suppose that what you cannot see or even conceive has for that reason no existence. If you can postulate the existence of a soul of which no one can have any knowledge, there should be no difficulty in postulating also the identity of the soul, whether it be merged in the Universal Soul or it retains a separate individuality.

Both Christianity and Hinduism have seen that man being by nature imperfect is not fit to appear immediately in the "Presence of God" or to become one with Him, regarded as the Universal Soul. The one has attempted to solve the problem by the device of Purgatory, the other by that of transmigration. But neither the one nor the other regards as hopeless the possibility of ultimate perfection. That is why it is completely wrong to say, as so many have said, that the Hindu system is an endless round of births and deaths. The idea of Purgatory presupposes a single life on earth.

Imperfect man then passes to an intermediate state the conditions of which are quite unknown and the duration of which is wholly indeterminate. Dr. Matthews explains that the underlying idea is one of purification and not that of giving imperfection a second chance. At first sight this last is just what the Hindu conception appears to be, but the true interpretation is the same as the Christian one. Transmigration is in theory a step towards perfection, but whereas the Christian hope is one of steady progress towards the goal, the Hindu idea is rather that of a slippery ascent of a mountain where at any given stage the climber may slide back further than he has climbed. This idea is based upon the Hindu conception of free will. Man is master of his fate. The notion of vicarious sacrifice and atonement seems to the Hindu to interfere with the action of free will, because salvation is made to depend not upon the effort of the individual but upon something over which the man has, and can have, no control. Or, to put it in more transcendental language:

> The Self or Atman is equivalent to Brahman. The individual soul is placed exactly on the same level as the Universal Soul, the natural consequence of which is that the individual partakes of the character of the One of which he is part and parcel.... He becomes really free, as free as the Supreme Being himself. Correctly speaking, he does not carry out the order of a different being, he takes the initiative in all matters, for it is as Atman or Brahman, who shapes the entire universe. At every step he does what he has decided to do.... What he wills in the stage of the Brahman, he does in the stage of the individual.[1]

The envelope which the Atman inhabits, though it is determined by what went before and will be determined by the present, is itself of small importance since it is necessarily very transitory. It is the hope of every good man to be born again into a state which brings him a step nearer his ultimate goal of Release. It is not really a question of rewards and punishments as they are understood in the West. The underlying conception is not the material advantage to be derived from social position, from wealth, or from the

[1] Chakravarti: *The Philosophy of the Upanishads*, p. 237.

opportunity of power. Nor does it suggest the hope of any immediate or definite spiritual reward; it is a step in progress, not the winning of a prize or the incurring of a penalty. For the doctrine of the three Gunas or Qualities here comes into play. The world is pervaded by Sattva (Light or Truth), by Rajas (Passion), and by Tamas (Darkness or Ignorance).

> These three bind down
> The changeless spirit in the changeful flesh,
> Whereof sweet soothfastness by purity
> Living unsullied and enlightened, binds
> The sinless Soul to happiness and truth.
> And Passion being akin to appetite;
> And breeding impulse and propensity,
> Binds the Embodied soul, O Kunti's son,
> By tie of works. But Ignorance, begot
> Of Darkness, blinding mortal men, binds down
> Their souls to stupor, sloth and drowsiness.[1]

These qualities are within the compass of every individual soul. In practice the more advanced were placed in a better position, and this perhaps led to the idea, now apparently discarded, that to be born again in a higher caste was an advantage. That, however, was a departure from the esoteric, philosophical standpoint, a concession as it were to popular comprehension. From the wider point of view every man has an equal opportunity but there is no promise of a continuous advance. The progress towards perfection is a difficult ascent and it is recognized that a virtuous man may yet be a backslider in a later incarnation which may, therefore, be something lower in the scale, and, having thrown away his advantage, he will have to recover his lost ground. On the same principle it is open even to the most vicious man, plunged though he be in Darkness and Ignorance, to attain to perfection by a super-saintly life; his previous imperfections have already been atoned for by his previous birth, and he starts again, with a handicap, no doubt, but with his past put away as it were with a clean slate.

While, therefore, it remains true that the envelope is of small importance, Hindu philosophy has not been able

[1] Bhagavad Gita, xiv (Edwin Arnold: *The Song Celestial*).

altogether to divorce the Atman from its temporary dwelling; it does allow that a life on earth is to some extent conditioned by the form it takes, but that form is neither a reward nor a punishment but an opportunity. Hence it is that the doctrine of Karma has a wider implication. For not only is it the determinant factor of a man's life in the present and in the future, but it is also the Hindu way of accounting for the existence of evil in the world, that baffling problem that seems so inconsistent with an all-wise, all-powerful, and all-loving God. The earlier form of Hindu philosophy, as already explained, does not postulate a personal God, but an abstraction, an Atman, the only Reality, without form or substance, transcendent and immanent, without qualities or attributes, of whom nothing can be predicated but that "it is." Hinduism seeks to solve the problem by the theory of Duality. Freedom does not necessarily imply perfection. The Universal Soul is indeed free from evil, but the individual Soul retains its individuality until it attains perfection and is fit to be merged in the Atman. Until that stage is reached man is necessarily imperfect, and whatever is imperfect must have in it something of evil. But imperfection and therefore evil is the result of a man's own deeds and according to his deeds so is his Karma. He is free to compass his own destruction as he is free to achieve his own salvation, and as long as there is free will, so long will there be the possibility of evil. "Error," says Professor Radhakrishnan, "is the denial by the ego of the supremacy of the whole." Evil, therefore, does not depend upon any outside Principle, by whatever name it may be called, neither does it depend upon an unseen Force whose actions are inscrutable and who permits it for ends that pass man's reasoning powers. It is inherent in man. It is what might be called "original sin," not in the sense that man has derived his sinful nature from something which happened to some primeval ancestor but because every man is born imperfect and imperfection is Evil. For the root of imperfection is ignorance and every man must at birth be ignorant. It is only during the course of his life that he can attain by his own effort to the perfection which is Atman or to the perfect knowledge of Atman which enables him to be purged of imperfection. Man was left to make what he could of the phenomenal world. What he made of it might be good or evil, in so far as he could control it. He could not control the elements, nor in those days the forces of Nature, and he never supposed that he could.

But evil in the world was not brought about by natural calamities. The conception of the Universal Soul superseded the older idea of gods who presided over different departments and whose caprice or anger might be averted by judicious sacrifices. Calamities such as flood or fire or storm were to be regarded simply as incidents in a phenomenal world and the phenomenal world under the doctrine of Maya was of very small account. The evil in the world, the evil that really mattered, was the "evil thoughts, murders, adulteries, fornications, thefts, false witness, blasphemies" which not only defiled the man but in the aggregate the whole world. These things determined the Karma of a man—these and of course their opposites—and the sum total of Karma became the measure of the world's progress towards salvation.

The case of infants and young people, however, presents a difficulty. No attempt is made to account for the inequality of the duration of human life. It can hardly have escaped notice that different spans of life are allotted to different individuals, that some live but a few months and others many years. That is a mystery which no one has ever solved. The Christian speaks of the inscrutable Will of God; the fatalist attributes it to some shadowy conception called Fate, but makes no effort to explain how Fate works or why. The Hindu simply accepts the fact and fits it into his scheme as best he may. But there is no special presumption of innocence of the infant on the ground that there has been no time for the development of evil or vice. One is tempted to say that the position is one of a neutral "non-proven." If the baby or the boy dies he will be born again and though he cannot have shaped his destiny by any actions in that existence, there may be a carry-over from the previous one, so that in any subsequent incarnation he is still able to make his way towards perfection or he may slide downhill to make up leeway in the following one. But that explanation does not satisfy the Hindu mind. It cannot credit an all-wise and purposive Spirit with the aimless creation of a life that leads nowhere, to be thrown on the scrap-heap as a photographer might throw away a spoiled negative. But if such a life has a purpose, what is that purpose? It is, like every other life, the outcome of Karma and Samsara. The span of such a life may be determined by past existence, particularly if, in accordance with the popular view, long life is to be considered a boon. But it cannot be called a probationary period for a new existence. According to one view, the infant expiates by its death the imperfections of its parents, much as the Christian might speak of the chastisement of God, not upon the baby but upon its parents. In that case the parents are working out their Karma by means of the child. The objection to this view is that Karma is a personal affair. I must work out my own Karma and you must work out yours. It cannot be transferred to someone else, because that would involve a vicarious sacrifice or atonement, to which, as we have seen, Hindu ideas are altogether opposed. To be consistent, therefore, Hinduism has fallen back on the explanation that the infant himself expiates by his death his own shortcomings in a previous existence. He is relieved of the burden which he carried and in his next existence he starts again with a clean slate; or, if that is too absolute a statement, his next existence will be purged to the extent that his death may have brought about an expiation. This doctrine, however, is not wholly consistent with the ideas inherent in Karma, because it deprives it of its forward influence. Nothing in a baby's life can go to the shaping of the future. But the doctrine is not illogical. Put in mathematical terms it amounts to this. If the Karma to be expiated amounts to five and the infant by its death has cancelled the whole five or only three, he starts again with a burden of nothing or two, as the case may be, his own life having contributed nothing on either side, so that the Karma of it would be represented by a nought.

The cancellation of Karma by the mere act of dying

presupposes that life in itself is a boon—and a boon of the highest value. That is the Vedic view and it is also, as I have said, the popular one. Long life is the frequent burden of prayer because men prize life above everything. But it is not the view of the Upanishads. They lay no great stress on the value of human life; each existence is merely a stepping-stone in the path of probation in a transitory world. But the Paramatman being without qualities or attributes, an abstraction, cannot be said to have a will in the sense of controlling the life of an individual. On the other hand, life being an opportunity, the longer that life lasts the greater the chance not only of purging demerit but also of acquiring merit for the next step forward. For the "path that leads to salvation," says Professor Radhakrishnan, "is like the sharp edge of a razor, difficult to cross and hard to tread. . . . Suffering is the condition of progress. . . . It is the ransom that son of man has to pay if he would attain his crown."[1] Thus the attainment of that perfection which fits a man to become one with the Universal Soul is difficult—so difficult that for the ordinary man it necessitates many incarnations; but it is not impossible, and hence the journey is not endless. It is just because it is so difficult that critics have fallen into the error of describing it as a wheel set in perpetual motion. The way of progress is a mountain path with zigzags and has many obstacles, but it leads to the top in the end. It is hard to see why the religion should be called pessimistic, unless it be pessimistic to reach forward to an ideal which is certainly difficult, though not impossible of attainment. There is more than a hint in the Hindu idea of the "strait gate and the narrow way," the authority for which no Christian would be inclined or would dare to deny. The system has been branded with pessimism partly because of what seems to be the extinction of individuality but mainly owing to this misconception of the endless cycle of rebirths and deaths. It may be added that this misconception is not to be found in the works of learned and thoughtful Hindus, who after all are best qualified to know what their religion signifies.

[1] *Philosophy of the Upanishads*, pp. 119–20.

## ESOTERIC HINDUISM

There is a further misconception of the doctrine called Maya, which is usually translated Illusion, but here it is due rather to the difficulty of expressing in one language the precise shade of meaning inherent in the other. "Illusion" is defined in the Oxford Dictionary as a "deceptive appearance, statement, or belief." But the Hindu, than whom no one has had a subtler brain, was not so foolish as to deny altogether the objective existence of the phenomenal world. To have done so would have involved him in all sorts of contradictions. For if the world were "such stuff as dreams are made on," if it could be blown out like a candle, like Alice in the Red King's dream, what man does or is in such conditions would be of little or no account. Of what use would it be to strive to live the virtuous life in order to attain perfection if that life had no more substance than a dream? For you cannot altogether dissociate life on earth from the phenomenal world. You cannot say that your conduct to your neighbour has no importance except in its reaction upon your own soul; you cannot pretend that your own existence is only "the baseless fabric of a vision," for that makes nonsense of the whole theory of Samsara. For if a man is to be judged by his actions (Karma) and if those actions have no objective reality, what is the use of striving after an ideal when all your actions are no more than a puff of smoke? It may satisfy the abstract reasoning of philosophers to argue that a phantom ploughman ploughs a phantom earth and sows a phantom seed to produce a phantom crop, but the Hindu philosophers were above all things logical (and practical) and they would have seen that such ideas were too far divorced from reality to obtain acquiescence; they would have seen further that to postulate a visionary world was to knock the bottom out of their whole scheme of things.[1]

The word "illusion" seems to have been used because there was no single English word which would convey the meaning of transitoriness and of relative unimportance inherent

[1] Cf. Schweitzer: *Indian Thought and its Development*. He carries the idea of Life and World Negation too far in assuming that Hinduism allows no objective existence to the phenomenal world.

in Maya. For the meaning of Maya is what the author of the Hebrews meant when he said that "here we have no continuing city." There is a hint of the same thing in St. Paul's outburst "O wretched man that I am, who shall deliver me from the body of this death?" The whole passage suggests that in essence he is enunciating a law of Karma. "Now if I do that I would not, it is no more I that do it but sin that dwelleth in me. I find then a law that when I would do good evil is present with me. For I delight in the law of God after the inward man. But I see another law in my members, warring against the law of my mind and bringing me into the law of sin which is in my members." The Hindu aim is to control all desire and all passion and that is an admission of an inherent imperfection or weakness which must be eradicated. It is "the sin that dwelleth in me." Every good man wishes to live the virtuous life; what prevents him and what is the perpetual stumbling-block is the existence of desire and passion or what St. Paul calls the "law of sin." The deliverance from the "body of this death," the moral death which is brought about by the law of sin, is equivalent to the Hindu conception of Release, and since the ideal can only be attained through the operation of Karma, the action which is the outward manifestation of a man's virtue or vice, the Hindu would answer St. Paul's question "who shall deliver me?" by saying that a man's destiny is in his own hands; it is he himself who must bring about his own deliverance. The Hindu recognizes that a man may be inherently and deliberately vicious; that there are men of whom it can be said that "they would not do good." But they are not without hope. In their next existence they will reap the consequences of their vice; but in that existence they can wipe away the stain, and, by practising virtue, they can advance a little on the road to perfection. There is no room in the system for such a conception as "everlasting fire"; no man is doomed to eternal damnation nor even, as Dr. Matthews has suggested, to extinction. It may no doubt be many centuries before such a one can attain to the ideal, but the Hindu mind, which cannot any more than any other grasp the conception of eternity, has yet a lively notion of it and is possessed of infinite patience. His powers of reasoning tell him that a million years are a very long time, but he can to some extent appreciate that they are but little as compared with eternity.

On the other hand, his ethical ideas do not always correspond to ours. When we are speaking of the cardinal sins or the cardinal virtues there is no doubt not a great deal to choose, but to these are added the special offences against caste. It is—or perhaps was, for times have greatly changed—as great a sin to marry outside the caste or to defile oneself with a low-caste woman or in other ways to offend against caste custom, as to steal or to commit fraud; sometimes, perhaps, even murder itself was a lesser offence. Such things as these we, with our twentieth-century notions and our ethical system based upon the New Testament, would class with the "washing of cups and pots" and other purely formal or ritual observances, and there are doubtless many Hindus to-day who would do the same. It is difficult for us—and perhaps even for them—to appreciate the intense grasp which caste had over the minds of those who framed the system. Nowadays it appears merely as an institution much of which has a baneful effect on the country and especially upon its material progress. But to an Indian, particularly in early times, an offence against caste would have appeared as an offence against society; and that not in the sense that theft is such an offence but rather in the sense that it threatens to disturb the whole order of society and to introduce chaos. Whatever view be taken—whether we attribute the institution to the desire for racial purity or to occupation or to something inherent in the Aryan family (Senart) or to the survival of aboriginal customs—there is no doubt that caste was, and still is, the very foundation of the Indian social fabric. If, being a carpenter, you married a blacksmith woman or if, being a Brahman, you married a Sudra woman, there was no reason why your neighbour should not do the same, and it is obvious that such marriages indefinitely repeated would take away the whole meaning and intention of caste and would therefore produce an entirely different social structure. Caste, moreover, was regarded as a divine institution so that a caste offence was a sin against God as well as against man. In judging these things, we should remember that the formal traditions against which Jesus inveighed were observed by the Pharisees and "all the Jews" and it took the Master Mind to see through them to the deeper things. Those who had the framing of the laws of caste, the priests, would very naturally interpret them to their own advantage and in doing so would probably be compelled by logic to continue the principle into other castes, so that a graduated scale would arise. It would be a more heinous offence to sin against the Brahman than against the Kshatriya, against the Kshatriya than against the Sudra, and so on, until you reached the stratum in which humanity was hardly thought to be human. Such conceptions were bound to lead to abuses; the priestly caste and the warriors claimed privileges that could not be justified and as they were also the dominant classes they could and did impose their claims upon a subservient people. The idea of caste had taken too firm a root; having accepted it, the sensitive people clung to it with an intense tenacity; nor until quite modern times does it ever seem to have occurred to them to dispute these extravagant claims. Though caste in its essentials is as strong—or nearly as strong—as ever, the attitude towards it has become modified partly by the long domination of the Mussulmans whose democratic ideas never took a really concrete shape but chiefly by contact with the West, with its wholly different ethical system, its ideas of social service, its conception of the inherent dignity of man, and its views upon equal opportunity for everyone.

It may, I think, without inaccuracy be said that the Six Systems of Philosophy were founded upon these main doctrines. It is true that they differ from one another in various ways but they come back to a predisposing cause; the doctrines of Samsara and Karma are the means whereby man can attain perfection in a world which has a real existence—using the word in the ordinary sense—but which is relatively illusory when compared with ultimate Reality. But this kind of religion was altogether too difficult for the uneducated masses; they wanted something more concrete to which they could offer worship. In this they differed very little from other peoples. The Israelites found it hard to practise the worship of Jahweh, who was represented by nothing that their minds could grasp and was to them an abstraction. They fell away, not permanently but at least often, into the worship of the gods of those by whom they were surrounded. The agnosticism of Buddha degenerated into the adoration of the man Gautama with his attendant satellites. Islam does not tolerate images and Mohammed is in no sense exalted to the position of a divinity; yet the Islamic world is extremely sensitive about the Prophet and any real or fancied insult to him, however unintentional, is apt to lead to riot and bloodshed. The icons of the Eastern Church and the images of the Roman have ever since the abortive attempt of Leo to abolish them betrayed the same tendency. It was, therefore, only to be expected that the abstractions of the Upanishads should in course of time give way to theistic conceptions in which Vishnu and Siva, Krishna and Rama could be worshipped in human form, and this movement, known as Bhakti or ecstatic adoration, was largely due to the teaching of Ramanuja, who lived in the eleventh century, and had as its High Priest the Bengali saint Chaitanya; it reached such heights that men began to believe that the way to salvation lay through the simple repetition of a name. On the way to Tirupati temple, a very sacred shrine barred to Europeans and situated on a hill seldom climbed by them, you can see the pilgrims in this state of exaltation, chanting ecstatically the name of "Govinda." It means little to them beyond a name and an ecstasy.

It is, however, no part of my purpose to follow Hinduism through its developments to the present time. But how did this sublimated philosophy arise out of the primitive Nature worship of the Aryans? For whatever we may think of the primitive origins, there can be little doubt that as Aryanism progressed, the religion began to spread over the country, mixed no doubt with primitive superstitions and primitive beliefs and customs but still distinguishable as a separate system. Professor Ghose, as we have seen, argues that Upanishadic speculations arose separately from the popular religion and in non-Aryan lands. His view is that the more refined intellects worked out a philosophical system of their own, leaving the masses to their grosser idolatries and superstitions. It is a possible view, though the author hardly claims for it more than the position of a reasoned guess; he calls it a "romance." We cannot therefore treat it as proved and established fact. Yet though we may not go all the way with him, it does seem that something of the kind did happen, whether we treat the Upanishads as Vratya or Aryan. In all ages and in most religions there have arisen thinkers who have set themselves to inquire and have produced theories, some of which have penetrated to the general public and are often accepted by them as axioms and some of which are above the heads of all but a select few.

The great gods of Nature: Indra, Agni, Savitar, and the rest seemed to the eclectic band too departmental. They seemed to act independently of one another and in certain aspects to be even antagonistic; the Maruts, the deities of the Storm, blotted out the beneficent Sun. If the Rain was withheld, that might mean that Indra was offended, but it might also mean that some other powerful god was standing in the way, and, to use a homely, modern phrase, was overzealous for his own department. Yet there was a certain cosmic unity which could not be denied. Day and Night came round regularly; the Sun shone, went down, and gave place to moon and stars, and this implied not the unco-ordinated efforts of different divinities but the existence of a single controlling spirit. Moreover, the Nature gods were busy only with their own natural functions; these no doubt could not but have an influence on the fortunes of the human race, but they left on one side all that ethical side of human nature which goes to make up a man. There was in such a system no reason why man should not indulge his passions and engage in an orgy of licentiousness of all kinds which was only to be restrained by fear of angering this or that divinity and might result in material calamity, if indeed the Nature gods condescended to take note of the misdoings of an

## ESOTERIC HINDUISM

individual. There was, however, some vague and probably not defined idea of individuality. The whole society was composed of individuals and the sin of any one of them contributed, as far as it went, to the aggregate of the whole. But that sin was only visited by some kind of material punishment, such as Job endured, the loss of cattle and wealth, the loss of children, the sufferings of disease. Such ideas could not satisfy. Even in the most primitive religions it was always recognized that a part of man must survive after the end of mortal life; there is nothing so universal as the belief in some kind of life after death. Clearly, then, that life must be something better than the present one and that, once the ethical ideas were grasped, could only be a progress towards perfection. But nothing more perfect could be imagined than the perfection of an all-controlling Spirit. Arguing, as they were forced to do, as everyone has been forced to do, from the analogy of human affairs and human conduct, the philosophers arrived at the conclusion that as God was embodied in the Universal Spirit and was manifested by the evident order of the Universe, the attainment of perfection could only be realized by approximation to that Spirit. And since they had also determined that this Spirit contained within itself the entire Order of Things, both material and spiritual, it followed that the spirit of man must be absorbed into that Spirit. This was pure monism. Later on there appeared schools which combated this conclusion and argued that man did not lose his individuality but existed in a state of perfection, as it were, side by side with the One Spirit. Thus arose the doctrine of Dualism, the Dvaita system, in opposition to the pure monism, the Advaita, the High Priest of which was Sankara.

At the same time it was recognized that man, being imperfect, could not hope to realize his object at a single stride. The allotted span of years, something under a hundred, was altogether too short to bridge the gulf between man and the Atman, between the Atman and the Paramatman. There must therefore be intermediate stages, and what was more natural than to suppose that man was born again in some other form, or possibly even in the same form, in

## HINDU CUSTOMS AND THEIR ORIGINS

which he could continue upon his road? And what, too, was more natural if the idea of vicarious sacrifice and atonement be excluded, than the conception that man himself was the architect of his own destiny and that he was to be judged by his own conduct? It was in some such way as this that the doctrines of the Atman, of Samsara, and of Karma took hold of intellectual India. The Upanishadic philosophy superseded the more primitive Nature worship; ethical ideas, once they were established, ousted the more material conception of the Vedic gods; Vishnu and Siva lost their Vedic attributes and became something cosmic and transcendental, the Preserver of all that was good in the world and the Destroyer of Evil and the Regenerator.

This transition was only gradual; men do not easily give up that to which they are accustomed, neither will they easily exchange for a somewhat frigid philosophy the ideas of a warmer and more attractive religion. But if the Vedic gods disappeared from the Pantheon or were transformed into something else, the Vedas remained, and the Vedas represented revealed religion. Not only were they divine, but they contained in themselves all that a man could want to regulate his conduct in this life. They are the rock foundation upon which everything else is built; to question them is like questioning the authority of the New Testament or the Koran. Hence, even during the time when doctrinal philosophy was at its zenith, there was still a reverence for the Vedic gods, and this persists even now in the various ceremonies at which propitiations are made of Indra and Agni, customs are observed which are clearly traceable to Vedic times and in which the incantations of the Atharva Veda are used. Such observances are, however, except for a minority, more a matter of ritual than of belief. The average educated man does not believe in the gods, though he goes through the prescribed ritual as a matter of course and because there is a vague belief or at least suspicion that to omit it or substantially to vary it might invalidate the whole ceremony.

But side by side with these higher forms of religion persisted the aboriginal cults and superstitions which are mainly

## ESOTERIC HINDUISM

responsible for the branding of Hinduism with the name of idolatry—an accusation about as just as to judge Catholicism by the tawdry images in its churches. The persistence of these cults indicates that at no time did the Aryan religion—and still less the philosophical speculations—ever really capture the popular imagination. The blending of the races led inevitably to the blending of the religion. The great temples grew up, dedicated to the greater gods, Siva and Vishnu in their various forms, to their female counterparts and to the deified heroes, Rama and Krishna, incarnations of Vishnu. With the coming of the bhakti movement—at any rate in the eyes of the masses—the religion lost all or nearly all of its esoteric meaning in ecstatic and unreasoning adoration, while in the villages still continued the worship of the minor "village deities, the Grama-devatas, particularly of those malevolently inclined goddesses whose special care was the physical ills of mankind. These were and are often accompanied by blood sacrifice and it is perhaps significant that even in so enlightened a State as Baroda, after a procession through the city and prayers by the ruling family, a ram is slaughtered which may be seen at a certain point in the road kept in readiness for the auspicious moment. Some of these aboriginal gods, especially those who, like Hanuman, probably represent old totemistic ideas, have been incorporated into the Hindu system and others have been added as the sons or other progeny of the greater gods; and these wherever they exist are treated with the same honours as the major gods. This multiplicity of gods and godlings has given rise to the idea of polytheism, which, however, is foreign to the true esoteric Hinduism. Properly viewed in that light they are only the aspects of the One God. Even the Hindu Trinity—the Trimurti—is only the expression of the same idea. It contemplates Creation, Preservation, and Regeneration which combine the great principles of Nature and therefore of the Universe.

Thus when Hinduism is spoken of as idolatry, there is only a measure of truth in the accusation; nor is it enough to protest that the Hindu does not worship the idols but only the principles which they represent. That is an accusation which applies equally to certain forms of Christianity, as anyone can testify who has seen the little dolls held out to be blessed by the Pope in the Vatican. It is true that these anthropomorphic conceptions are pressed to the extreme limit; the gods eat and sleep, are married and beget children. It is, moreover, difficult to believe that the villagers who are not representative of Hinduism but rather of the aboriginal cults with their demon worship and their village deities, are only worshipping the indwelling spirit when they cart some weird-looking puppet to the boundaries of a village, in order to get rid of the particular disease with which they are afflicted and in the hope that the goddess will transfer her attentions to their neighbours. It can hardly be denied that such practices are idolatry in its grossest form. But it is an entire misconception to suppose that the purer esoteric Hinduism has any part or lot in such worship. Most of what is seen is nothing but the shell; it may be affirmed that very few believe in it. Hinduism, properly so-called, appeals, unlike Judaism, less to the emotions than to the intellect. Its limitations are the limitations of man's reasoning powers and the very difficulty which has so often been found in defining it is due to this cause. Its intellectualism—its insistence that knowledge is the way of Salvation and that ignorance is the cause of all backsliding—is indeed its weakness, for that is a state of mind that very few are either inclined or will seek to attain.

# Index

Aboriginal towns, nature of, 41
Aborigines—
    totem cults, 63
    inferiority of, 75
*Aghnya*, 137–8
Agni, born in wood, 160
*Ahimsa*, 150
Aiyanar, village constable, 149
Apastamba, 173
Apis, 139
    fusion of, with Osiris, 149
Aryans—
    gradual invasion of, 42
    superior civilization of, 42
    intermarriage of, 44
    mixture with other races, 44
    filtration of, 76
    penetrate Vratya-land, 89
    inadequacy of, theory, 91
    date of invasion, 132
    killed and ate cattle, 138
Asia—
    claim to spirituality, 18
    early superiority of, 19
Asramas—
    explained, 32–3
    four stages of life, 100, 172
Association, effect on national character, 22–3
*Aswamedha*, horse sacrifice, 140
Atharva Veda, 57
    composition of, 91
    a Vratya document, 92, 212
Atman, 201
*Ayusha Vardhana*, 162

Bants, totemism of, 58
Barley, emblem of fertility, 161
Barnett on Marathas, 155
Beans, male half of fertility, 159
Belief, foundations of Hindu, 195
Berriedale Keith—
    on aboriginal civilization, 40

Berriedale Keith—*continued*
    on caste, 61
    on sanctity of cow, 137
Bhakti, 209, 213
Brahmans—
    colour of, 52
    tradition of divinity, 119
    glorification of, 122
    causes of supremacy of, 123
    privileges of, 124
    degenerate type of, 125
    oppose British rule, 127
    European dislike of, 129
    criticism of English by, 130
    and English education, 131
Breasts, touching the, 177
Buffalo, Dravidian animal, 144
Bull, sacred to Siva, 145
Burial in Rig-Veda, 189
Burning of dead, 190

Caste—
    gradual establishment of, 42
    occupations of, 48
    in Tamil, 60
    analogy of Greece and Rome, 71
    Dutt's theory, 72
    recapitulation, 73–4
    divisions of, explained, 78
    origin of, 79
    religious key-note of, 80
    strength of, in villages, 83
    among Vratyas, 99
    order determined, 99
    originally four, 117
Cattle, over-population of, 144
Child marriage, 182
    reason for, 183
Climate, influence on national character, 14
Cobra, sanctity of, 146
Colour—
    false guide to classification, 11
    as basis of caste, 38

215

Compass—
  invention of, 27
  points of, in rites, 157–64
Cow—
  killing of, sacrilege, 134
  divine because useful, 134–5
  preservation of useless, 135
  an imported animal, 135
  exempt from sacrifice, 137
  Egyptian sanctity of, 139
  a corn spirit, 140
  in Rig-Veda, 141–2
  sanctity not Aryan, 142
  a deity of fertility, 145
  summary, 152–3
Creeds, key-note of, 13
Cults, intermingling of, in rites, 168

Danyas, 56
Dasyus, 37
Dean Matthews on Purgatory, 197
Doctrines, contradictory, in Hinduism, 102
Dravidians, entry into India, 36
Dutt—
  on divisions of society, 51
  on aboriginal influences, 53
  on sacerdotal power, 121
Dvaita system, 211

Earth Goddess, 163
Edwardes on Marathas, 155
Ethics, Hindu conception of, 207
Europe, the darling of Nature, 28
Evil spirits, belief in, in India, 66
Exogamy, 57
  peculiar to Hindus amongst Aryan peoples, 74

Fauna, importance of, 92
Fertility spirit embodied in all cattle, 152
Fire, charm against demons, 63
Frazer, explanation of tabu, 65

*Garbha dhana*, Maratha rite, 157

Garuda—
  vehicle of Vishnu, 58, 149
  a totem, 59
Gayatri, 178
Ghose on Eastern Empire, 87
Gonds, touching forehead with blood, 180
Grama devatas, 213
Gunas, 176

Hair—
  shaving the, 69
  parting the, 161
  magical properties in, 171
Hieun-Tsang on outcastes, 111
Hinduism—
  a blend of two creeds, 103
  tolerance of, 156
Horse, draught animal of the gods, 140

Implements, meaning of, in ceremony, 168
India—
  in early times, 32
  topography of, 61
Infants, position of, in Hindu system, 202
Initiation—
  years of, 173
  ceremonies common to primitive peoples, 180
Interdining, prohibition of, 64
Intermarriage of Aryans, 39
Iranian, division of castes, 70–1
Iron as a charm, 69

Japan—
  climate of, 29
  effect of Russian War, 30
  seclusion of, 30
*Jatakarma*, Maratha rite, 162

*Kanyadana*, Maratha rite, 187
Kapus, totemism and exogamy of, 58

# INDEX

Karma—
  operation of, 102
  working of, 115
  implications of, 201
  meaning of, 196
Kitchen—
  Roman analogy, 67
  sanctity of, 66–8
  and marriage, 68
Knots, symbolism of, 170
Komatis, totemism and exogamy of, 58

Latitude—
  importance of, 13
  choice of 35th degree, 14–15
Lingam, emblem of Siva, 149
Longitude, relative unimportance of, 13
Lothrop Stoddard on the Aryan theory, 37
Lyall on exogamy, 62

Mágadha—
  wrongly derived from Magadha, 96
  a Court jester, 96
  in the Code of Manu, 97
  a true Vratya, 98
Magic, Dravidian, 56
Mahabharata, 52
Marathas—
  a mixed race, 77
  origin, 155
Matas, symbol of number eleven, 163
Materials for girdle in initiation, 175
Maya, 205
Meriah, sacrifice of Khonds, 146
Mohenjo-Daro, excavations at, 41
Moksha, 198
Monkey, a sacred totem, 146–7

*Nama-karana*, a ceremony, 165
Names, significance of double, 165

Nandi—
  Siva's bull, 58
  guardian of temple, 150
Nature gods, their functions, 210
Nesfield on origin of caste, 51
No-castes, 45
  as argument against Aryan theory, 111
North—
  trend of empire towards, 17
  material civilization of, 18
  invasions from, 19

Occupation—
  caste develops on lines of, 48
  as guide to marriage, 48
  no guide to persistence of caste, 53
O'Malley on Aryan theory, 37
Oraons, rites of, in Bengal, 160
Oriental, connotation of, 11
Outcastes—
  *ascripti glebae*, 109
  misleading word, 111

Paraiyans—
  aboriginal origin, 113
  victims of tabu, 114
  degradation of, 115
Paramatman, 234
Pariah, derivation of word, 112–13
Patriotism of Brahmans, 132
Peacock, totem of Bhils, 147
Pharisees, unfair treatment of, 128
Pollution—
  in the Acts, 65
  Brahman use of silk cloth, 69
Priests, claims and instances, 78
*Punsavana*, Maratha ceremony, 158
Purusha-Sukta, 117

Rajas, 200
Rajasuya, rite of consecration, 89
Rapson, on Marathas, 155
Release, doctrine of, 199
Re-marriage, objection to, explained, 61

217

Renaissance, 17
Rivers—
    sanctity of, 151
    embody water spirit, 152
Roman Empire, 29
Rudra—
    identified with Siva, 147
    in Rig-Veda, 148

Sacred thread—
    initiation ceremony, 172 sqq.
    symmetry of, 177
Sacrifice, importance of, 136
Samoa—
    burying dead animals, 58
    animals as vehicles for gods, 58
Sapta Rishis, 188
Sashti, worship of goddess, 167
Sati, explanation of, 101, 184
Sattva, 200
Script, influence on contact, 23–4
Sea—
    effect on contact, 25
    early navigation, 25–6
    European discovery by, 26
    coast-line of Africa and South America, 28
    coast-line of Europe, 28
Seasons for initiation, 173
Senart—
    on Aryans, 43
    on occupational theory, 51
Serpent, worship of, 119
Seven steps, meaning of, 187
Shaving the head, 171
Shraddha, 189
    kinds of, 191
Sin, Hindu conception of, 185
Sind, discoveries in, 41
Siva—
    destroyer and regenerator, 148
    deity of fertility, 149
Slater—
    Dravidian element in Indian culture, 49
    occupational theory of caste, 49–53

Slater—*continued*
    on Brahmans, 118
    on cow sanctity, 143
South—
    the determining factor, 16
    India, the product of, 33–4
    purity of races in, 47
    Brahman ascendancy in, 47
    the place of Death, 164
State, Eastern conception of, 126
Sudras, colour of, 52
Sun and Serpent, worship of, 119
Suta—
    a bard priest, 95
    a true Vratya, 98
Sutikagni, Maratha ceremony, 163

Tamas, 200
Timur, 19
Topography—
    of Europe, 20
    influence on national character, 20
    of Asia, 20–1
Totem, definition of, 57
Totem tribes in Australia, 60
Totemism in primitive tribes, 57
Transmigration, 96, 211
Tropics, influence on character, 22

Udambara tree in Maratha ceremonies, 159
Universal Spirit, evolution of, 211
Untouchability—
    economic disadvantage of, 104
    palliation of, 105
    survival of, explained, 105
    Slater's theory, 106
    objections to Slater, 107
    not due to occupation, 108
    not Aryan, 110
Upanishads, non-Aryan, 100

Vaisyas—
    colour of, 52
    meaning of, 90
Varna, 39
*Varna-ashrama-dharma*, 98

# INDEX

Vratya—
  meaning of, 87
  not Brahman, 90
Vratya-land—
  constitution of, 88
  popular religion, 94
Vratya-stoma, mass conversion ceremony, 88

Washburn Hopkins on date of Mahabharata, 52
Water, importance of, in rites, 165
Weaving imported from Egypt, 120
Whitehead on village deities, 56

For Product Safety Concerns and Information please contact our EU
representative GPSR@taylorandfrancis.com
Taylor & Francis Verlag GmbH, Kaufingerstraße 24, 80331 München, Germany

www.ingramcontent.com/pod-product-compliance
Lightning Source LLC
Chambersburg PA
CBHW062226300426
44115CB00012BA/2232